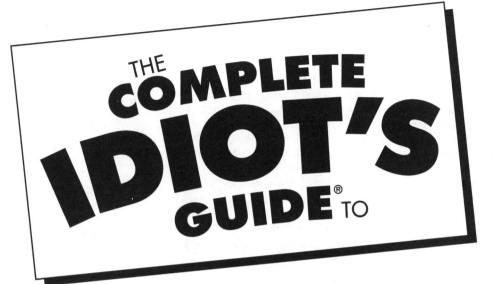

# THE COMPLETE IDIOT'S GUIDE® TO

# Online Marketing

## by Bill Eager and Cathy McCall

A Division of Macmillan USA
201 W. 103rd Street, Indianapolis, IN 46290

**The Complete Idiot's Guide
to Online Marketing**

**Copyright © 1999 by Que Corporation**

International Standard Book Number: 0-7897-2037-x

Library of Congress Catalog Card Number: 99-61224

Printed in the United States of America

First Printing: *September 1999*

02   01   00   99        4   3   2

## Trademarks

## Warning and Disclaimer

**Executive Editor**
*Greg Wiegand*

**Acquisitions Editor**
*Angelina Ward*

**Development Editor**
*Kate Shoup Welsh*

**Managing Editor**
*Thomas F. Hayes*

**Project Editor**
*Leah Kirkpatrick*

**Copy Editor**
*Molly Schaller*

**Indexer**
*Larry Sweazy*

**Technical Editor**
*Bill Bruns*

**Proofreader**
*Maribeth Echard*

**Interior Design**
*Nathan Clements*

**Cover Design**
*Michael Freeland*

**Illustrator**
*Judd Winick*

**Copy Writer**
*Eric Borgert*

**Layout Technician**
*Eric S. Miller*

# Contents at a Glance

# Contents

## 6 Your Ad Strategy and Ad Placement 97

## 7 Ad Creation: What Kind of Internet Ad Should You Use? 111

## 10  How to Use (but Not Abuse) Email Marketing   167

## 11  Marketing with Newsgroups   191

**xi**

# About the Authors

**Bill Eager** is an Internet and technology pioneer. Bill has spent 15 years researching, writing about, speaking about, and implementing electronic communication systems. Bill has written 10 books about the Internet and technology, including *The Information Payoff*, *The Information Superhighway Illustrated*, *Using the Internet*, and *NetSearch*. Bill regularly gives presentations and keynotes about technology at national conferences. He has led workshops for executives of corporations, including JD Edwards, Novartis, TCI International, Jeppesen, and Citibank. Bill has helped some of the nation's leading companies, including Kaiser Permanente, Columbia Healthcare, RE/MAX, INVESCO, and Kryptonics, design and implement interactive Web sites that provide services to employees and customers. Bill can be reached via email at eager@rmi.net; check out his Web site at http://www.beager.com/~eager.

**Cathy McCall** has spent nearly 20 years marketing online, interactive, and e-commerce products and services. In a dozen years with Standard & Poor's, Cathy grew the information and software product lines to a multimillion-dollar business that garnered industry awards and premier leadership status. With the advent of the Web, she directed marketing and investor-relations efforts for an Internet startup that built high-performance e-commerce products and other business applications.

## Dedication

*We dedicate this book to Bill's parents, Pat and Gerry; Cathy's family; and everyone who uses technology for good causes and teaches us it's whom you love, not who loves you, that really matters.*

## Acknowledgments

*We would like to thank Angie Wethington for believing in this idea from the very beginning; Angelina Ward for her professional support and great ideas; and Kate Welsh, an excellent development editor.*

# Tell Us What You Think!

As the reader of this book, *you* are our most important critic and commentator. We value your opinion and want to know what we're doing right, what we could do better, what areas you'd like to see us publish in, and any other words of wisdom you're willing to pass our way.

As the Publisher for the Consumer team at Macmillan USA, I welcome your comments. You can fax, email, or write me directly to let me know what you did or didn't like about this book—as well as what we can do to make our books stronger.

*Please note that I cannot help you with technical problems related to the topic of this book, and that due to the high volume of mail I receive, I might not be able to reply to every message.*

When you write, please be sure to include this book's title and author, as well as your name and phone or fax number. I will carefully review your comments and share them with the author and editors who worked on the book.

Fax:      317-581-4666

Email:    consumer@mcp.com

Mail:     Executive Editor
          Consumer Group
          Macmillan USA
          201 West 103rd Street
          Indianapolis, IN 46290 USA

# Introduction

The quickest way to describe online marketing is to say, "It's here now!" Some 150 million people from around the world use the Internet today. There is almost a 50-50 split of men and women online. In other words, the online world has quickly become a medium that marketers cannot ignore. And your marketing budget must include the Internet. Indeed, spending on online advertising campaigns is expected to surge to $6.5 billion by 2002, up from $906 million in 1997, according to a report by Veronis, Suhler & Associates.

But using this medium is not as simple as, say, using television, radio, or newspapers for reaching customers and prospects. Various techniques and options are available for online marketing. There are myriad advertising options: content sponsorships, direct email campaigns, newsgroup participation, virtual communities...the list is huge. And the "data" side of online marketing is phenomenal. You can capture detailed information about your customers and prospects and use this information to enhance marketing efforts and better serve your customers.

The odds are pretty good that you or your company already has a Web site (or soon will have). You can use online marketing to simultaneously leverage the content that already exists on your Web site, bring an increasing number of qualified leads and customers to your site, and enhance the relationship your customer has with your company. It sounds like a lot—but it's all possible!

This book provides the information you need in order to understand the sometimes-complex world of online marketing. It also offers case studies from companies who use the medium effectively. In addition, you'll find numerous instructions, checklists, and practical advice you can use immediately to make your online marketing efforts both successful and cost-effective. We hope you enjoy reading the book and using the information as much as we enjoyed putting it all together.

## *Fabulous Features*

This book uses a few "standard" *Idiot's Guide* features that make it easy for you to learn. These include the following:

### Check This Out

You'll find these "Check This Out" sidebars scattered throughout the book. They highlight important notes, tips, warnings, and other tidbits that will help further your education about online marketing.

### Techno Talk

We shun long-winded technical explanations because they tend to be boring and don't help you do your job. Nevertheless, on occasion we use Techno Talk sidebars to explain complex technical terms or concepts in "plain English."

### Note

This "cross-reference" box points you to other parts of the book that contain related information.

# Part 1

# Why You Need to Market on the Internet

*Everyone tells you that the Internet and the online world are the hottest things since sliced bread. But is the Internet really a good place to invest your precious marketing dollars? The chapters in this section provide an overview of the Internet from a marketing perspective. You'll learn about the people who use the Internet and how you can determine whether your target market is online. You'll find out how you can do research (online, of course) to discover how your competition uses the Internet for their marketing efforts. You'll also discover ways in which you can use the Internet to enhance your marketing strategy—whether that strategy focuses on branding your products and services, retaining existing customers, or obtaining new customers. Case studies and examples will show you how various companies use online marketing to reach out to their customers.*

# Chapter 1

# The Pot of Gold: The Internet Is Not a Fad and Why You Should Care

---

### In This Chapter

➤ How many people use the Internet, and how that applies to you

➤ How to use the global nature of the Internet to your advantage

➤ How marketing in cyberspace differs from marketing in the real world

➤ The advantages of using multimedia for marketing

➤ Why the Internet is perfect for both mass communications and target marketing

---

The Internet? Of course! That global, network of networks that connects millions of people all around the world. Who hasn't heard of the Internet? There are endless stories in newspapers and on the radio and television. Everyone, it seems, has an email address, and the phrase *dot com* has become part of everyday conversation.

This chapter **is not** going to hype the Internet. Plenty of people already do that. Instead, let's examine why the Internet is an important tool for mass communications, and specifically for marketing. This chapter starts with a broad overview of the scope of the Internet and focuses on how the unique nature of the Internet provides practical applications for you—the Internet marketer.

# The Internet Sets New Standards and Creates New Rules

The Internet is the most important, and potentially most effective, communication and marketing medium the world has ever seen. Do you think that's a bold statement? Read on. One of the first criteria for a mass medium is that it has the potential to reach a very large audience. Well, the Internet hits this in spades. The following figure shows the Yahoo! home page. Yahoo! consistently ranks as one of the most visited sites on the Internet, receiving more than 25 million users each month. The value of this traffic is reflected in Yahoo!'s stock price, which has edged over $200 per share!

*With millions of visitors every month, Yahoo! has proven that the Internet is indeed a medium that reaches a mass market.*

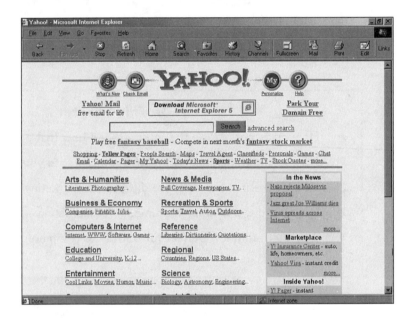

### Online Population

Even so, given that the global population might exceed 6 billion people, the online population will account for less than 5% of the world population.

As the next figure illustrates, approximately 150 million people now use the Internet globally, with projections surpassing 300 million users by the year 2005 (which is not that far away, really). If these numbers prove true, that's an incredible 82,191 new users every day for the next five years!

In fact, it is amazing how quickly the Internet has become a mass medium. In four years, the Internet has grown to reach an audience of 50 million users—it took radio 38 years to achieve the same numbers (see Table 1.1)!

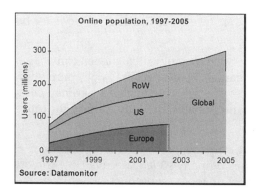

*Datamonitor predicts that over 300 million people will have Internet access by 2005 and that the Asian and South American user market will generate a substantial percentage of the overall growth.*

### Table 1.1   The Internet Has Reached 50 Million Users Faster Than Any Other Form of Mass Communication

| Medium | Years to Reach 50 Million Users |
|--------|--------------------------------|
| Radio | 38 |
| Television | 13 |
| Internet | 4 |

**More on Demographics**

Chapter 2, "Who's Out There and What Are They Doing? Profiles of Internet Users," takes a closer look at the demographics of the Internet. You'll learn more about the specific characteristics of the people who log onto the Net. This information will help you as you make decisions about using the Internet to reach your customers.

# How Does the Global Nature of the Internet Affect You?

When you launch a Web site or use Internet marketing, you can reach a global marketplace. And, if you have products or services that can benefit (and be sold to) people all over the world, the Internet becomes a new sales channel that has the potential to dramatically enhance your revenues. This is great news for both small and large companies.

Small companies or companies that are geographically isolated can actually realize even more benefits than large companies. That's because large companies generally have established international offices and sales channels. For a small company, the Internet usually becomes the first, and possibly the only, vehicle for international exposure and sales.

For example, the Coloso Footwear Company, based in Guanajuato, Mexico, is a manufacturer of children's footwear. The company's Web site, available in both Spanish and English, offers detailed information about its products for customers, as well as information for prospective dealers.

*Based in Guanajuato, Mexico, the Coloso Footwear Company uses the Internet to reach a global audience.*

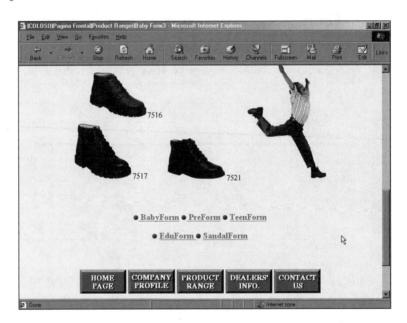

### Recognizing the Potential

Chapter 3, "Internet Marketing 101," provides more details on the types of companies and products that might realize the greatest benefits from Internet marketing.

Here's another example: We once met a business owner in Grand Prairie, Canada, population 28,000. This town is approximately 500 miles north of Calgary. His firm sells designer eyewear in Grand Prairie and does quite well because there is little competition from the large eyewear chains. He plans to use the Internet to expand to reach a national, and even international, audience.

# The Issue of Language

Because the Internet reaches a global audience, you need to consider language. Although it might be hard to believe (especially as you surf Web sites), not everyone in the world speaks or reads English. From the marketing and advertising point-of-view, you need to determine whether you are trying to reach an audience that is more comfortable with a language other than English.

Because Canada is a country where people speak both English and French, it is not surprising to find that many Canadian Web sites offer the user a choice of these two languages. Air Canada, for example, starts its home page with only two links—English and Français. Choose your language and get going!

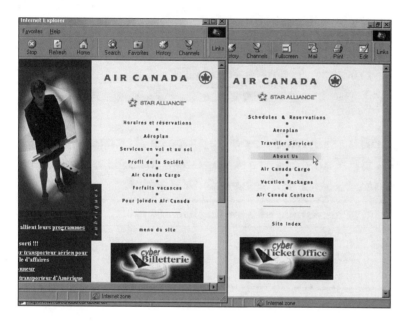

*Side-by-side browser windows show that the Air Canada site is fully replicated in both English and French.*

International companies realize that it is important to reach people in their native language. These companies have Web sites that offer the user a selection of languages. The next figure shows how Compaq Computers enables Web users to jump to home pages for Compaq sites in various countries. These Compaq "mini-sites" are usually displayed in the language of that country.

If you are smaller than Compaq (and most companies are), you can target your international expansion to specific countries or regions where one language might take priority. From a purely "numbers" point-of-view, Spanish, German, and Japanese would reach the largest non-English-speaking/reading audiences. Table 1.2 shows the breakdown of non-English language usage on the Internet.

*International companies, such as Compaq, create Web sites in many languages, and sometimes maintain Web sites for every country where they have an office.*

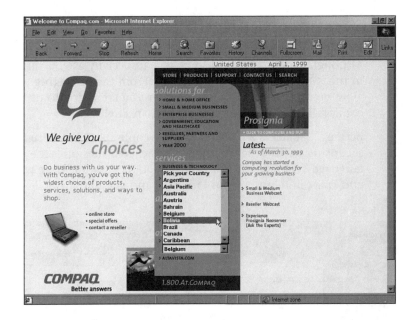

## Table 1.2   Spanish, German, and Japanese Account for More Than 50% of Non-English Language Usage on the Internet (Source: Network Wizards)

| Language | Percentage of Non-English Users |
| --- | --- |
| Spanish | 20.5% |
| German | 20.4% |
| Japanese | 18.4% |

Indeed, many companies recognize the tremendous potential audience of Spanish-speaking people, both in the United States and other countries. CNN created CNNenEspañol to reach the large Spanish-speaking population, as seen in the following figure.

Regardless of how big your company or organization is, you need to consider the value that you (and your customers) receive from a bilingual site. Going bilingual with a Web site is a big decision, because you must create every page on your site two times—and every time you change or update your site, you need to be sure that the second language is updated as well. If your site is small (under 25 pages) and is relatively static (it changes only once every couple of months), then it is not too difficult to be bilingual.

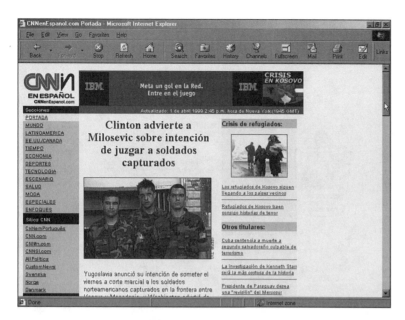

*CNNenEspañol provides daily news and information in Spanish.*

# The Internet Is Virtual

The word is *cyberspace*. It sums up one of the unique characteristics of the Internet. All your marketing, advertising, surveys, images, and information exist in a place that is not real (well, it exists on the hard drive of a computer).

If you make and sell a product, the product exists in the real world. People might go to the grocery store where they see, touch, and buy the product in a package that is carefully designed with logos and branding. If you own a restaurant, a video store, a day-care center, a college—these businesses all exist in the real world. The buildings themselves, with signs and an address in the telephone book, are part of the marketing.

One of the terrific possibilities with cyberspace is that you can actually have a business, or a store, which has no brick-and-mortar counterpart. The entire business exists only in cyberspace...on the computer hard drive. Think of the potential. You eliminate tremendous overhead—leases, electricity, desks, and often personnel. Impossible? Not at all. Many companies now exist only in cyberspace. If there is a real product, the company needs only to have a system for distribution of the product.

One of the early companies to jump into this type of business was Virtual Vineyards, a Web site that today offers a variety of consumable products, as shown in the following figure. Peter Granoff, creator of Virtual Vineyards, states his mission: "My goal is simple—to find outstanding food and wine selections from superb producers and offer them to you for purchase here at Virtual Vineyards. I also want you to have fun while you are shopping and perhaps learn a little bit about food and wine along the way."

*Virtual Vineyards—a true cyberstore—makes it easy to locate and purchase the perfect wine.*

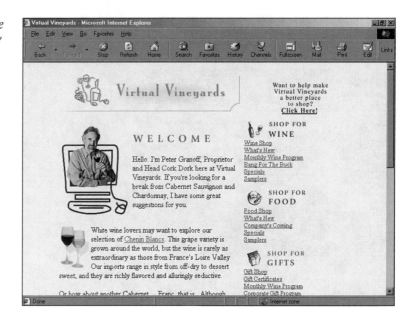

Clearly, other companies are also having great success with the operation of virtual businesses. The Web site 100Hot.com (yes, at http://www.100hot.com) monitors traffic to various Web sites and then ranks sites based on home page views. Every day there is a list of the most visited (or hot) sites in different categories. During one week, the Web's 10 most popular shopping sites included Amazon.com and CDnow—both completely virtual stores—as seen in Table 1.3.

### Table 1.3  The Web Site 100hot.com Provides a List of the Most Popular Shopping Sites

| Ranking | Site | URL | Product/Service |
|---|---|---|---|
| 1 | Amazon.com | http://www.amazon.com | Books, music |
| 2 | OnSale Inc. | http://www.onsale.com | Auction of electronics |
| 3 | Ticketmaster Online | http://www.ticketmaster.com/ | Tickets |
| 4 | EBay Auction | http://www.ebay.com | Online auctions |
| 5 | Egghead Computer | http://www.egghead.com | Software |
| 6 | CDnow Inc. | http://www.cdnow.com | 300,000 music items |
| 7 | Classifieds2000 | http://www.classifieds2000.com/ | Classified ads |

| Ranking | Site | URL | Product/Service |
|---------|------|-----|-----------------|
| 8 | Virtual Flowers | `http://www.virtual flowers.com/` | Flowers |
| 9 | MovieLink/ 777-Film Online | `http://www.777film. com/` | Movie reviews and information |
| 10 | N2K Inc. | `http://www.n2k.com` | Music content |

Notice that the products and services are pretty diverse, ranging from flowers to books to electronics to tickets. Other sites on the top 100 list have included Land's End, The Disney Store, K-Mart, and JC Penney. There are also lesser-known companies on the list, such as the WigOutlet (`http://www.wigs.com`), which sells wigs, and Wristwatch.com (`http://www.wristwatch.com`), which sells, surprise, wristwatches.

# It's On 24 Hours a Day, and Can Last Forever

What are the hours of your business? Nine to five? Maybe you've got an answering service or customer support system for after-hours calls. Nevertheless, most businesses in the world still operate on a standard, eight-hours-a-day schedule. If your business is consumer oriented—such as a dry cleaner, a pet store, a real-estate firm, or a doctor's office—you have some weekend hours. Generally, businesses large and small require that their customers be available during these limited office or business hours.

Increasingly, this is a bad way to conduct business. Hectic schedules make it difficult for most people to be a "customer" during business hours. Even business customers are increasingly unavailable for sales and marketing messages or calls during the week. Just think about how much of your week you spend leaving or receiving voice mail messages.

Enter the Internet. It never closes. Open 24 hours a day. If someone wants to learn about your products and services, if they want to ask questions about your products and services, if they want to buy your products and services, they can do it when their schedule permits. The Internet also lets the customer (who, remember, is always right) have self-service access to the information and services he or she wants. There has been an evolution toward empowering consumers to make decisions at their leisure.

In the 1970s, people were introduced to the concept of self-service access to gasoline—pump it yourself. In the 1980s, we discovered bank cards and were given the ability to have self-service access to our money, 24 hours a day. Now you can also use your telephone, and increasingly the Internet, to access your bank accounts at your leisure. For the next 10 years, we will see an ever-increasing use of the Internet as a means to providing customers with self-service access to information, services, and purchasing.

*In the market for a new Ford, but aren't sure where the nearest dealer is? The Ford Web site (www.ford.com) helps you find a dealer and provides a map and driving directions.*

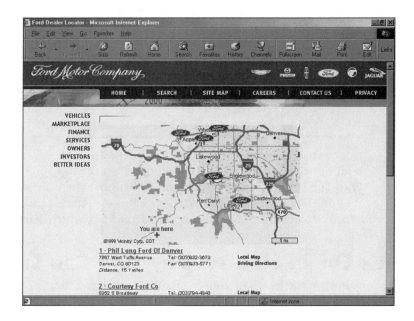

The "always-on" aspect of the Internet plays another important role. If you have an exotic flower store in Hawaii, and your customer is in Germany, there is a significant time-zone problem—ten hours. You are asleep when they want to buy their anniversary flowers. The Internet enables your business, your organization, your store to be "always open." Try doing that with any other form of mass communication. Indeed, the incredible growth of electronic commerce is partly fueled by the fact that people like to shop at home, when they want to.

## The Internet Creates a Level Playing Field—Sort Of

It might not be completely level, but the Internet makes it much, much easier for small businesses to compete head-to-head with much larger companies. For example, say you want to go to Paris. You've never been there but you'd like to stay in a charming bed and breakfast. Go to Yahoo!. Search on "bed and breakfast paris." Get a list of choices. **Chateau de Jonvilliers—Recently renovated 18th Century chateau near Paris, Versailles, and Chartres. Now a bed and breakfast** (in English and French). As the figure illustrates, you can use the Chateau de Jonvilliers Web site (www.chateaudejonvilliers.com) to see pictures of the rooms, check the rates, and make a reservation.

If you always stay in Hilton hotels, you can visit http://www.hilton.com and find out about the Paris Hilton. We don't have access to the marketing budgets of either the Chateau de Jonvilliers or Hilton Hotels Corporation, but it's probably safe to say that Hilton spends much more money on marketing in general, as well as on the Internet, than does the bed and breakfast. Yet both provide an opportunity for visitors from around the world to easily visit their sites and make reservations.

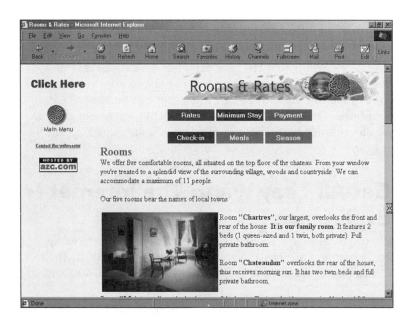

*The Internet makes it possible for small businesses to market to a global audience.*

Now, it is true that the Hilton Web site might get more visitors than the bed and breakfast, but that is because Hilton is an internationally recognized name with properties all over the world. Hilton might also spend more money promoting its Web site both online and with other collateral marketing materials. But clearly, without a Web presence, the smaller bed and breakfast would have very little chance of reaching people from around the world.

The same is true of other small and medium businesses. If you have a product or service that would be attractive to an audience that stretches beyond the physical location of your office or store, then the Internet is a cost-effective way to reach that audience. Often, small companies have a certain advantage. Without the committees and approval processes that frequently occur in large companies, small firms can quickly create and modify their Web sites and marketing efforts.

# Interactive Means Two-Way

Television is probably the most passive of all media. You sit and watch. Sometimes, with radio, the disc jockey asks questions or has contests and you can call in to the station to participate...if you can get through on the telephone. With publications, you turn the page. Sometimes, if you see an ad that you like, you can send in a reader response card (also called bingo cards because of all the numbers); the company then mails you information about the product. This is a form of interaction, but a very slow one.

Well, users of the Internet can interact with the information that they see on their screens. Computers (and therefore Web sites) are great at providing responses based upon the choices that the user makes. Your customers, and potential customers, have an opportunity to interact with your information (and your company) at the very moment that they are engaged with the information. It is "instant gratification."

At the simplest level, interactive means that the user can click on various text or graphic choices on a Web page to move from one part of the site to another. The user "interacts" with the choices that you present. More interaction can be created when the user is given several options. Then, based on the selection that each user makes, the site delivers custom-tailored information. So, in a sense, you are delivering information to an audience of one.

# Let the Senses Get All They Want: The Internet Is a Multisensory Experience

Another great, overused word is *multimedia*. On a daily basis, most people use five senses (touch, taste, smell, hearing, and sight). Although touch, taste, and smell are not yet available via PC, computers are great at delighting the senses of vision and hearing.

Let's be honest: Plain text is boring. On the Web you can take text and color it, enlarge it, or animate it. Text itself takes on a life of its own. Now add images. We all love pictures (don't you have a photo album?). Although trite, it's true that a picture "speaks a thousand words." You want to see the new features of that automobile? You want to see what the living room of the house for sale in Canada looks like? Easy.

The Internet has taken images to a new level. Sites can use live images by connecting video cameras to the Internet. And a sense of 3D can be added with surround videos or virtual reality, in which you use your mouse to move through a space. Microsoft was one of the first companies to take advantage of the surround video format, in which you use your mouse to click an image and rotate the image for a complete 360-degree view. You can also zoom in and out and change the speed of rotation. Microsoft added this feature to its auto site, CarPoint (`http://carpoint.msn.com`), and it provides a very effective means of showing automobiles.

**More on Interactive Advertising**

Chapter 7, "Ad Creation: What Kind of Ad Should You Use?" provides more techniques and advice for the creation of interactive advertising.

Don't stop now! Let your customers use their ears. What new computer doesn't come with speakers? Because audio can easily be digitized, it can also be distributed over the Internet. When you combine images and sound, you have multimedia. Let the user select what he or she wants to experience, and you have interactive multimedia.

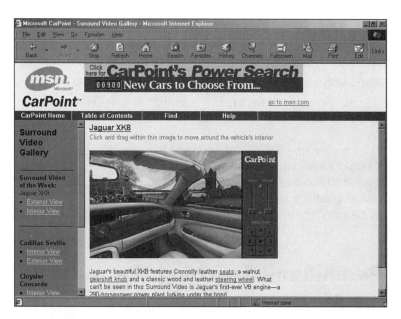

*The CarPoint Web site enables you to experience a little virtual reality as you use your mouse to explore a 360-degree view of automobiles.*

# What About Marketing in Cyberspace?

Most marketing efforts exist in the real world even if only for a limited time. A billboard stands over the highway and drivers see it. Your Yellow Pages ad is in a book. Newspaper and magazine ads take up physical space in the publication. Even radio and TV ads "exist" for 30 or 60 seconds.

Most traditional marketing and advertising reach out and hit people in the face. When you watch television or listen to the radio and an ad begins, you have four choices:

➤ Turn the channel.

➤ Hit the mute button.

➤ Go to the bathroom (unless you're in your car).

➤ Watch or listen to the ad.

With publications, it is similar. If you're reading an article that sits next to an ad, it's hard not to see the ad. You might not read every word, but you see the ad. There has been tremendous research and effort put into techniques that ensure the success of traditional advertising. For example, right-facing ads in magazines draw more attention than those on the left. Radio commercials in "drive time" cost more than other times because more people are in their cars listening at that time.

But what about the Internet? How the heck can you ensure that people hear or see your message? There are several techniques to get people to see your information, your marketing message, on the Internet.

➤ You have a Web site in which you have information for target markets.

➤ You strategically place your Internet advertising and marketing on sites that reach your target audience and then bring people to your Web site.

➤ You place your information on multiple Web sites people visit frequently.

➤ You send electronic mail messages or Internet newsgroup announcements to people and invite them to come to your Web site.

Remember how easy it is to ignore that TV ad? You might hit mute, but the ad still runs. With the Internet, it takes a fraction of a second (basically, a mouse click) for a user to move from your ad or site to something else (and with cyberspace, there is always something else). At any time, a potential customer might be able to choose from 20 radio stations or 60 cable channels, but with the Internet they have millions of choices.

# The Marketing Pendulum—Reaching the Individual and the Masses

There are, of course, many ways to market products and services. Broadly speaking, there is a pendulum that swings from marketing to individuals to marketing to a large number of people (also known as mass marketing).

In 1906, Alfred Carl Fuller began walking door-to-door in Connecticut to sell his handmade, twisted-wire brushes. And, as they say, "the rest is history." The Fuller Brush Company has been extremely successful. Mr. Fuller represents one side of the pendulum for marketing: one-on-one marketing. You take your message to one person at a time. This gives you the advantage of custom-tailoring your presentation to the needs and desires of that very small audience, one person. One-on-one marketing remains one of the most effective ways companies successfully reach their customers. It is, of course, very time-consuming and expensive. (As the next figure shows, The Fuller Brush Company has entered the electronic age with a full-featured Web site— one that still offers valuable information to individual buyers, but also reaches a global market!)

As the pendulum swings toward the middle, there is "target marketing." With target marketing, a message is created for a group of people. This group is larger than one person, but smaller than "the whole world." Say, for example, that you've got a hot, new rock club in Atlanta, Georgia. You create a radio commercial for people in their 20s and you air it on a rock-n-roll radio station in Atlanta. You're now reaching a lot of people who fit your "profile" for the perfect consumer of your product—the nightclub. Simple enough.

On the other side of the pendulum is mass marketing. The world really did not have great opportunities for either target or mass marketing until we had mass media— vehicles by which a message is sent to a large number of people simultaneously. Print publication was the first form of mass media. Consider this: Between 1700 and 1900, there were about 2,000 almanacs issued in the United States—Benjamin Franklin created his famous and profitable *Poor Richard's Almanac* in 1732. But it really wasn't until the 1880s that publications with a large subscriber base and advertising really appeared.

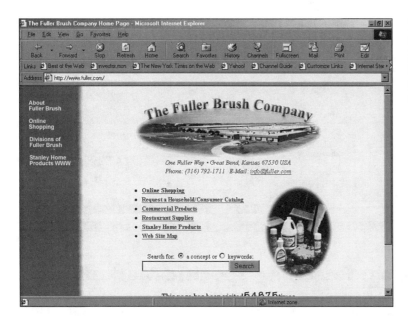

*The Fuller Brush Company that exemplified one-on-one selling now uses the Internet to reach customers—and a mass market.*

You might ask, "Why the 1880s?" It was at this time that the industrial age offered brand-name products for sale to the national market. Also, the increasing literacy and redistribution of income across groups of people in the United States created a market for mass circulation.

In 1883, Cyrus Curtis began the 10-cent *Ladies' Home Journal*. By selling advertising, Curtis could sell the magazine very inexpensively, even less than it cost to produce. As a result, the publication reached sales of nearly a million by the end of the century, and the concept of mass media reaching out to a large audience and using advertising as a revenue stream was born. *Ladies' Home Journal* continues to reach a large audience with its Web site (see the following figure). Indeed, *LHJ* tells potential advertisers exactly what the readers can expect when they use the Web site:

> *Ladies' Home Journal* (LHJ Online) provides clear and meaningful information to women around the world in an innovative and entertaining way. LHJ Online, through the use of the World Wide Web, helps our customers improve and enjoy their lives.

*One of the nation's first popular magazines, Ladies' Home Journal, has made the leap to the Internet.*

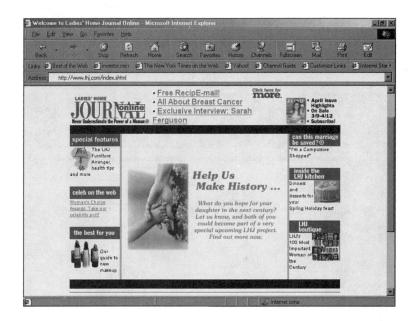

# Target Marketing: Reaching Specific Markets

In 1922, AT&T launched WEAF, its radio station in New York City. It broadcast what was perhaps the first paid commercial announcement, a ten-minute speech for a real-estate firm, The Queensborough Corporation. The ad cost $50. In the 1950s, television became a mass medium with three commercial television networks (you know them: NBC, ABC, and CBS).

What is very interesting, and important, is that all types of mass communication continue to have more and more competition. The number of magazines in circulation has increased from 700 in 1870 to more than 20,000 today. Television and cable channels are up from three in 1950 to more than 100 today. And Web servers (these are the computers that house Web sites—each server can have multiple Web sites) have skyrocketed from 270 in October of 1993 to more than 10 million today!

Information overload? Perhaps not. Two things are happening:

➤ First, an increasingly large, global audience, means that each publication, each network, each Web site can now focus on a smaller, more targeted audience and still reach a large number of people.

➤ Second, there is increasing demand on the part of consumers and business users to have information and entertainment tailored to their interests. Naturally, advertisers want to use mass media that targets specific groups of people. Also known as target markets and narrowcasting, this is an effective way to reach a group of people who share common interests.

We have Nickelodeon, where children can enjoy programs for children and advertisers can reach them. There's ESPN, where sports enthusiasts can watch sports and advertisers can sell products and services to people who like sports. Magazines are even crazier. There's *Campaigns and Elections*, the magazine for political professionals; *MBA Style*, focusing on the MBA job search and career-wear for men and women, and *Cruise Industry News*, a quarterly print magazine targeting people in the cruise industry.

But the Web represents the perfect medium for target marketing. If your company has a product or service designed for a specific purpose or audience, the Web can be a very effective marketing vehicle. For example, the Leading Authorities Speakers Bureau Web site (`http://www.leadingauthorities.com`) helps companies and organizations locate speakers who meet their needs.

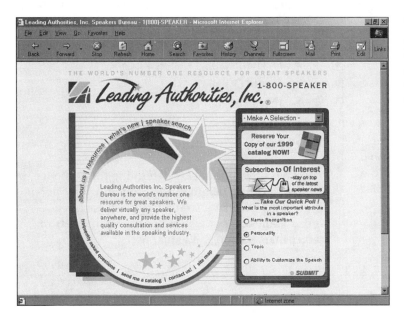

*The Leading Authorities, Inc. Web site reaches its target market with a Web site that helps companies and organizations find speakers.*

Not only do targeted cable channels, publications, and Web sites reach a specific audience, they also offer smaller companies an affordable vehicle for advertising to and reaching their target market.

So what's the best way to spend valuable advertising dollars? There are no "wrong" answers here, but some choices are more cost-effective than others are. If you are marketing a product that all the people in the world might enjoy (perhaps soda pop), then NBC and *People Magazine* and the CNN Web site are the way to go. But if you have an electrolyte-building sports drink, perhaps *Runners World* magazine and the ESPN Web site would be better.

# You Can Have It All: Market to the Masses, Market to the Individual

Who said you couldn't have your cake and eat it, too? From a marketing perspective, the Internet offers the best of all worlds. You can use both your Web site and your advertising to reach a mass market, a target market, or even one individual—all at the same time!

There are actually several ways that you can accomplish this. One of the best techniques is to design your Web site in such a way that from the home page, each target market or individual can quickly select choices that bring them to the information they desire. For example, the IBM Web site home page has the following links:

➤ Business Partners

➤ Developers

➤ Home Office

➤ Investors

➤ Small Business

➤ Job Opportunities

The Web user can quickly determine the audience to which he or she belongs, and jump into that portion of the Web site. So the site itself reaches a broad audience, but also supports the interests of target markets and individual users.

**Check This Out**

**More One-on-One Marketing**

Chapter 14, "Precision, Targeted, One-to-One Marketing," provides more information on how you can use Internet technologies for effective one-on-one marketing.

---

### The Least You Need to Know

➤ The Internet provides a cost-effective vehicle for global marketing.

➤ Consider the importance of language when you market to international audiences.

➤ Use the interactive aspects of the Internet and online services to help your customers locate information they need.

➤ Provide a multimedia experience with visuals and audio.

➤ Consider how you can market to both a large audience and individual customers.

# Chapter 2

# Who's Out There and What Are They Doing? Profiles of Internet Users

> **In This Chapter**
>
> ➤ Use demographic information to make decisions about Internet marketing
>
> ➤ Profile(s) of Internet users
>
> ➤ Global trends in Internet usage
>
> ➤ Learn how people use the Internet
>
> ➤ Conduct your own Internet market research

Webster's New World Dictionary defines *demography* as "the statistical study of populations"; that makes *demographics* the statistics that provide insight into groups of people. This chapter examines the demographics of the Internet. What types of people use the Internet? How many people use the Internet in different countries? Usage patterns are also examined to lead to an understanding of *how* people use the Internet. In other words, do users just madly surf the Net, or do they look for specific types of information? In addition, we offer some tips on how you can cost-effectively conduct your own market research.

## Why Are Demographics Important?

Demographic information has become a useful—indeed, *critical*—tool for the marketing profession. Why? Because if you can understand the quantity and types of people that use a communications medium (that is, the Internet), you can determine both how to reach your target market (existing and new customers) and how you might want to tailor your message for those individuals.

Demographic trends are equally important. In other words, your target audience might not be using the Internet today, but if the trends suggest they will be within 12 months, you should start planning your tactics. From a marketing perspective, there are two "big picture" aspects to Internet demographics:

➤ Demographics of people who use the Internet

➤ Demographics of people who use individual Web sites

The first represents users of a specific type of technology or media; the second represents users of specific types of content. To understand the distinction and importance of both, let's use an analogy.

### *The Television Analogy*

Statistically, 99.9% of the households in the United States have a television set. So, demographically speaking, everyone watches TV (and don't tell me that you don't!). The percentage of households that have cable television is a little less—approximately 65%. So, that means television involves two different technologies: broadcast channels and cable channels. (This doesn't even include technologies such as Microsoft's WebTV, which enables you to use the television to access the Internet.) Let's get back to our analogy. The broad technology here is television. And, statistically, we know that everyone watches TV—much like we will soon examine the "big picture" demographics of Internet users.

Now, what about individual TV viewers (or Web site users)?

We still need to determine what your target audience is watching and what Web sites they visit! Clearly, not everyone who watches cable TV tunes into the Animal Planet cable channel, but given the fact that the tag line for that channel is "The all animals, all the time television channel," you can probably assume that the people who watch it like, well, animals. So if your company makes dog food or offers safari trips, Animal Planet would be the perfect place to advertise.

What does all this mean? You want to begin your Internet marketing strategy by understanding the technology demographics. Is your target market using the technology today and/or will they in the future? After you've answered that, then you move into the area of content—how can you effectively reach your audience on the Internet? Which Web sites will they be using? The next few sections help you sort out these issues.

## The United States Leads in Internet Usage

The United States continues to lead the world in several areas related to the Internet, including the number of people who have the necessary hardware to use the Net and the sheer number of users who access it.

It was only a few years ago that the "average" Internet user was predominantly male, 24–35, above average income, and very interested in technology. Now, as the number of people in the U.S. who have Internet access continues to rise, we find that the demographics of Net users continues to move closer to the demographics of the population at large.

Of course, to get onto the Net you need a personal computer (at least that's how most people access the Internet). According to Jupiter Communications (http://www.jup.com) research, approximately 50% of U.S. households now own personal computers, but only 30% of these households are online. By the year 2002, the number of households with both PCs and online access will jump to 60%. These projections are consistent with research by International Data Corporation (http://www.idc.com), which projects an annual growth rate of online users in the U.S. to be at 28.5%. By the year 2002, IDC projects that 136 million users will access the Web in the United States. Clearly, if you've got half the population using the Internet, it is a medium that can effectively reach most target markets.

# The Internet Is Now a "Necessity"

America Online and Roper Starch Worldwide conducted a survey of 1,000 people in the U.S. who subscribe to online and Internet services from home. Fifty percent of those surveyed said that the Internet is a necessity, and two-thirds of Internet users would rather give up their phone or TV than Internet access!

In a press release, AOL Senior Vice President Marshall Cohen noted, "This study demonstrates that this new medium has firmly established itself among all age groups, from senior citizens to young adults, and is rapidly penetrating the everyday lives of people in all walks of life." Other interesting facts from this survey include the following:

➤ 71% of the online consumer population has been online for less than three years and 29% has been online for a year or less.

➤ 77% believe it has made their lives better.

➤ 71% of the online consumer population regularly or occasionally go online to get information about products to purchase both online and offline.

➤ 87% say they go online to communicate with friends and family.

➤ 65% of the interactive population is over age 35, is more likely to have graduated from college, to be married, and to have children under age 18, and represents a higher median household income than the American public at large.

➤ 26% of online users check email on vacation.

It's quite interesting that the Internet might actually have more allure than television. According to a Simmons online usage study, 37.1% of active Web surfers say they watch less television than they did before they got access to the Internet. Only 4.9% reported watching more (these people need to get a life!). The study also discovered that two-thirds of the people who access the Internet spend at least 10 hours a month online. This is one reason that many Internet service providers don't mind offering a $19.95 unlimited access package, because they know that the average user is not going to be online all day long. According to the Simmons study, of other communications media (such as print magazines, newspapers, and radio), television experienced the largest audience loss.

# A Few More Numbers

Many companies do research about Internet demographics. Sometimes the statistics are the same; sometimes they're not. A couple of factors influence the results of demographic studies:

➤ **The size of the sample (the number of people who are surveyed)** This can make a big difference. If you ask 10 people whether they like red cars or blue ones, all 10 (100%) might say red. Ask 1,000, and the statistics might be different. Generally, the larger the sample size, the more accurate the statistics.

➤ **The group of people whom you ask to take a survey** If you ask only people at the shopping mall whether they like shopping, the answer might be a resounding yes. But it would be better to ask a more diverse group (and, for that matter, random) if you are trying to find out what the general population thinks about shopping.

Of course, there are many other variables in surveys, as well. Consider, for example, that the manner in which a question is phrased can influence the answer. Nevertheless, if you look at the big picture, the general statistical trends between Internet surveys are fairly consistent.

Survey.Net (http://www.survey.net) is a Web site that conducts ongoing online surveys on different topics. (You can participate!) One survey, The Internet User Survey, asks some basic demographic questions, as shown in the following figure. As of this writing, about 3,500 people had taken the Internet User Survey.

*Survey.Net lets you participate in an ongoing demographic survey of Net users.*

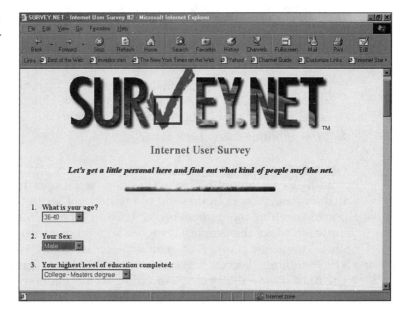

Some of the results are shown in Table 2.1 (all answers that represented less than 2% of the sample have been exempted). The results of some questions, such as "How do you access the Internet?" and "What do you use it for?" total more than 100% because you can select more than one answer in the survey.

## Table 2.1    Demographics of Internet Users

| Age: | 3.4% | *13–15* |
|------|------|---------|
| | 5.3% | *16–17* |
| | 14.5% | *18–21* |
| | 17.5% | *22–25* |
| | 16.9% | *26–30* |
| | 12.2% | *31–35* |
| | 8.6% | *36–40* |
| | 6.8% | *41–45* |
| | 6.3% | *46–50* |
| | 3.8% | *51–55* |
| Sex: | 62.5% | *Male* |
| | 34.6% | *Female* |
| | 2.8% | *No Answer* |
| Highest level of education completed: | 24.6% | *College—Bachelor's degree* |
| | 23.3% | *Some college* |
| | 17.8% | *College—currently enrolled* |
| | 12.3% | *College—Master's degree* |
| | 9.1% | *Some high school* |
| | 8.4% | *High school graduate* |
| | 3.2% | *College—PhD* |
| | 1.4% | *No Answer* |
| What is your average annual family income? | 17.2% | *No Answer* |
| | 9.8% | *$41k–$50k* |
| | 8.1% | *$51k–$60k* |
| | 7.1% | *$10k–$20k* |
| | 6.5% | *$81k–$100k* |
| | 6.3% | *$61k–$70k* |
| | 6.1% | *$26k–$30k* |
| | 5.9% | *$21k–$25k* |
| | 5.6% | *$71k–$80k* |
| | 5.5% | *$30k–$35k* |
| | 5.4% | *$36k–$40k* |
| | 4.8% | *Under $10k* |
| | 4.2% | *$101k–$120k* |
| | 2.5% | *$151k–$200k* |
| | 2.1% | *$121k–$150k* |
| What is your marital status? | 53.7% | *Never been married* |
| | 35.0% | *Married* |
| | 6.1% | *Divorced* |
| | 3.5% | *No Answer* |

*continues*

## Table 2.1   Demographics of Internet Users (Continued)

| On average, how much email do you receive? | | |
|---|---|---|
| | 21.9% | *3–5/day* |
| | 16.1% | *6–10/day* |
| | 14.8% | *1–5 a week* |
| | 14.2% | *1–2/day* |
| | 10.8% | *11–20/day* |
| | 5.1% | *21–30/day* |
| | 3.2% | *31–40/day* |
| | 2.2% | *41–50/day* |

To summarize, we see a fairly young group of users. Sixty-one percent of users are between the ages of 18 and 35, largely college-educated, more men than women, slightly more than 50% of the people have purchased something online, and most people use either a local Internet service provider for access or America Online.

Another series of online surveys of Internet users is conducted by the Georgia Tech Research Corporation. The 10th survey had 5,022 participants, was conducted from October 10, 1998, through December 15, 1998, and was endorsed by the World Wide Web Consortium (a group that develops common standards for the evolution of the Web). Not surprisingly, the profile of the average Internet user in this survey remains a highly educated, fairly upscale individual. The survey posed a wide variety of questions (too many to add here), some of which might have relevance for your specific business. For example, they asked people about their concerns related to Internet security. You can access the survey results at `http://www.gvu.gatech.edu/user_surveys`.

**Check This Out**

### Conduct Your Own Research

Chapter 11, "Marketing with Newsgroups," provides information about how you can do a little market research of your own by using newsgroups to discover how popular specific topics and product categories are on the Internet.

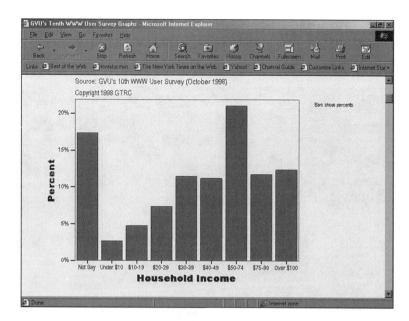

*The GVU survey posts results online, including bar charts such as this one about the annual income of users.*

# The Internet Gender Gap—Is There One?

According to Media Metrix (a research company), the male-female ratio of Internet users hit 50/50 for the first time in 1999. This is a big leap from three years ago, when 82% of Internet users were men. Another research firm, Forrester Research, has come up with some statistics about how men and women use the Internet (see Table 2.2).

## Table 2.2    Men and Women ARE Different

| Use of the Internet | Men | Women |
| --- | --- | --- |
| Visit company or product sites | 50% | 37% |
| Research products or services | 49% | 41% |
| Read newspapers and magazines | 32% | 26% |
| Shop | 24% | 16% |
| Play games | 16% | 19% |
| Visit family sites | 11% | 15% |
| Bank | 13% | 10% |
| Trade stocks | 5% | 2% |

Indeed, if you take a look at the types of sites and content available on the Web, sites increasingly target either both men and women, or women only. In fact, there are entire Web-based communities that focus exclusively on women; Women.com (www.women.com) and iVillage (www.ivillage.com) are two examples. These sites offer useful information on a broad range of subjects that include parenting, relationships, shopping, careers, and fitness. Wall Street believes that women and the sites that cater to them are valuable. Indeed, when iVillage went public, its shares opened at an incredible $95.88.

*iVillage is a Web site that targets the large number of female Web users.*

# Let's Not Forget Kids

Women represent a statistically important market segment (actually, the world population is composed of slightly more than 50% women), but there are other large market segments that include both sexes. One of these is children. Ask any parent who has a five-year-old and a computer whether the child likes to use the PC; we guarantee the answer will be "yes." (Perhaps it's not the scientific method for market research; it's my gut feeling and results from informal surveys.) Children are fascinated by computers. They enjoy the hand-eye coordination experience and the multisensory, audio-video-images aspects of the media. Indeed, the sale of software directed at children under the age of four grew by 50% in 1998, and was worth $13 million at the end of the year, according to PC Data, a market research firm.

But what about the Internet? As seen in Table 2.3, eMarketer (www.emarketer.com) predicts a surge in the number of children who surf the Net.

### Table 2.3   Growth of Numbers of Children on the Net

| Year | Millions of Children Online (Ages 3–17) |
| --- | --- |
| 1998 | 8 |
| 1999 | 18 |
| 2000 | 22 |
| 2001 | 30 |
| 2002 | 38 |

Again, the trend in increased usage by this age group is closely matched by an increase in the number of sites that have content or products for the members of this age group. Indeed, you can find and purchase a wide range of children's products including clothing, books, toys, and music. Disney, Toys 'R Us, and Nickelodeon all have extensive Web offerings for children. Another good one is Tiger Electronics' Web site (they make Furbys) at `http://www.game.com/furby`, which is designed for children (when you visit this site, your mouse pointer turns into a Furby, funky music starts playing, and you can talk to Furbys, read stories, or send your friends an electronic Furby postcard—now that's FurCool!).

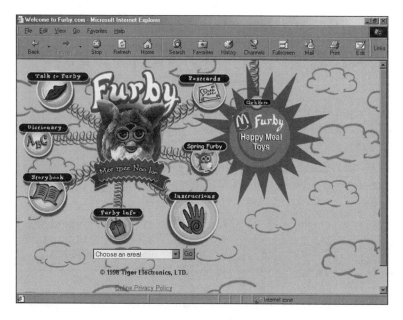

*The Tiger Electronics Furby site is created with kids in mind.*

# Seniors on the Net

The Internet does not discriminate according to age. More than 13 million U.S. adults over the age of 50 have Internet access today, and their numbers are growing rapidly, according to a study conducted by SeniorNet and Charles Schwab, Inc. The research was based on random telephone surveys of 600 adults, age 50 years and over. This number of online seniors represents approximately 16% of the total U.S. online population. Also of interest, 70% of the seniors who own a home computer also use the Web. The study took a look at usage and found that 72% of the seniors use email, 59% research issues, 47% conduct travel research, 53% access news, and 43% tap into weather information.

@plan is another online market research firm that added a few more pieces of information to the over-55 group. According to @plan's research, Internet users over the age of 55 are highly educated, affluent, and have a higher tendency to purchase products online. Compared to younger surfers, they found that this group is 85% more likely to purchase business equipment, 37% more inclined to make book purchases, and 27% more inclined to invest online. They also have the money to spend; 45% earn more than $75,000 annually, and 50% have investment portfolios that exceed $100,000.

When you think about it, seniors represent a great online audience. Many seniors (especially retired) have extra time with which to explore the Internet. They also enjoy communicating with friends and family. The Internet is also a great way to create an extended family and meet new friends. For example, the Golden Hub Senior Center, based in Fredericksburg, Texas, is a site where seniors meet, exchange ideas, and participate in activities. Information about current events and services are all available on that Web site.

# Not Only Are There Lots of Users, They're All over the World

Let's not forget the rest of the world! One of the important—and powerful— marketing traits of the Internet is that it is a global medium. And, the number of international users continues to rise rapidly.

Marketing professionals around the world now use the Internet to get a leg up on the competition. Likewise, users from around the world surf the Internet to locate information, products, and services.

**Rule of Thumb**

Countries with more host computers have more Web sites and probably more Internet users.

Let's take a look at some statistical evidence about the global reach of the Internet. There are several types of statistics: One identifies the number of host computers that each country has connected to the Internet. Generally, a *host computer* is a computer that is connected 24 hours a day to the Internet. Host computers usually house (or host) one or more Web sites, and these sites can either be sites that the general public can access, or private sites that might provide access only for employees of a company. Table 2.4 lists the number of host computers on the Net from a few selected countries.

**Table 2.4    Although Most Internet Host Computers Are in the United States, There Are Millions in Other Countries (Statistics by Network Wizards)**

| Country | Host Computers |
| --- | --- |
| Australia | 750,327 |
| Brazil | 163,890 |
| South Africa | 140,577 |
| Russian Federation | 130,422 |
| Poland | 98,798 |
| Mexico | 83,949 |
| Argentina | 57,532 |
| Chile | 22,889 |
| India | 10,436 |
| Egypt | 2,043 |
| Belize | 262 |
| Vatican City | 9 |

A second way to consider the global reach of the Internet is to assess the number of households and users that have Internet access in any specific country. Table 2.5 provides a sample of the number of users in different countries. Notice that the United States represents a significant percentage of users.

Check This Out

**Statistical Skewing**

Many people access the Internet from a school or from their business, so the total number of Internet users per country might be much more than the number of households.

**Table 2.5    Countries Around the World Are Experiencing Growth in the Number of Internet Users**

| Country | Percentage of Population or Households Online | Number of Users | Source |
|---|---|---|---|
| Australia | 18% of households | 4.2 million users | Australian Bureau of Statistics |
| Canada | 39% of adults online | 9.7 million users | CBC/Nielsen |
| Ireland | 11% of households | 250,000 users | Information Society Commission |
| Spain | 6.6% of households | 2.25 million users | Asociación de Usuarios de Internet |
| United States | 30% of households | 50 million users | IDC |

# How People Use the Internet

Internet growth and demographic statistics have told us a lot. We know millions of people representing a variety of demographic groups and target markets use the Internet today. We've also learned a few things about usage patterns—for example, that 59% of seniors use the Internet to research issues, that 37% of women use the Internet to visit company or product sites, and that 49% of men research products or services.

It's the usage patterns that provide the information you need to make marketing decisions. If you know how people use the Internet—what type of content they access—you can focus your online marketing efforts and advertising in those areas. One striking example of effective target marketing comes from the Super Bowl. Did you watch the Super Bowl? If you did, you probably saw a variety of ads for Web sites. According to Media Metrix, the companies that advertised during the Super Bowl saw a 48% increase in traffic to their sites compared with the Sunday before the game. Overall, men represented 81% of the visitors to the sites advertised during the Super Bowl (no surprise here). And traffic to football-related Web sites was estimated to be 2.7 million unique visitors the week following the NFL playoffs.

What is particularly interesting is how the companies that advertised Web sites during the Super Bowl actually received a double whammy—they got attention during the game, and they got people to come to their Web sites. Of course, a 30-second commercial during the Super Bowl is not an inexpensive marketing proposition. However, if your company makes a product or service for men, you might want to consider advertising on one of the Web sites that caters to football fans—ESPN, NFL, or SuperBowl.com.

In addition to sports, news and weather are also big draws on the Internet. Pew Research Center has done research about how people use the Net. Two years ago (when only 23% of U.S. adults were wired), technology stories represented the most popular online news stories. New research shows that the most popular online news attraction these days, however, is weather. They suggest this is a result of the fact that the Internet users now represent a broad cross-section of the American public. In their most recent survey, 64% of those polled went online to get news at least once a week. Again confirming the connection between traditional media and the Net, 41% of those people who got online news stories said they went online to get additional information about a story they saw in traditional media. Table 2.6 shows a breakdown of the types of information that people access when they get online news.

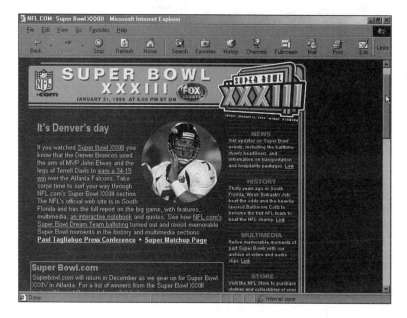

*Web users could go to www.superbowl.com to get live updates and player information during the Super Bowl.*

### Table 2.6 Pew Research Survey Showing Percentage of Online Users and the Types of News They Access

| Category | Percentage of News Users |
| --- | --- |
| Weather | 64% |
| Technology | 59% |
| Entertainment | 58% |
| Business | 58% |
| Sports | 47% |
| International | 47% |
| Health | 46% |
| Science | 43% |
| Politics | 43% |
| Local news | 42% |

*The popularity of online news makes sites such as MSNBC good vehicles for reaching Internet users with advertising (and stories).*

## News on the Net

Like the world, the Internet is "on" 24 hours a day, and users can access up-to-the-minute news at a variety of locations. In fact, thousands and thousands of newspapers, radio stations, and television stations (the traditional news outlets) now have Web sites. Table 2.7 shows some of the best national news Web sites; you might consider these sites when you develop your marketing media plan.

### Table 2.7   Popular Web Sites for News

| Television News | Web Site |
| --- | --- |
| ABC | http://abcnews.go.com |
| Bloomberg | http://www.bloomberg.com |
| CBS | http://www.cbs.com/navbar/news.html |
| CNN | http://www.cnn.com |
| CNN en Español | http://www.cnnenespanol.com |
| FOX | http://www.foxnews.com |
| MSNBC | http://www.msnbc.com |

| Radio News | Web Site |
| --- | --- |
| NPR | http://www.npr.org |
| MIT Station List | http://wmbr.mit.edu/stations/list.html |

| Newspaper News | Web Site |
|---|---|
| American City Business Journals | http://www.amcity.com |
| New York Times | http://www.nytimes.com |
| USA Today | http://www.usatoday.com |
| Wall Street Journal | http://www.wsj.com |
| Washington Post | http://www.washingtonpost.com |

### Local News Is on the Web

There is a very good chance that local newspapers, television stations, and radio stations have Web sites. Go to your favorite search engine and type the name or station call letters that you're looking for.

# Growth and Future of Electronic Commerce

Because this chapter is all about statistics and growth trends, we feel it's important to take a look at what's happening with electronic commerce. More than likely, if you have a Web site or are planning your Internet marketing strategy, you are, or will be, selling a product or service online. In fact, there's nothing wrong with having one of the goals of marketing be to increase sales.

Let's take a look at some of the trends in the world of electronic commerce. First, electronic commerce can be divided into two large categories:

➤ Consumer electronic commerce

➤ Business-to-business electronic commerce

The growth in the number of dollars spent online in both these sectors is going to be phenomenal. eMarketer (http://www.emarketer.com) offers a variety of reports on electronic commerce. In a recent study, projections for consumer spending online will rise from $1.8 billion in 1997 to $35.3 billion in the year 2002. Meanwhile, Forrester Research (http://www.forrester.com) predicts business-to-business commerce will reach $842 billion in 2002, up from $16 billion in 1997.

If you have products and services for consumers and want to sell them online, you are not alone. According to the National Retail Federation, in 1996 only 8% of retailers had an Internet site. This grew to 20% in 1997, and jumped to 26% in 1998. So even though the economic pie is getting larger, more companies want a piece of it. Indeed, Keenan Vision predicts that the number of merchants with an online presence will jump from 45,000 in 1999 to almost 6 million by the year 2003.

But where do people spend their online money? Well, you can literally purchase anything from automobiles to groceries via the Web. Big and small companies want to get on board. Macy's wants to have 10% of their sales online by the year 2000; Bloomingdale's now has 3,000 products available via the Web. At the Yahoo! online shopping center, there are more than 2 million products available from more than 27,000 stores!

*Bloomingdale's has some 3,000 products available online.*

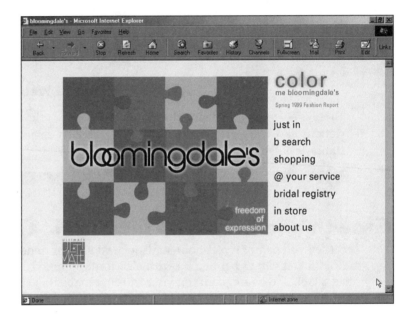

We will probably see some changes in Web shopping patterns over the next couple of years. Jupiter Communications' analysis for 1998 shows that the single largest shopping category was computer hardware—not difficult to believe when you realize that Dell Computers sells approximately $14,000,000 worth of computer equipment on its Web site EVERY DAY!

Table 2.8 shows some of the big shopping categories for 1998. The future? Predictions from eMarketer suggest that in the year 2000 the top four e-commerce categories will be travel, financial/insurance, entertainment/sports, and groceries—yes, groceries. eMarketer predicts that by 2002, some 7 million households will purchase groceries online. Don't believe it? Go to the Wild Oats Web site at http://www.wildoats.com and start shopping.

### Table 2.8   Computer Hardware Led the Shopping Categories in 1998 (Jupiter Communications)

| Category | Percentage of E-Dollars |
| --- | --- |
| Computer hardware | 30.1% |
| Travel | 29.6% |
| Books | 9.2% |
| Other | 31.1% |

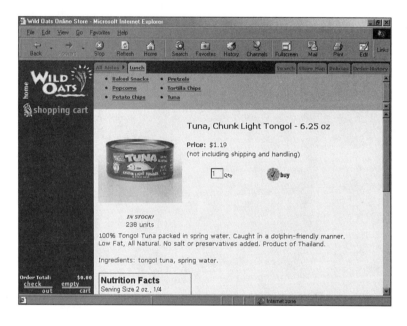

*A variety of food and health products is available at the Wild Oats Web site.*

When you combine the incredible growth in electronic commerce with the increase in competition, the importance and value of Internet marketing become even more significant. To effectively capture your piece of the combined consumer and business-to-business market, worth some $858 billion, you need to have effective online marketing.

## The Least You Need to Know

➤ An equal number of men and women are using the Internet today.

➤ The number of children who go online will reach 38 million by 2002.

➤ News and weather represent two of the most popular topics for Internet users.

➤ Electronic commerce is growing rapidly for both business and consumer purchases.

# Chapter 3

# Internet Marketing 101

> **In This Chapter**
>
> ➤ How marketing is different from advertising
>
> ➤ The marketing strategies that work for obtaining new customers or retaining existing customers
>
> ➤ The products and services that are best for Internet marketing
>
> ➤ How to analyze the marketing efforts of your competition

This book is about marketing on the Internet, but to be successful with Internet marketing, it is important to understand the scope, tools, and techniques of marketing. This chapter provides the groundwork for understanding how marketing tactics can be used on the Internet to obtain new customers, retain existing customers, and change perceptions.

## Who Should Market on the Internet?

It is a safe bet that your business has a listing, if not an ad, in the Yellow Pages. But not every business buys billboard or television advertising to promote the company, products, or services. So, the first question you might have is, "Should I market on the Internet?" We think that before you can answer this question, you need to answer a few other questions:

➤ Can I reach my target audience?

➤ Will I achieve my marketing goals (acquire new customers or retain existing customers)?

➤ Are my company's products and services suitable for Internet marketing?

➤ Are my competitors marketing on the Internet?

Ideally, your answer to each of these questions would be a resounding yes. However, it might be that simply having your competition on the Internet is reason enough to have a Web site and market on the Internet. The previous chapter provided information about the demographics of Internet users, which can help you answer question number one; this chapter helps you answer the other three questions.

# So What Is Marketing?

A textbook definition of marketing encompasses the entire process of creating and executing a plan to develop and sell your product or service. Marketing can play a role in product definition and development, packaging, pricing, promotion, and distribution—in other words, all aspects of successfully getting a product or service into the marketplace. If you calculate the expense of all these efforts, marketing costs average more than 50% of the total cost of consumer goods!

Product, pricing, promotion, and distribution are the four Ps of marketing (yes, I know distribution starts with a D). What does all this mean? Well, marketing plays a key role in the success of your company's products and services in the marketplace.

For most businesses, the role of marketing is more limited in scope because they can't afford to have a gigantic marketing staff (not that they wouldn't want to). Every company, from one-person shops to multinational conglomerations, has a function or department known as "Marketing Communications." The larger the company, the more individuals and departments can be devoted to specific aspects of marketing. For example, you might have an advertising department, a trade show department, a public relations department, and so on. Alternatively, you might personally be in charge of all these areas of marketing.

We like to think of marketing communications as a big umbrella. Under this umbrella, we put two categories:

➤ Branding

➤ Customer care

Everything that is done in all realms of marketing is designed to help you and your company achieve one of three goals:

➤ Acquire new customers

➤ Retain existing customers

➤ Change or create perceptions

Table 3.1 shows a breakout of whether the various aspects of branding and customer care enable you to meet the goals listed previously.

## Table 3.1 Marketing Communications Matrix

| Marketing Communications | Acquire New Customers | Retain Existing Customers | Change or Create Perceptions | The Internet Can Help |
|---|:---:|:---:|:---:|:---:|
| **Branding** | | | | |
| Packaging | ✕ | ✕ | ✕ | ✕ |
| Advertising | ✕ | ✕ | | ✕ |
| Direct mail | ✕ | | | ✕ |
| Trade shows | ✕ | ✕ | ✕ | ✕ |
| Public relations | ✕ | ✕ | ✕ | ✕ |
| Investor relations | | | ✕ | ✕ |
| Government relations | | | ✕ | ✕ |
| **Customer Care** | | | | |
| Event management | ✕ | ✕ | | ✕ |
| Customer service | | ✕ | ✕ | ✕ |
| Training | | ✕ | ✕ | ✕ |
| Product education | | ✕ | ✕ | ✕ |

The bottom line is that the Internet is a tool that helps you in all aspects of marketing communications.

*Campbell Soup company uses the Internet to effectively brand its products, reinforcing both product packaging and name recognition.*

*Campbell Soup also uses the Internet for customer care with product education (online recipes) and customer service (feedback forms).*

## What Can a Brand Do for My Company or Products?

For starters, a brand can help improve your bottom line both with investors and customers. In the "old days" (actually, as far back as the Egyptian dynasties of 3000 BC), the branding of cattle became an honored technique and art by which the ownership of specific livestock was recognized. In a similar fashion, branding as it relates to marketing is the process by which your company (corporate branding) or your products (product branding) are established in the minds of your customers, your investors, and your employees. By *establish*, we mean more than just "they remember the name." Everybody can remember "Disney." But the brand "Disney" delivers a message about company direction and leadership that says "good family entertainment." Customers recognize brands, and they often choose products and companies that have brand-recognition over those that do not.

Branding is a strategy. It establishes a viewpoint in the customer's mind about your company or product's message. Tactically, you support your branding strategy with advertising (newspapers, magazines, radio, billboards, Internet, and TV); and collateral materials which are print pieces, direct mail, telemarketing, and trade shows.

## Brand, Identity, and Image

Okay, we're on a roll! Let's try one more. Branding is different from your corporate image or corporate identity. You can control corporate branding, product branding, and corporate identity, but you have less control over your corporate image. Table 3.2 clarifies these differences.

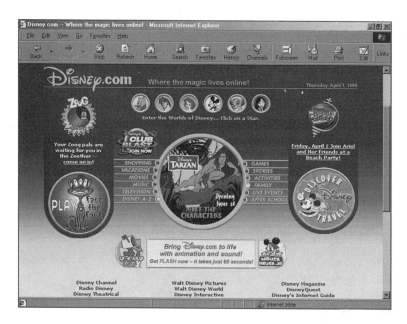

*Disney uses branding to effectively convey its position as a leader in family entertainment.*

## Table 3.2   Brand, Identity, and Image

| Brand | Identity and Image |
| --- | --- |
| Corporate Brand | The strategic direction of your company understood by employees, customers, and investors |
| Product Brand | Reinforces the name (quality and benefits) of a specific product |
| Corporate Identity | The visual representation of a company identified by logos and tag lines |
| Corporate Image | The general perception that consumers and the public have about your company |

Consider Microsoft as an example. As shown in Table 3.3, there are distinctions between the company's corporate and product brands, and the company's image and identity. Of course, the best of all worlds is when these four separate elements of marketing all reinforce one another.

## Table 3.3   Microsoft's Brand, Identity, and Image

| Brand | Identity and Image |
| --- | --- |
| Corporate Brand | A multinational leader in software creation and distribution |
| Product Brand | Microsoft Word, Microsoft Excel, and so on |
| Corporate Identity | Software that sets you free ("Where Do You Want To Go Today?") |
| Corporate Image | A large company that has a leadership position; Bill Gates and his empire |

## But My Company Is Too Small to Brand

Not true. There is not a single company, even a company of just one person, that is too small to effectively use branding. A hospital can brand itself. So can a grocery store, or a men's clothing store, or a car dealership. Even if you have only one product, you can brand it; in fact, you can use branding to establish yourself as a leader in a product category.

For example, with over 1,000 outlets and serving coffee to more than four million people a week, Starbucks Coffee used its brand, first, to establish a leadership position in selling quality coffee products at outlets. Then, it took the established brand into the retail market (you can probably find Starbucks products at your grocery store).

*Starbucks uses its well-known brand name to expand both its product line (ice cream, chocolate, bottled drinks) and distribution channels (convenience and grocery stores).*

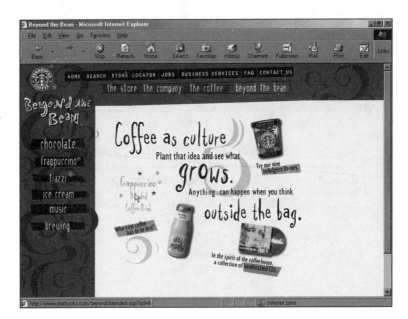

In fact, sometimes a product brand can become more powerful than the name of the company that makes the product. You have probably heard of the Slinky (that wonderful little toy that crawls down stairs). More than 250 million Slinkys have been sold, but do you know the name of the company that manufactures the Slinky?

You don't have to be a mega-company and spend millions of dollars to achieve effective branding. Branding involves knowing what makes your company or product stand above or apart from the competition (sometimes known as your *differentials*), and then consistently sending this message to your employees, investors, and customers.

What about the Internet? Branding is especially important on the Internet! In a matter of 10 seconds, a Web surfer can move through 10 different Web sites. Your brand needs to be strong enough that it stands out, shouting "My company! My product!" whenever people see it on the Internet.

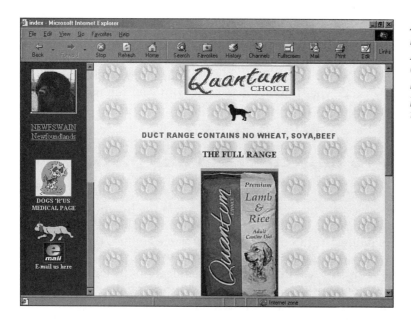

*Any size business can benefit from branding. Branding for Quantum Choice, a dog food made by a UK-based company, focuses on the all-natural ingredients.*

## A Brand Checklist

Following are some points that might help you reinforce an existing brand or bring a new brand to market.

➤ **Your company brand is more important than the product brand.**

   ➤ What sentence describes your company's vision, which is shared by employees, customers, and investors? A great exercise is to use your network to ask employees to write one sentence summing up the vision of your company, and see how close these statements are. If they are all over the board, you might need to work on establishing your company brand internally before you work on external branding.

   ➤ Does your mission statement reflect the corporate brand (and can you use it as part of the branding process)?

   ➤ What are five attributes of the company that differentiate you from the competition?

   ➤ What are five attributes of the company that most customers recognize as your strong points?

➤ **Your product brand is more important than the company brand.**

   ➤ What are some of the differentials of your product over the competition?

   ➤ How many products in the marketplace compete with your product? Obviously, the more products that are competing for "mind share," the more difficult and expensive it becomes to build a product brand.

➤ Does the product name reinforce the product attributes (for example, the way that *Pizza Hut* says *pizza*)?

➤ Does the product name already have name recognition, or are you building it from scratch? If you are just starting on branding a product name, then you need to integrate your Internet marketing with your full marketing plan.

# What Products Are Easy to Brand and Market on the Net?

Any type of product or service can have effective branding on the Internet. With branding, you focus on establishing, enhancing, or maintaining name recognition—and the name you are branding might be your company name and not the name of a specific product. For example, Chiquita has an extensive Web site. You can learn about the history of the company, see stickers for bananas, learn nutritional facts, learn interesting facts (did you know the inside of a banana peel can be used to polish leather shoes?), play games, download recipes, access press releases and annual reports, and discover employment opportunities.

Even though we learn that there are about 400 varieties of bananas, Chiquita's site doesn't actually *sell* them. Instead, Chiquita is focusing on branding and retention—the theory being that if the branding is successful, you might buy more Chiquita bananas the next time you go to the grocery store.

Chiquita's branding strategy seems to have worked (on the site, Chiquita notes that "When asked to name one brand of bananas, more consumers say 'Chiquita' more than any other brand"), and it has statistics to prove it (see Table 3.4).

### Table 3.4   Chiquita Brand Awareness Around the World

| Country | Brand Awareness |
|---|---|
| Germany | 100% |
| Italy | 98% |
| U.S. | 98% |
| Belgium/Luxembourg | 96% |
| Netherlands | 96% |
| Austria | 95% |
| Sweden | 94% |
| Greece | 93% |
| Switzerland | 93% |

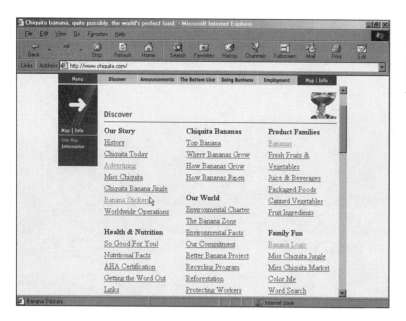

*The Chiquita Web site offers a lot of information about fruits and bananas to reinforce both the company and product brand.*

*Information-rich* products and services (that is, any products that the customer is likely to research before buying) are perfect for Internet marketing when it comes to enhancing sales (acquiring new customers). With information-rich products and services, you can easily use the Internet to convey a lot of detailed information for the prospective customer. Remember, with the Web, your prospects are coming to your site because *they* want to. They might be trying to make a purchasing decision, comparing your product to one of your competitors'. With most types of advertising, you have a limit to how much you can say about your product or service—the radio spot is only 30 seconds long; the quarter-page newspaper ad allows for only 200 words. Not so with the Internet. Talk up a storm!

What are some examples of information-rich products and services? Most technology-related products fall into this category, in that there are technical specifications that distinguish one product from another. California-based Telenetic Controls has a digital heating and air conditioning thermostat with telephone control operation—the TeleTemp 2000. The Web site enables potential customers to read about the features of the thermostat, and provides detailed operating instructions.

*Low-tech* products, such as houses, can also be information rich. Real-estate companies have harnessed the Net to provide prospective home buyers with all types of information about current listings: pictures of houses' exteriors and interiors, floorplans and room dimensions, neighborhood maps, taxes, and more.

**49**

*Learn detailed informa-tion about the benefits, features, and operation of the digital thermostat, an information-rich product.*

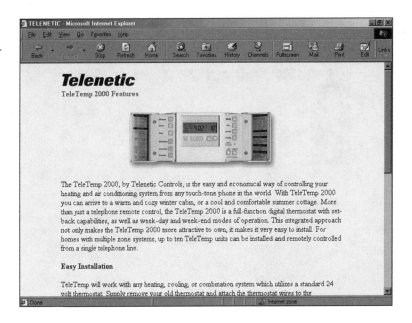

*There is a lot of useful information (text and images) that can help prospective customers evaluate a new home at the RE/MAX Web site.*

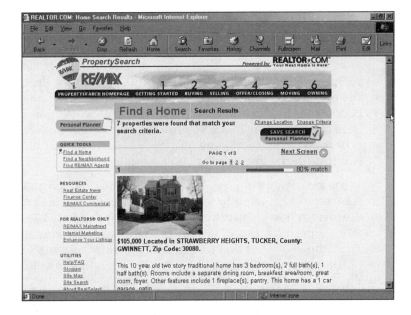

Another type of product that is perfect for Internet marketing (and sales) is one that is not widely available. In the case of this type of product, a Web site can represent a unique opportunity for the customer to acquire something that he or she could not get anywhere else. For example, the Hawaiian Greenhouse Web site at http://www.hawaiian-greenhouse.com helps you purchase Obake Anthuriums, Gingers, Birds of Paradise, and Dendrobiums—flowers that are not widely available.

Likewise, the Sundance Catalog site (yes, you'll find Robert Redford on the home page) at http://www.cybermart.com/sundance presents a wide range of gifts by artisans that you couldn't get anywhere else (unless you get the catalogs).

# Branding Your Company

As we have seen, many companies (both with consumer and professional products) focus on branding their company name. They do this in many different ways, with slogans that you hear again and again, advertising, and now Web sites and online marketing. Think about BASF, General Electric, Microsoft, and Sony. Although they might also brand individual products (Sony Playstation, Microsoft Excel, and so on), the focus is on the company. They want you to identify the company as the best company for any product in a given industry. That way, when you go to purchase software or a television set, you look for products by that company.

Indeed, their Web strategy reflects this approach. They promote a Web site for the company, not for products. First you go to the company Web site, and then select a product or product category. Table 3.5 shows how these companies use a Web marketing strategy that first brands the company, and then the products. In fact, even the URL (Web address) for the company becomes part of the branding process—and slogans are repeated on the home page.

## Table 3.5   Companies That Connect Products, Slogans, and Web Sites

| Company and Slogan | Web Site Address | Product Categories |
| --- | --- | --- |
| BASF "We don't make a lot of the products you buy, we make a lot of the products you buy better." | www.basf.com | Product search (BASF has thousands of products), Our Business |
| General Electric "We bring good things to life." | www.ge.com | Appliances, electrical products, leasing and loans, lighting, wiring devices |
| Microsoft "Where do you want to go today?" | www.microsoft.com | Backoffice, Developer tools, Office family, Windows family |
| Sony "Live in your world, play in ours!" (for Playstation) | www.sony.com | Music, movies, and TV shows; electronics, Playstation |

When should you brand your company more than your products? Corporate branding focuses on the strategic direction of your company—where you are headed, and what makes your company stand apart from the competition. Generally, business-to-business products, especially high-ticket items that run into thousands or hundreds of thousands of dollars, are branded with a company name. That's because your

**51**

customers are buying your products based on the knowledge and belief in your company, that all of your products and services are superior, and that you have excellent customer service.

*Large companies such as General Electric often brand the company with their Internet site, and then let users navigate to products and product categories.*

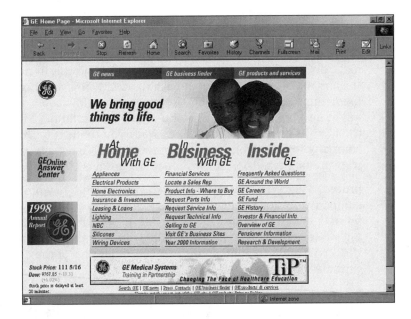

BASF is a great example, making thousands of products that range from chemicals to coatings to fibers to polymers. BASF's customers are other businesses that use these products. Advertising and branding focuses on the company itself. The slogan, "We don't make a lot of the products you buy, we make a lot of the products you buy better," provides awareness for the general public, and name recognition for people who make purchasing decisions in these companies.

# Branding Your Products

Other companies decide that it is to their advantage to brand products. If they have products that can be closely tied with the name of the company, then they can simultaneously brand both the company and the product. For example, America Online is the name of both the online service and the company. Wal-Mart is the name of the company and the store. Dodge Ram gets a double whammy, as you remember both the company that makes the truck and the truck itself.

You can, of course, also focus on branding only the product. A good company or product brand has many benefits. It reinforces the product in the customer's mind, but it can also help you weather a crisis. Remember the Tylenol cyanide-laced tampering case in 1982? Clearly, it was the proactive crisis management techniques that Johnson & Johnson used that helped prevent widespread panic. But the brand name had very strong recognition as a quality product. The company used the brand to help both retain existing customers and to create (and perhaps change) perceptions. Branding at work!

Even today, McNeil Consumer Products Company maintains this branding strategy for Tylenol. They have an extensive Tylenol Web site (http://www.tylenol.com) that stands alone rather than being part of a larger site for all of McNeil Consumer Products Company. The same company also makes Nicotrol, the smoking cessation product; as with Tylenol, you go to http://www.nicotrol.com rather than to a larger site. That's because McNeil Consumer Products Company knows that consumers are more familiar with the brand of the product than with the brand of the company.

To help with the branding process, these companies create slogans for the individual product and reinforce those slogans by putting them on the Web site. For example, who can forget 7-Up as the "un-Cola"? Well, go to the 7-Up site (http://www.7up.com), and you can click on links labeled "Historical Un Facts" or play "Fun Un Games." In this way, branding process for the product is carried throughout the Web site.

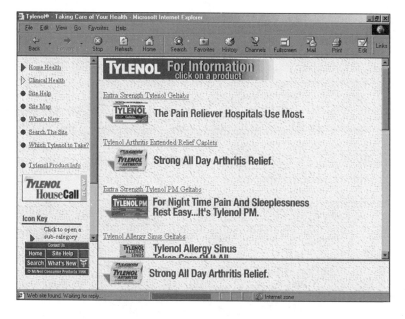

*McNeil Consumer Products Company focuses on Web sites that brand its products— such as Tylenol.*

When should you brand your product(s) instead of your company? Well, it might sound obvious, but when you want customers to remember the product more than the company when they make a purchasing decision. Product branding focuses primarily on name recognition of a product. You might connect product benefits or superiority to this branding, but the name is the main thing. This is often because when your customers are purchasing the product, they are in a situation where competitive products sit side by side as in a grocery store. Many consumer products, such as Sprite, Cheerios, Crest, and Listerine, are heavily branded. Clearly, it is better if your customer remembers the name of your product as they are about to grab an item off the shelf. Table 3.6 shows a few products where the company has created Web sites to brand the product instead of the company.

## Table 3.6    Companies That Brand Products

| Company | Product | Web Site |
| --- | --- | --- |
| Dr. Pepper/7-Up Inc | 7-Up | www.7up.com |
| Mars Inc. | Snickers Candy Bar | www.snickers.com |
| McNeil Consumer | Tylenol | www.tylenol.com |
| Southland Corporation | 7-Eleven Stores | www.7eleven.com |
| Time Inc. New Media | People Magazine | www.people.com |
| Tricon Global | Pizza Hut Restaurant | www.pizzahut.com |
| Warner Lambert | Listerine | www.listerine.com |

Anything—services, stores—can be branded. Pizza Hut, for example, wants you to think about its restaurants when you are driving down the highway, which is why its Web site is located at http://www.pizzahut.com instead of http://www.triconglobal.com. (Tricon Global is a Dallas-based company that has sales of almost $8.5 billion, and is the parent company for Pizza Hut, KFC, and Taco Bell.) Tricon Global doesn't really care whether the people who go to its restaurants remember its name. However, Tricon Global also has a corporate Web site that provides information for other target audiences, such as the investment community. The Pizza Hut site is linked to this corporate site, which is smart because potential investors might be interested in linking to the Pizza Hut site for more information about that restaurant chain, or vice versa. The bottom line? Brand your product if it is important, but make it easy for people to learn about your company.

*Southland Corporation brands its franchise, the 7-Eleven stores, not the company.*

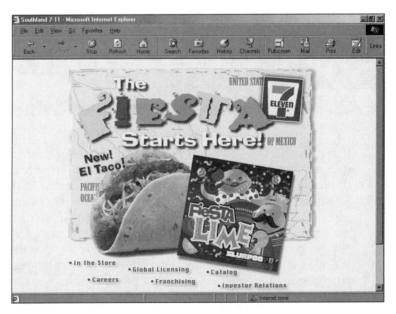

# Acquiring New Customers

This is probably the area that most people consider when they think about marketing. After all, who doesn't want to attract new customers and increase sales? Branding helps acquire new (and repeat) customers because your prospects remember your company name, product name, and attributes. You can also use other marketing tactics to elicit a spectrum of responses from a prospective customer. On one end of the spectrum, your prospect simply recognizes your name for future reference (as a rule-of-thumb, it takes approximately 20 impressions before someone remembers a new name, meaning that a prospective customer must see your name 20 times before he or she remembers it). At the other end of this spectrum, your customer places an order for one of your products or services.

When you use advertising to acquire new customers, be sure that you have a "call to action." In other words, you want your prospective customer to *do* something, such as

➤ Entering his or her email address and phone number (for a contest, to receive an email newsletter, and so on)

➤ Filling out an online survey or personal profile

➤ Printing out information about your products

➤ Sending in an email or form-based request for more information

➤ Requesting a follow-up call by a sales representative

➤ Placing an online order

These are examples of actions in which a prospective customer could engage in after viewing your Web site. For example, at the Clinique Web site, users can fill out a questionnaire that helps them determine their skin type. Then, Clinique offers to "remember" this information so it can recommend products in the future. Free samples are also offered as an incentive. The call to action is the request of fairly detailed user information (21 questions) that can be used for future marketing efforts.

*Clinique asks users to fill in personal profile information in exchange for information about products from which the user would benefit and product samples.*

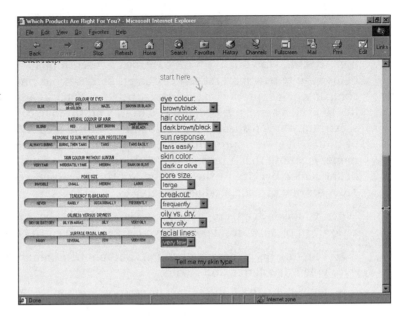

## Customer Retention

Customer retention focuses on getting return business from the customer. This can be more important than getting new customers. Existing customers have tried your products and services and hopefully like what they find; you want to keep these customers coming back. You can do this by helping customers answer questions or solve problems they might experience. This can be as simple as providing a phone number that they can call, or you can proactively tell customers about new products or special offers. Online stores have learned how to effectively use the Internet to get return business.

The online music store CDnow publishes an email newsletter (also known as an e-zine) that includes information about new music releases and discounts. I receive an email message titled *THE CDNOW UPDATE—William Eager's Edition*, that contains links that bring me directly to pages where I can learn about and purchase new products online.

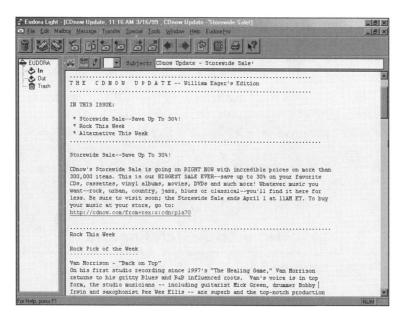

*CDnow uses an email newsletter to foster customer retention and increase sales.*

# Size Up Your Competition's Net Presence

If you are in business, you have competition—be it local, national, or international. It's that simple. Successful marketing depends upon your ability to have your customers and prospects think more about your product than the products your competition offers. Therefore, it's important that you know how your competition is using the Internet to attract *their* customers (your potential customers). You can use this "competitive intelligence" to fashion your own online marketing strategy.

The good news is that you can use the Internet itself to conduct your research about the competition. First, find out how many competitors you have out there in cyberspace. We guarantee you won't be alone. A Forrester Research study shows that there are five popular methods by which people locate a Web address and learn about companies on the Internet. Table 3.7 shows these methods and the percentage of people who use them. As you can see, search engines are by far the most popular method.

### Table 3.7   How Internet Users Locate Web Sites

| Method to Locate Web Sites | Percentage of Population |
| --- | --- |
| Search engines | 57% |
| Email messages | 38% |
| Other Web sites | 35% |
| Word-of-mouth | 28% |
| Magazine ads | 25% |

Let's use the tools that your customers use to learn about your competition. Table 3.8 lists three popular search engines with results for searches for a type of company (a flower store in Boston) and a type of product (a water filter). Let's use them to hunt for some information about your competition. The goal of this exercise is threefold:

➤ Find out how many Web sites potential customers are presented with when they use the most popular method of locating companies and products on the Net.

➤ See whether the companies or products that you consider to be direct competition have a Web presence.

➤ Some search engines display banner ads for companies that match search criteria, so you might find some of your competitors' online ads.

## Table 3.8   Finding Sites with Search Engines

| Search Engine | Flower Shop in Boston | Water Filter |
|---------------|----------------------|--------------|
| Snap | 0 | 7035 |
| AltaVista | 2 | 7555 |
| Yahoo! | 14 | 13 |

Despite the fact that these searches asked for only those entries that exactly matched the phrases entered, both Snap and AltaVista still found thousands of Web sites that match *water filter*. That's because the phrase could still be part of a wide range of choices, such as *water filter system* or *water filter camping*.

The phrase *flower shop in Boston*, however, is much narrower. In fact, a user might try many variations, such as *Boston flowers*. The goal of your search for this exercise is to narrow down the results to the sites that truly are competitive.

Here are a few tips to help with the search process:

**Check This Out**

**Start the Engine**

We'll learn more about how search engines provide results and how your site can get listed in search engines in Chapter 8, "The Role Search Engines and Directories Play."

➤ Be as specific as possible. For example, if you have a Lexus auto dealership in Dallas, type in Lexus dealership Dallas not Lexus or auto dealers.

➤ Try a couple of different searches with phrases that describe your products or services.

➤ Type in the exact name of your known competitors.

➤ Use the advanced search options provided by many search sites (you'll usually find a link for an advanced search on the search site's home page).

Table 3.9 is left blank so you can use it for your own research. Try several different search phrases.

## Table 3.9 Competitive Search Checklist

| Search Engine | Search A: # of Sites | Search B: # of Sites |
|---|---|---|
| AltaVista<br>http://www.altavista.com | | |
| Excite<br>http://www.excite.com | | |
| Go<br>http://www.go.com | | |
| HotBot<br>http://www.hotbot.com | | |
| Infoseek<br>http://www.infoseek.com | | |
| Lycos<br>http://www.lycos.com | | |
| Snap<br>http://www.snap.com | | |
| Yahoo!<br>http://www.yahoo.com | | |
| Webcrawler<br>http://webcrawler.com | | |
| Number of direct competitors found to have Web sites: | | |

### The Least You Need to Know

➤ Decide whether it is better to brand your company or your products.

➤ Use your Web site (even your address) to enhance your branding.

➤ High technology and information-rich products are perfect for Internet marketing.

➤ Determine whether you are acquiring new customers or retaining existing customers (or both) with your Internet efforts.

➤ Use search engines to find out what your competition is doing on the Internet.

# Chapter 4

# Marketing in Cyberspace: Unique Aspects of Internet Marketing

---

### In This Chapter

➤ Key similarities and differences between online and offline marketing

➤ The importance of selection and registration of your site's Web address (or domain name)

➤ The vocabulary and metrics that help you evaluate the cost of Internet marketing efforts

---

By and large, marketing principles are similar across industries, disciplines, and media. Nonetheless, there are unique characteristics, special considerations, and even simple language differences from sector to sector.

Just as accountants need to master different ways to account for depreciation in manufacturing companies or depletion in oil and gas companies, we need to understand a few topics unique to Internet marketing.

## It Works Both Ways

The Internet has returned power to the consumer. He (or she) chooses when he visits, what he views, how often he stays, and what he buys—all at his convenience. And he expects you to be right there with him.

For the first time, businesses can interact with customers one-to-one, not just to deliver information or drop off a brochure. Collecting and acting on customer input and feedback are easier than ever before. Businesses now have the ability to respond to the market, build new products, and provide better service with agility and creativity. And this is all happening in real-time. The expectation is that everything is current, you reply immediately, update information in seconds, and refresh data.

# Hit the Bull's-Eye: One-to-One Marketing

This can be the most useful opportunity the Internet affords you. It's become clear that targeting is essential for success in digital marketing: the need to attract users, engage their interest, be sure they return, learn about their preferences, and relate back to them with a personalized product or service

An analysis of 95 Fortune 500 consumer marketing companies with product- or service-related Web sites shows that most still treat interactive media like any other traditional marketing channel. What's left on the table is the unparalleled ability to develop and manage your customer relationships. Don't miss the opportunity to identify each user individually, tailor services for each, and deliver exactly what he wants.

**Holy Grail of Marketing**

Chapter 14, "Precision, Targeted, One-to-One Marketing," provides more details about how you can implement personalized marketing.

# To New Heights: Accountability

Results for Internet marketing can be measured, and user activity can be monitored, with a greater accuracy than with virtually any other media. Whether online or offline, you can't manage your business unless you can track it. And with the Internet, you can learn when your customer arrives, who he (or she) is, how he shops, what he wants, and how he wants to do business with you.

# What's in a Domain Name

Let's talk about something you will find nowhere on the planet except on the Internet: the domain name. A domain name is the place where your customers will find you, your home page, your Internet name. Yahoo! chose www.yahoo.com as its domain name. A domain name is more than just your Web site address (also known as a *URL* for *Uniform Resource Locator*). It is your brand; it is your signature online, and should appear on every business card you hand out, every invoice you send, and every proposal you deliver. So invest in the process of choosing your domain name. Engage your colleagues in the break room. Talk it up with friends at the ball game. When you've got your top five or eight names, say them out loud. Go ahead, say your URL and "dot com" after it to see how it sounds. If you're not proud to say it and excited to send your customers there, you won't be able to build a successful business around it.

*The Happy D Ranch Worm Farm has a great Web site at www.happydranch.com. But when you read the domain name, you have to take a minute to ask yourself, "What's a dranch?"*

The biggest decision in this process is whether you choose your company or product name as your domain name. No easy answer here. If you are a service company or have a large inventory of products, it is easier to stick with your company name. If creating brand awareness or developing recognition or loyalty around your product is your goal, think about how to represent that product in your domain name. There are a few other options. Say you have a company that makes hats, "Johnson's Hat Factory." Try

➤ Any reasonable variation of your company or product name. (www.hatfactory.com)

➤ Your company slogan or tag line. (www.hatsoff.com)

➤ A trademark. (www.smarthat.com)

➤ Wordplay. (www.onyourhead.com)

Avoid

➤ Characters that are hard to find on a keyboard, or a URL that is too long. (www.johnsonshatfactory.com)

➤ Any address too confusing for the average person to remember. (www.johnsonshf.com)

*The Joy of Socks company promotes a wide variety of hosiery and other foot apparel on its site.*

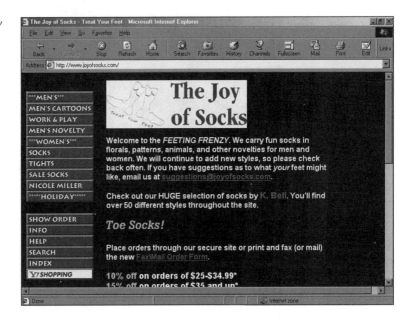

# What Does "Dot Com" Mean, Anyway?

The very last part of a Web site address (the .net or .com) is known as a *top-level domain*. These define either the type of organization or the geographic location of the address. There are seven top-level domains (shown in Table 4.1).

### Table 4.1   Domain Name Extensions

| Name | Type of Organization |
| --- | --- |
| .com | Commercial |
| .edu | Educational |
| .gov | Government |
| .int | International |
| .mil | Military |
| .net | Network |
| .org | Organization (commonly nonprofit groups) |

Obviously, most businesses are going to have a URL that ends in .com. In fact, because there are so many .com sites, most people just expect that your addresses ends in .com. Unfortunately, the exponential growth of the Web means that many of the **good** names are taken; we need more suffixes. Although no final decisions have been made, proposals have been submitted for several new top domains (see Table 4.2).

### Table 4.2 Proposed Domain Name Extensions

| Name | Type of Organization |
| --- | --- |
| .arts | Cultural and arts |
| .firm | Business |
| .info | Information services |
| .nom | Personal names |
| .rec | Recreational |
| .store | Stores |
| .web | Organizations related to the Web |

# How to Get Your Domain Name

After you've decided what you want your domain name to be, acquiring that domain name involves two processes:

**1.** First, you should conduct a search to determine whether that name is already taken.

**2.** Second, you need to formally register and pay for this name so you own it.

Following is an overview of the process of locating, registering, and activating a new Internet domain name (more detailed instructions follow):

**1.** Perform a search at www.networksolutions.com to find out whether the domain name you want is available.

**2.** Contact your Internet service provider and arrange for domain name service (see the following Techno Talk).

**3.** Review Network Solutions' registration policies and billing procedures.

**4.** Fill out a registration template.

**5.** The template is processed (you are notified if there are any problems).

**6.** You receive email that tells you the process is complete.

**7.** The information for your new domain is added to InterNIC's Whois (the lookup) database (so other people don't register your name).

**8.** Network Solutions sends you an invoice (you can also pay online with a credit card).

*Check This Out*

**Network Solutions**

Network Solutions, which offers InterNIC registration services, is the company that currently registers most of the domain names (and the important .com names). You'll find this company on the Web at http://www.networksolutions.com.

9. Network Solutions sends you a renewal notice 60 days before the two-year anniversary of the registration.

### Techno Talk

### Domain Name Service

In reality, the "address" of a computer on the Internet consists of a string of numbers (such as **192.45.24.3**), called the *Internet Protocol (IP) address*. Domain names provide the "plain-English" versions of these addresses, making them easier for people to remember, but the Internet itself uses IP addresses.

Therefore, for you to be able to use a domain name, the Internet must use computers known as *name servers* to translate domain names into their corresponding IP addresses. This process is known as *resolution*. Most Internet service providers have name servers, so they can provide this important names-to-numbers translation.

If your ISP does not have domain name service, InterNIC will not process your registration, which means no one will be able to use your domain name to find your site on the Internet. (They could, however, use your IP address; however, IP addresses are awfully hard to remember, and just don't resonate the way "microsoft.com" does.)

## Searching for Domain Names

### Check This Out

### Two-Year Registration

You can pay for a two-year registration. After the two years are up, you can renew the registration for another two years, ad infinitum.

Most of the great names that end in .com have already been taken, so your first order of business is to see whether the name you want is available. You could sit at your computer with your browser and type in names such as www.groovy.com (this is actually a real address). Unfortunately, this would take a long time, and besides, even if you don't find a site that uses the domain name you want doesn't mean that someone doesn't own that name. (That site might just not be up and running yet.) The better route is to go to the Network Solutions Web site and perform a quick search. To search for a domain name, perform the following steps:

1. Go to http://www.networksolutions.com.

2. Type your proposed domain name in the **Search the Database of Registered Domain Names Using Whois** field (Whois is a database that contains domain names and who owns them).

3. Click **Search**.

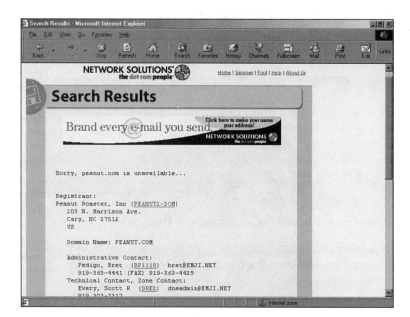

*A search for* peanut.com *shows that someone already owns the domain name.*

## Check This Out

## Other Options for Your Domain Name

You must type the name with the top-level domain after your name. For example, you could try dog.com, dog.org, or dog.net (all taken, in case you were wondering). Also, you do not need to use the http://www for the search.

### Be Creative with Domain Names

You might need to try several names before you find one that is available. Sometimes combining words (such as dogsmile.com) works.

### Purchasing the Name from Another Business

If the name you want is taken, you might be able to purchase the rights to buy the name from the current name holder. If a name you try has already been taken, Network Solutions tells you who owns the name, and provides an address and phone number you can call to try to buy the rights. Also visit www.domainsauction.com to bid on names that may be taken but fit well in your branding strategy.

After you've found some available domain names that might work for you, be sure to search the Web to compare them with other domain names already on the Web. You might come across companies or products whose domain names are too similar to the one you want to use. Be sure it doesn't sound like or look like a competitor's or like some unsavory destination that is far afield from where your customers want to be. This is a judgment call. Remember, it's your decision, but you should have your eyes wide open.

## Registering Your Domain Name

After you decide on a name that is actually available, you need to register it. To do so, perform the following steps:

1. Go to http://www.networksolutions.com.
2. Click the **Register a Domain Name** link.
3. Follow the onscreen instructions and forms for your registration.

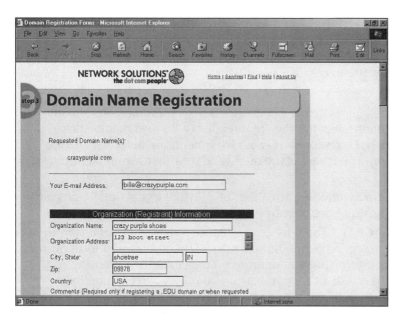

*When you find an available domain name, the Network Solutions Web site helps you complete the registration process with a series of onscreen forms.*

Choosing and registering your domain name is an important part of your branding and, ultimately, of your online presence, so you should invest in the process. We've given you a road map that helps you do it yourself, but if you are interested in hiring a third-party provider to handle the details, there are a number of options for you.

# Counting, Counting, Counting: Internet Marketing Terms

There are many terms and concepts that are unique to marketing on the Internet. Understanding these terms helps you when you're talking to your Internet service provider or advertising agency about the success of your site and your marketing efforts. Let's learn a few terms that specifically relate to measurement of traffic, costs, and revenues.

**Registration Fees**

As of May 1, 1999, the registration fee for domains in .com, .org, or .net runs $210 (U.S.). This fee covers the cost of the initial registration and updates to your domain name record for two years.

➤ **Clickthrough**   The act of clicking on a banner or other ad that takes the user through to the advertiser's Web site. Used as a counterpoint to impressions to judge the response-inducing power of the banner.

➤ **Clickthrough rate (CTR)**   The response rate of an online advertisement, typically expressed as a percentage and calculated by taking the number of clickthroughs the ad received, dividing that number by the number of impressions, and multiplying by 100 to obtain a percentage:

20 clicks/1,000 impressions = .02×100 = 2% CTR

Historically used as a measurement of an ad's effectiveness based on the idea that online promotions do what they're intended to do—get you to click. Recently, clickthrough rates for banner advertisements are dropping and are being questioned by advertisers as the only valid measurement of ad pricing and effectiveness.

➤ **Clickstreams**   The electronic path a user takes while navigating from site to site (or while navigating from page to page within a single site).

➤ **Cost per action (CPA)**   The price paid by an advertiser for each action that a content site delivers. An *action* might be a sale, a lead, a successful form fill-out, a download of a software program, or an e-commerce sale of a product. The action, price, and terms of a CPA purchase are mutually agreed upon by the advertiser and content site. Such a purchase typically involves a back-end tracking system that enables the content site to view clicks and actions every 24 hours. (See also *Cost Per Sale.*)

➤ **Cost per click (CPC)**   The price paid by an advertiser to a content site. When buying on a cost-per-click model, the advertiser and content site have mutually agreed that the content site will continue to display the advertiser's ad creative until a certain number of clicks have been delivered—the amount purchased. This pricing model typically ranges between 10 cents CPC up to $2 CPC and, as with other forms of online advertising, is dependent on content, audience reached, and targeted delivery (untargeted being lower priced, targeted to an affluent audience being at the high end of the rate scale).

➤ **Cost per sale (CPS)**   The price paid by an advertiser to a content site for each sale that results from a visitor who is referred from the content site to the advertiser's site. This type of buying model is typically tracked with cookies, where the cookie is offered on the content site and read on the advertiser's site at the success page after successful completion of one transaction/sale. (See also *Cost Per Action.*)

➤ **Cost per thousand (Roman numeral M) impressions (CPM)**   The price paid by an advertiser for a content site displaying its banner 1,000 times. In traditional media (TV, radio, and print), CPM is also used, but it is based on viewership.

➤ **Effective frequency**   The number of times an ad should be shown to one person to realize the highest impact of the ad without wasting impressions on that individual.

➤ **Effective reach**   The number of people who will see an ad the most effective number of times.

➤ **Exposures**   See *Impression.*

➤ **Hit**   A downloaded file as recorded in a server log. A hit is probably the least valuable and most misunderstood metric around. A *hit* does not imply a pair of eyeballs or even one eyeball; rather, a hit is a downloaded file, which refers to any graphic or any page. Therefore, a page with 8 graphics would equal 9 hits.

➤ **Impression**   A unit of measure. One set of eyeballs glancing over one banner counts as one impression, whether they are the same pair of eyeballs or not.

➤ **Opportunity to see (OTS) (also known as pageview)**   A *pageview* is an OTS, but not necessarily an impression. The page can be downloaded, but if the banner is located at the bottom of the page and the visitor does not scroll down, the banner is not seen.

➤ **Pageview**   When a browser retrieves a Web page. Pageviews are often used to track the number of impressions a banner gets.

➤ **ROI (return on investment)**   All businesspeople understand this concept; it's evaluated to make decisions about virtually every activity, whether buying a backhoe or leasing a plane. And every ad agency has adopted this concept as the NEW measurement of a campaign's efficacy, finally overcoming some of the shortfalls of the clickthrough. It will be a different calculation for your business than it is for your neighbor's, but calculate we must.

The RelateNetwork from Creativision offers software that tracks the user's activity *after* the clickthrough. Reports tell you how many orders each advertisement or link generated, along with the actual sales revenue.

➤ **Visit (also session)**   A completed visit to a Web site by a surfer/viewer/visitor.

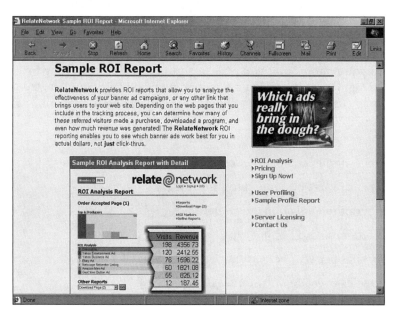

*RelateNetwork software tells you which ads and links brought new revenue to your site.*

# New (and Not-So-New) Marketing Stuff

There are a few more definitions that you should add to your Internet marketing dictionary. These terms and their concepts relate more to your marketing strategy:

➤ **Attrition (also known as churn)**   Occurs when a customer terminates his or her relationship with a service provider. Marketing efforts usually focus on minimizing churn because the cost of bringing a customer back is usually much greater than the cost of retaining the customer in the first place.

➤ **Banner ad**   Typically a rectangular graphic element that acts as an advertisement on the Web and entices the viewer to click on it to access further information, typically on the advertiser's Web site.

➤ **Customer segment**   A group of prospects or customers who are selected from a database based on characteristics they possess or exhibit.

➤ **Database marketing**   Strategic tool that provides for the collection and analysis ("slicing and dicing") of self-reported customer information used to profile, retain, and improve service for those customers. The goal is to segment customers, predict their behavior, and lead them to a call-to-action such as an order, reply, or inquiry.

➤ **Data mining**   Activity of searching large volumes of data to construct models for patterns that accurately predict customer behavior. A *data warehouse* is a database that stores consumer data collected from a variety of sources.

➤ **Interstitial ad**   A class of ad that pops up in a window between page loads. The window can display for a given time and then go away without annoying the viewers by requiring them to close the window manually.

➤ **Lifetime value of the customer**   Okay, so this concept is as old as the hills. But this is truly the heart of the matter. This proposed method to calculate a customer's value to you requires that you make assumptions, and then plug in the numbers. Cheri Sigmon of Justin Thyme Marketing offers this template; try to calculate your own customer's value by filling in numbers appropriate for your business.

    A.    Average sale = _____

    B.    Number of sales per year per customer = _____

    C.    Number of years customer buys from you = _____

    D.    Number of referrals from customer = _____

    E.    % of referrals who become customers = _____

    F.    Gross sales per year per customer (A × B) = _____

    G.    Gross sales over life of customer (F × C) = _____

    H.    Referrals who become customers (D × E) = _____

    I.    Gross sales from referrals (G × H) = _____

    J.    TOTAL VALUE of satisfied customer ( G + I ) = _____

➤ **Opt in/Opt out**   An adjective that describes marketing promotions that give visitors an opportunity to join in or not. Campaigns can be launched via email and on the Web site. The industry is a bit defensive about the fast growth of the call for consumers to volunteer to receive advertisements or other marketing programs. Concerns arise that email will begin to smell like junk mail and get thrown in the garbage.

➤ **Sponsorship**   A form of advertising in which a content site such as a chat, forum, newsletter, and so on is sponsored by an advertiser that targets the same audience as the content publisher. Sponsorship might prove more valuable than other types of advertising because the viewer has come to the page to read the content and also sees the "advertising." Table 4.4 indicates that sponsorship will be an increasingly popular form of Internet marketing.

## Table 4.4   The Mix of Advertising Today and Tomorrow

| Percentage of Revenue Forecast | 1998 | 2003 |
|---|---|---|
| Banners | 60% | 40% |
| Sponsorships | 30 | 40 |
| Interstitials | 10 | * |
| Next-generation ads | N/A | 20 |

*Source: Jupiter Communications*
*\*Next-generation ads include interstitials in 2003 estimate.*

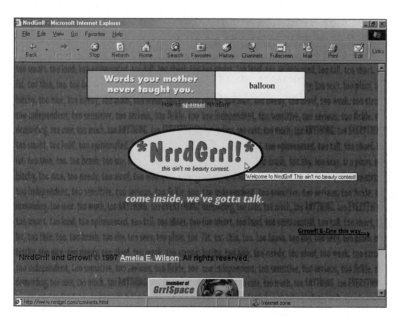

*Sites such as NrrdGrrl!, for women ages 15–35, encourages sponsorship as an advertising opportunity.*

73

➤ **Stickiness**  The state of being sticky. A measure used to gauge the effectiveness of a site in retaining individual users. The term is typically used to describe all features, content, navigation, and use of multimedia technologies used to extend a user's visit. Just a new adjective to describe a well-designed and conceived site.

➤ **Target marketing**  Concept that uses extensive data about customers' wants and behaviors to craft a narrowcast version of each marketing message. The objective is to understand each customer well enough to customize exactly the product or service that he needs. This is not a new concept; it's only gaining popularity because the Internet offers better data collection and user behavior measures that make targeted marketing easier.

# Use What You Know

How exactly can you take these concepts and apply them to your Internet marketing strategy or Web site? Here are a few ideas:

➤ Define your goals.

➤ Chart a course to achieve them.

➤ Measure as best you can.

➤ Do the math on what you're willing to pay to get and keep a customer.

Statistics and metrics continue to change. You must interpret the numbers, tweak them, and interpret them again. Cost per-anything is mushy. This is a buyer's market, and you should be prepared to negotiate everything.

The Internet has changed things for one-to-one marketing. It's like customer loyalty programs on steroids. Take advantage of the tools that make it easy to identify your best customers, differentiate and segment by needs and value, interact with them so you know what they've done and can predict what they probably will do, and then customize what you deliver.

# Who Measures What?

We've taken an initial look at how to measure and analyze ad effectiveness and site traffic to improve the return on investment in your online business. We've learned that there are many ways to talk about this topic, but no common language that explains how these disparate facts and figures work together. But there's a move afoot to bring order to the chaos.

The Future of Advertising Stakeholders, otherwise known as FAST, is a broad-based industry group that focuses on accelerating the development and use of digital advertising, and standards for advertising. FAST (http://www.fastinfo.org) has more than 600 individual members that work in the following industries:

➤ Advertising

➤ Advertising agencies

➤ Online media companies

➤ Technology enablers

One of the goals of FAST is to accelerate the use of digital advertising through a series of voluntary guidelines. Here's a broad summary of the progress of the FAST committee:

➤ Move toward a single measure that compares to other media. Something close to *opportunities to see* (OTS).

➤ Identify a way to exclude international and under-18 audiences from audience reports, because domestic adult is the category against which ads are bought.

➤ Consider the viewpoint of the ad, the site, and the user in a single standard.

➤ Introduce best practices and ethical standards such as full disclosure, user confidentiality, and an independent audit capability.

---

### The Least You Need to Know

➤ A well-conceived choice of your domain name is a critical component of your branding strategy.

➤ Measuring the success of your marketing plan is as important online as it is offline.

➤ Success online will be measured more by your ability to move customers to action and less by the number of eyeballs that see your site.

---

# Part 2

# Nuts and Bolts Internet Marketing

*One of the characters on the television show* The A Team *used to say, "I love it when a plan comes together." The chapters in this section will help you create the plan you need for successful Internet marketing. Getting people to your site is what it's all about, and we'll show you how it's done. First we'll look at techniques for integrating your "real-world" marketing efforts with those online—after all, online marketing should be one aspect of your overall marketing strategy. Advertising represents one aspect of your marketing plan; you'll find out how to develop an advertising strategy. When it comes to ads, the Internet offers more choices than any other type of medium. You'll learn about each of the options, ranging from "old-fashioned" banner ads to ads that use animation and interactivity to engage the user. Finally, you'll find out how you can modify your site to ensure useful listings on popular search-engine sites such as Yahoo!.*

# Chapter 5

# Integrating Real-World and Internet Marketing

---

### In This Chapter

➤ How to blend the Internet into your overall corporate and marketing objectives

➤ How event marketing, press releases, and giveaways connect your marketing efforts

➤ Develop a comprehensive marketing plan

➤ Specific tactics to promote your business online and execute on that plan

➤ Create a detailed marketing budget

---

## There Is No Such Thing As Internet Marketing

That's right. Even if you're in an online-only business such as America Online, priceline.com, or eBay, your marketing efforts cross many boundaries. The Internet is simply another channel. Just how you choose to wisely and profitably exploit it depends on the following:

➤ What you sell

➤ Who your customers are

➤ Why your customers buy from you

# Create a Single Plan for Online and Offline Marketing

There's no such thing as "Internet marketing" because your marketing plan is a single, integrated document. It contains both online and offline tactics that you've identified as crucial to your success. Just as in traditional marketing, the key is in the mix of ads, public relations, direct mail campaigns, and so on, that help you achieve your goals. Let's look at the components of your integrated marketing plan.

## Conduct Environmental Analysis

Take a long, hard, honest look at your company and its products. What are its strengths and weaknesses—especially relative to the competition? What new opportunities lie ahead? Are there possible upgrades to your products, or an expanded direct sales force? Identify threats on the horizon, both real and those you can only imagine—such as new regulatory constraints or pressure from new, offshore competitors.

This evaluation helps you showcase your strengths and optimize your competitive advantage both online and offline. Shortfalls relative to the competition can be minimized and plans set in motion to correct them.

## Establish Marketing Objectives

How do you measure your success? How do you know when you've achieved your goals whether they are short-term or long-term? Your marketing plan needs measuring sticks so that when you hit specific numbers or goals, you know you've made a home run. There is a variety of ways to measure. Choose your yardstick (or yardsticks), as shown in Table 5.1.

### Table 5.1    Ways to Measure the Success of Marketing Efforts

| | |
|---|---|
| I. New Revenue Streams | Dollars of new revenue |
| | Number of new units sold |
| | New customers |
| | Additional products sold to current customers |
| II. Productivity Gains | Fewer sales calls before closing a deal |
| | Shorter service calls |
| | Less time spent in the production process |
| | Fewer customer support calls |
| III. Cost Savings | Fewer overnight deliveries |
| | Fewer copies (paper, toner, binding materials) |
| | Less faxing |
| | Online delivery of four-color literature and SEC documents |
| | Reduction of long-distance phone expenses |

Consider a real-world example. A Web site is developed for a full-service investment banking company with a corporate finance department in the headquarters location and more than 20 brokerage offices around the country. The business case for this site was based on cost savings. We asked the client to identify monthly expenses associated with communicating with shareholders, potential customers, employees, and partners in underwriting syndicates. Then, assumptions were made as to the percent of each expense we thought we could eliminate using the Web site as a communication vehicle to route memos, share annual reports and prospectuses, promote upcoming Initial Public Offerings, and so on. The data associated with these expenses indicated payback in less than seven months, justifying the cost of the Web site with the savings in just these few categories.

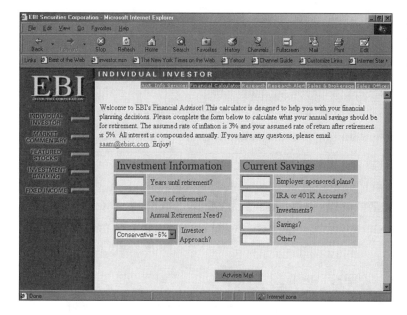

*EBI Securities has a Web site that provides services to customers, as well as cost savings to the company.*

# *Define Your Strategies and Tactics*

Strategies and tactics are a lot like benefits and features, because most people use these word pairs interchangeably. But these concepts are, in fact, very different. Your products' *benefits* can be defined as the improvements your customer enjoys when using products, such as reduced cost to harvest the wheat crop when using agricultural equipment. *Features*, on the other hand, are the characteristics of products that help a customer fulfill those needs, such as the lightning-fast speed and broader swaths cut by the combine.

For your marketing plan, you can think of *strategies* as your business goals—for example, increasing brand awareness or increasing sales by 20%. Your *marketing tactics* are the specific efforts that help you accomplish those goals, such as buying ads on the radio or attending three industry trade shows during the year. And tactics always tie back to support the business goals. Here's an example that shows how marketing tactics support strategy:

**Corporate Goal**
Generate $5 million in incremental revenue next year.

**Strategy 1**
Develop new, lower-tier market.

**Tactic 1**
Reduce price and build new product with trimmed-back features so as to lower the price point for customers with smaller budgets.

**Strategy 2**
Increase industry awareness of your brand.

**Tactic 2**
Publish articles and white papers for trade publications.

**Strategy 3**
Upsell new products to existing customer base.

**Tactic 3**
Direct mail campaign offering one-time discount on premier product to existing customers.

# Your Internet Marketing and Web Site Checklist

This questionnaire takes another valuable perspective on the planning process and guides you through questions that help define a good Internet marketing plan.

## Marketing and Web Site Checklist

**A planning guide for successful Web site development and Internet marketing**

**Vision of the Web Site**

Mission statement:

The mission statement provides an overview of the purpose of your site. This statement describes in one or two sentences what you hope to accomplish with the site.

### Audience Analysis

**A.** Identify all target audiences (internal, external, customers, suppliers, vendors)

1. _____

2. _____

3. _____

4. _____

**B.** What is the primary business problem being addressed by this project for each audience?

**C.** What action(s) do you want the visitor to take during or after visiting the site?

### Business Strategies, Goals, and Objectives

**A.** What is the fundamental business objective for the site?

**B.** What are the specific goals that my company has for providing information and services online (that is, save money, increase sales, improve productivity, customer service)?

**C.** How do I evaluate the success of the Web site?

**D.** Goals for specific departments (check those that apply):

___ Create an awareness of products and services

___ Provide useful information to a target audience

___ Generate a database of information about people who visit

___ Reduce printing, mailing, and distribution expenses

___ Enhance customer service by answering questions online

___ Generate new sales leads

___ Let customers and the media know about new product developments and press releases

___ Enhance investor relations

___ Provide information and services to employees

### The Competition

**A.** Who is the competition?

**B.** How do competitors currently reach your target markets?

**C.** Do competitors have a Web presence; and if they do, how do they use it?

### Implementation

**A.** What is the target date to have my Internet presence up?

**B.** What is a realistic expectation for an annual budget for the site?

**C.** What additional resources does my company need to make this a success (such as accounting, legal, marketing)?

**D.** Will the Internet team and/or employees need training?

## Technology

Which of the following technologies and media would be appropriate?

\_\_\_ Text-based content

\_\_\_ Ability to search the site for specific content

\_\_\_ Secure logon for selected clients and/or employees

\_\_\_ Registration process that collects information from users

\_\_\_ Audio, video, or multimedia

\_\_\_ Forms for users to send in questions and order literature

\_\_\_ Electronic commerce for online sales

\_\_\_ Users can enter data that's added to a database (that is, purchase orders)

\_\_\_ Users have online access to databases (for example, account information)

\_\_\_ Enable users to access different types of files (that is, spreadsheets, documents)

## Marketing of the Web Site

Which of the following marketing strategies will I plan to ensure success of the Internet strategy?

\_\_\_ Press releases

\_\_\_ Business cards

\_\_\_ Fax all prospects

\_\_\_ Internal announcements

\_\_\_ Telemarketing

\_\_\_ Add Web address to all print media and advertising

## Internet Marketing Efforts

**A.** What is my annual budget for marketing on the Internet?

**B.** Am I successfully listed in search engines? Which ones?

**C.** What sites should I consider for banner advertising?

**D.** Will I use any online games or contests to attract customers?

**E.** What happens when someone clicks on a banner ad?

**F.** What types of data do I want to collect from visitors to my site?

**G.** How can we use email for marketing?

**H.** How can we use newsgroups for marketing (what newsgroups are relevant)?

# Offline Tactics Move Online

Internet marketers crow about the new marketing tactics that can be executed only on the Web (more about those in Chapter 13, "Money-Saving Marketing Tips"). But, for the most part, offline marketing activities can be ported to the Internet with a few modifications. Let's examine some old-fashioned offline tactics that have jumped on the Internet bandwagon.

In most businesses, sales keep the doors open. Traditionally, many marketing functions exist solely to support the sales effort in any way possible. Maybe your site already has evolved into an e-commerce site where your products can be purchased online. Whether the sales function has moved to the Internet or not, marketing online can help.

## *Tell a Story with Literature*

The most obvious tool from the offline world that has made a slick, effective move to the Internet is the brochure. Yes, that expensive, four-color glossy has leapt into the online world. You can either present your brochures on your Web site using standard HTML (Web pages), or using Adobe's PDF file format—which actually presents the literature onscreen in a format that duplicates the real-world literature. PDF files have several unique advantages, including the fact that users can search the documents, print entire documents (while maintaining those documents' formatting), enlarge or reduce pages, and view a table of contents. Figure 5.2 shows how one company uses PDF files to put its product literature online.

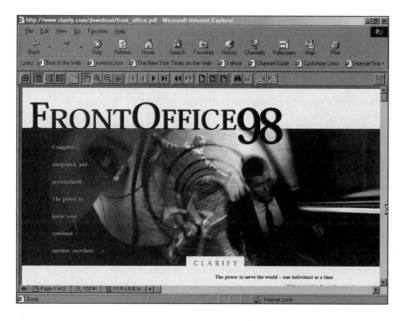

*Clarify Inc. uses PDF files to present a two-page, online brochure about its eFrontOffice suite of sales-management software on its Web site.*

## Target Marketing and Database Management

In previous chapters, we've discussed the principles of one-to-one marketing. Find your customer, distinguish his particular needs, interact with him, and, finally, customize your marketing message. Just like a direct mailer sent through the good-ol' U.S. Postal Service, online marketers can solicit preferences from targets and deliver the sales message just for them.

*Caviarteria offers a free catalog in exchange for information used to create a database of prospects and customers.*

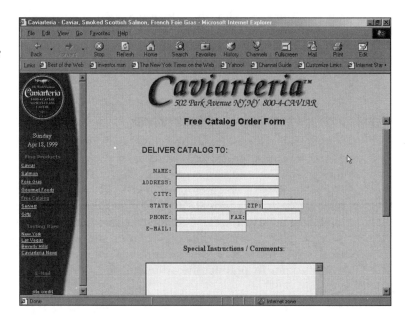

## Who Can Refuse Free Samples and Giveaways?

Thanks to the beauty of downloading, Internet marketing can take advantage of a tactic made famous in consumer packaged goods and the cosmetics industries.

Everybody loves a free sample. You've seen those nice ladies in the grocery store, decked out behind a little table with a fancy apron and tiny cups and spoons filled with goodies—she holds out a sample to you, spilling over the top with new flavors, all on special this week. You might even get a coupon, even though you'd probably have tossed the new product into your cart without one.

How many women pass the cosmetics counter at your local department store without checking out the "gift with purchase"? But how else would you discover the latest lipstick shades if you hadn't tried the free sample the clerk slipped into your bag?

Online marketers offer freebies, too, and online coupons are picking up steam. Companies whose products can be downloaded offer samples directly from their Web sites. Examples include software companies that let you download trial versions of their software; the movie industry, which lets you download sample movie clips; and the music industry, which lets you download samples from music CDs.

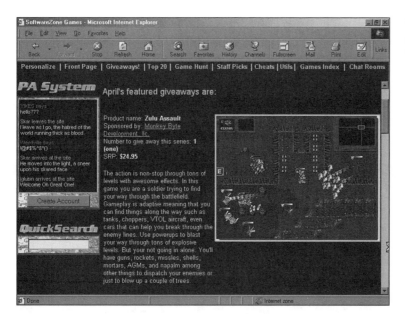

The SoftwareZone sells digital games and offers weekly special giveaways.

CDnow lets users play samples from the songs of various artists before they make a purchase.

# Get Noticed with Press Releases

Press releases represent a great opportunity for both your Web site and your company to get noticed. Press releases can get "picked up" by both national and local media, after which your story is heard by customers and investors alike.

The traditional press release outlets such as Business Wire (http://www.businesswire.com) and PR Newswire (http://www.prnewswire.com) also make your release available via the Internet. On the Internet, a release can include links to Web pages that users can quickly access, or even photographs. Other Web sites, such as the NASDAQ site (http://www.nasdaq.com) or Microsoft's Investor site (http://investor.msn.com), also pick up these releases. Indeed, many companies put out press releases that specifically cover activities of their Web sites—the number of visitors, new e-commerce features. Use your Web site as a vehicle for company publicity!

*PR Newswire puts all of its press releases up on the Internet. Releases can also include links to Web pages.*

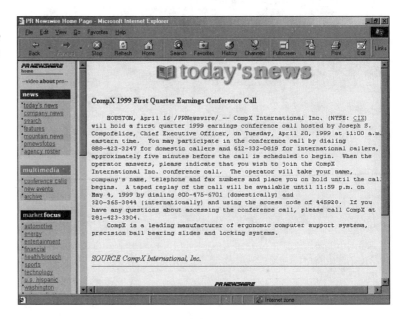

You can also subscribe to press release services that distribute your release to all content sites that have requested news. Just as in traditional media, these organizations and e-zines are often industry-focused. For example, Environment News Service (ENS) presents late-breaking environmental news on such issues as lawsuits, international agreements, demonstrations, science and technology, public health, and air quality.

Another way (although it is more time-consuming) to get your message to the media is to send your information directly to media contacts at specific newspapers, magazines, radio stations, and TV stations. Lucky for you, Internet publisher Paul Krupin created the U.S. All Media E-Mail Directory, which is a publication that contains nearly 12,000 email addresses of contacts in magazines, newspapers, syndicates, radio, and TV in the U.S. and Canada by type of medium, contact name, and title.

According to estimates by Mr. Krupin, 15 to 20% of the media in the United States actively use email public relations. Clearly, what you do not want to do is "blast email" or spam all of these individuals with your release. Editors hate junk mail as much as you do. You should very carefully target your information to those individuals and organizations that can really use and have an interest in your message. To learn more about the directory, go to `http://www.owt.com/dircon`. There is also a link to a page where you can access the Web pages for more than 3,000 magazine Web sites.

*There are more than 3,000 magazines that also have Web sites where you can find useful information to get your story some print—this one is for Four Wheeler enthusiasts.*

# Publicity in Online Publications

The power of press coverage should not be underestimated—it can build your credibility with customers and prospective partners of all kinds. Plus, this is one line item on which you needn't spend tons of cash; a little brainpower and a few creative ideas are all that you need.

Many Web-centric online publications have arisen in these frothy days, and all reporters are looking for content, trends, and new information. You can provide that information. Your articles, product comparisons, and white papers, for example, can make it easy for an e-zine to cover you as an industry expert and your product (or company) as a force to be reckoned with.

A number of online publications have set up *virtual press rooms*, where you can publish your news and reporters track the topics. Check out eZines Database (`http://www.dominis.com/Zines/`) for a comprehensive guide to online publications.

# Plan Event Marketing and Investor Relations

Don't forget that conference companies have also expanded into the Internet. If you are a sponsor, exhibitor, or speaker at an industry event or seminar, be sure to ask about and exploit any opportunities to promote yourself and your company on the exhibition's Web site. Here's another opportunity: Most event planners sell cassettes of speeches and panel discussions after the conference. Why not place a "sound bite" (a small audio clip) of your speech on your Web site? You cultivate your reputation as an industry leader, inspire the customers with your expertise, and promote your products.

The lilting tones of the CEO, often accompanied by his or her CFO, are music to the ears of investors. The phrasing, pace, and tone are sometimes as important as what is said. The Internet offers that additional audio (and video) dimension to a conference call between a company and the investors and analysts betting on its success.

## Provide Customer Service

You already know how important support is to your business; not surprisingly, the Web can help you in many ways. For example, you can collect data and conduct market research with surveys and questionnaires to develop and enhance products, reduce the cost of customer service and ensure customer satisfaction with online educational tools, and inform your customers with product support materials.

*GlaxoWellcome delivers educational, medical, support, and promotional information for its migraine drug, Imitrex.*

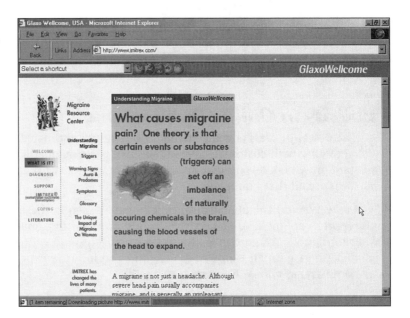

## Shout Your URL from the Rooftops, Literally

Okay, this will be fun. Get the juices flowing and figure out every single marketing item that your company currently has, or products that can be branded with your Web site address. Have an office pool to see whose list is longest. The goal is to put your address everywhere. Period. Table 5.2 provides some initial ideas.

### Table 5.2　Brand Your Web Site in Many Locations

| Brand | Location |
| --- | --- |
| Corporate Identity Materials | Business cards<br>Stationery<br>Invoices<br>Fax covers<br>Trade show booth<br>Giveaways |
| Cross-media Promotion | Billboards<br>Awnings<br>Ads in print, TV, newspaper, radio<br>Direct mailers |
| Product Marketing | On packaging<br>On the products themselves<br>On product literature, warranty cards, and instructions |

## *Merchandise Your Address*

Consider the tactic of exclusivity. If you join the club, you are put into a small group that gets access to the golf course, the celebrity T-shirt, or your favorite singer's online chat with fans. Or you can try the "you must be present to win" tactic. This gets the customer in the door (or to your Web site) without requiring a purchase but with the hope that he finds something there that he can't find anywhere else. It works for the members of the Dave Mathews fan club and with the extra track on the movie soundtrack CD; it can also work in cross-media promotions for the Internet.

Look at those brilliant folks at DreamWorks and PDI. Not only were they able to create magic with the cartoon movie, *Antz*, backed by the biggest voices in Hollywood, but they assembled a powerful combination of merchandise to accompany the release of the movie on videocassette and offer these products for sale via the Web at http://www.antzstore.com.

## Look Who's Using Cross-Promotion

Integrated communications. Multimedia marketing. Strategic marketing messaging. Cross-media marketing is a must for a well-conceived marketing plan. For some businesses, that might simply mean that the Web site is listed in the yellow pages ad and the Sunday newspaper supplement. For some, that might be the right marketing mix.

Others do it up right. It is a tradition that a few companies shoot the entire year's marketing budget with a single TV spot during the Super Bowl with the opportunity to attract 130 million viewers. In 1997 and 1998, online car broker Autobytel.com gave it a shot. Not only did the spot raise consumer awareness, it also led to sales.

"Our servers lit up," said Anne Benvenuto, Autobytel's senior vice president of marketing. "In 1998, after our commercial aired at the end of the first half, visits to our site were up 1,700% during halftime. Purchase request activity was up 104% after halftime, and 78% after the game."

The e-tailers are also using the cross-promotion idea. Bloomingdale's, New York's famous department store, has launched an aggressive in-store campaign to promote its online catalog. What's more, the Web site guides visitors through each store throughout the country, as well as to their next sumptuous meal—in each store's restaurant.

*Bloomingdale's cross-promotes merchandise and services both onsite and online.*

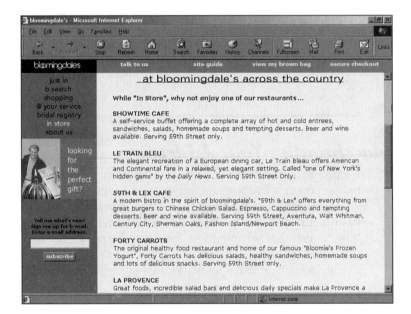

# Foundation of the Marketing Budget

"How much should I spend on marketing?"

This has to be the most important question. Unfortunately, there is no single answer. There is no single percent-of-sales. There are no industry standards.

In his theories on guerrilla marketing, Jay Conrad Levinson defines three different targets:

➤ **Your first target market**   This is the largest of the three markets but will generate the least profits for your company—is absolutely everybody in your geographic area, giving no thought to how well they fit your customer profile. We'll call this target market "the universe."

➤ **Your second target market**   One that will generate substantial, but not gold-medal, profits—is your prospects, those members of the universe who fit your customer profile.

➤ **Your third target market**   This is the tiniest of the three, but can (and should) generate by far the highest profits of them all—is your existing customers.

Levinson's rule of thumb for budgeting: 30% of your marketing budget goes to prospects, 10% to the universe, and 60% to customers. As you begin to draft your budget spreadsheet, keep these and a few other basic concepts in mind:

➤ **Marketing is an investment in the future of your business**   Keep your eyes on the prize and continually match up your marketing goals to your business goals. Marketing helps you stay in business, ahead of your competition, and in front of your customers and potential customers.

➤ **Set forth a budget for the next 12 months**   You need to make a commitment and plan for it. There is a delicate balance between giving a marketing program a chance to succeed and giving a marketing program so much time it sucks you dry. Conventional wisdom tells you to stick to it. Twelve months gives you four quarters to set forth a plan, and to outline the dependencies, critical paths, and benchmarks that will help you measure your success.

➤ **Mix it up**   Be prepared to create a marketing mix of several tactics you are willing to fund. Consider all the potential ways to influence your target markets and allocate your budget among them. Don't put all your eggs in one basket.

Your budget will contain three essential components:

➤ **Component one is the categories where your marketing dollars are spent**   These include advertising, direct mail, public relations, market research, sales support, print collateral, multimedia collateral, trade shows, events, conference, seminars, corporate identity, launch programs, and investor relations.

Notice that each category can contain both online and offline components. We suggest that you allocate between them within each category to leverage vendor and partner relationships. For example, white papers you produce for the print version of a trade magazine can be reposed on your Web site, in an industry association newsletter, and in online e-zines.

➤ **The second component is timelines**   Schedules and project timelines are essential to good planning. But in a budget, you must be sure to preplan for expenditures that drive subsequent events. For example, if you speak at an industry conference in October, be sure to allocate advertising dollars (or the equivalent) in the weeks preceding the event. This sounds elementary, but adding online activities to your existing offline efforts has made your budget process a bit more confusing.

➤ **The third component is resources**   Think of two kinds of resources you need to accomplish your tactics: dollars and people. The dollar-based expenditures are pretty easy to nail down. It becomes more difficult when you try to quantify the time and labor you and your people invest in Internet marketing.

**93**

Consider putting resources toward these areas of expertise:

➤ Graphics/design (consistency with look and feel)

➤ Web development (build databases, for example)

➤ Technical/infrastructure (maintain computer network)

➤ Financial analysis (build and measure site performance)

# It's in the Numbers: Creating Your Marketing Budget

By now, it should be obvious that you have to spend some money on your Internet efforts. There are two sets of numbers you need to create to finalize the budget.

➤ First, you'll need estimates or proposals from your vendors and the media outlets. How much will it cost to enhance your Web site with your new ideas? How much will it cost to run banner ads on the three most popular search engines for two months? If you don't know how much things cost, it is difficult to create a budget.

➤ The second set of numbers represents the dollars that you can allocate to your Internet (and offline) marketing efforts.

Leverage all of your existing relationships with media, ad reps, meeting planners, and so on. Find out what additional opportunities they offer in the online world, and be sure your budget reflects the opportunity to repropose or reuse all of your existing content and graphics between brochures and the Web site—between print ads and online ads.

For example, investigate the opportunities to expand your current advertising mix. Go to your media outlets (newspapers, radio, TV, yellow pages) and ask for information on online opportunities bundled with other, more traditional forms of advertising. Most media outlets have Web sites and offer advertising or content sponsorship opportunities. The following figure shows opportunities presented by the *Seattle Times*.

You don't have to be an accountant to realize that it is important to create a detailed marketing budget and follow the budget and the ongoing success of your campaigns. You probably already have a budget process and spreadsheets in place. However, if you are looking for new ideas or a fresh take on how to model your marketing budget, there are a number of software programs available to help you. Here are two for your consideration:

➤ **Marketware Technologies' ROI it!** (www.marketware-tech.com)  ROIit! 98 is a software program that helps with marketing program analysis, including return on investment (ROI). The software uses analysis that involves ROI, breakeven, response percentage, sales lead percentage, and other analyses for a particular marketing program.

➤ **Comshare's BudgetPlus** (www.comshare.com)  You can create a single database that allows comparisons of actuals, forecasts, and budgets. Link your topdown plans with bottom-up budgets to integrate your organization's strategic plan, annual budget, rolling forecast, and variance analysis. BudgetPlus helps provide analytic reporting through your network or Web browser access.

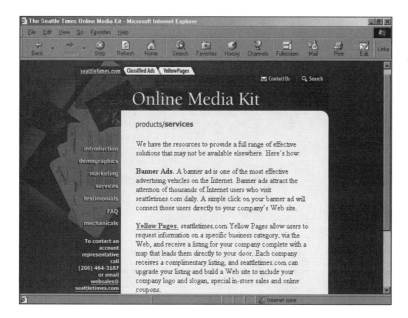

*The* Seattle Times *offers special packages of online, print, and Yellow Pages advertising.*

Remember, the key to building a successful marketing plan and budget is to align the Internet with your corporate objectives, and overlay the opportunities of the Internet with your existing business plan. Consider these suggestions to help you complete your budget:

➤ Focus on the prospect's needs, not what your product does.

➤ Show that you understand your customer and his business.

➤ Be judicious during the sales process and qualify your prospect as you go.

➤ Fine-tune your message with as much clarity as possible.

➤ Be clear and compelling with your message and call to action.

➤ Make customer satisfaction just one more product feature included in every sale.

The following worksheet helps you identify costs associated with specific Internet marketing efforts. Some of these costs will be outsourced to consultants or companies that you hire or pay, and others will be absorbed with in-house talent.

| Internet Activity | Monthly Expense | Annual Expense |
| --- | --- | --- |
| Internet access | _____ | _____ |
| Web-site hosting | _____ | _____ |
| Web-site development | _____ | _____ |
| General enhancement | _____ | _____ |
| Advertising tie-ins | _____ | _____ |

*continues*

| Internet Activity | Monthly Expense | Annual Expense |
|---|---|---|
| Media planning and placement | _____ | _____ |
| Internet advertising development (creative) | _____ | _____ |
| Banner ads | _____ | _____ |
| Sponsorships | _____ | _____ |
| Contests | _____ | _____ |
| Customer followup | _____ | _____ |
| Email support and response | _____ | _____ |
| Additional phone lines | _____ | _____ |
| Tracking and analysis | _____ | _____ |
| Site public relations | _____ | _____ |
| Print materials | _____ | _____ |

## The Least You Need to Know

➤ Your marketing plan is a single document with both online and offline components.

➤ You can modify offline tools such as four-color brochures, direct mailers, and free samples and deploy them online.

➤ Press relations are equally effective online; just be prepared to create copy as well as the news.

➤ Put your Web site address on everything, everywhere.

# Chapter 6

# Your Ad Strategy and Ad Placement

## In This Chapter

➤ Review guidelines that help develop an appropriate ad strategy.

➤ Evaluate whether to use partners such as agencies, consultants, and software providers to help with your ad plan.

➤ Understand the role of ad networks, ad auctions, and third-party ad server companies.

➤ Look at different kinds of advertising options such as sponsorships and interstitials.

Advertising is one aspect of marketing. There are others, such as tradeshow participation and direct mail campaigns. But advertising is the one we usually think of first, perhaps because we live in a world where ads seem to be everywhere. In this chapter, we will explore options for successful and cost-effective online advertising ranging from ad networks to ad auctions.

# Strategy Development

Let's recap a process by which you can clarify your marketing strategy and figure out whether advertising should be included in the marketing mix. The process involves four stages:

➤ Discovery

➤ Requirements

➤ Implementation

➤ Analysis and modification

The first stage, discovery, enables you to review your existing customer base and examine customers' needs and how your products meet them. In this stage, you take a fresh look at competition and see whether you need to reposition your offerings. In the next stage, you define the functional, technical, and creative requirements of the marketing plan. This design will guide your execution because you will set out measurable, quantifiable goals and a budget by which you can achieve them.

The implementation phase launches the actual production of your advertising plan and its components. The last phase, analysis and modification, is where you test, track, retool, adjust, and modify the campaign. Be sure to circle back and measure your results on an ongoing basis.

# Should You Advertise on the Internet?

Generally, if you buy newspaper, radio, or cable advertising or conduct direct marketing campaigns, you're probably a pretty good candidate for Internet advertising. The Web is best for highly focused, narrowly targeted messages.

Do you need a minimum budget just to get in the game? Most people will tell you no. If you manage your own ad sales, you can very easily seek out and contact the few sites that are a perfect match for your targets. But it's easy to be intimidated. As you can see from the Nielsen ratings in the following figure, the top advertisers represent a Who's Who of companies on the Internet.

*Nielsen/NetRatings broadcasts the top advertisers every week.*

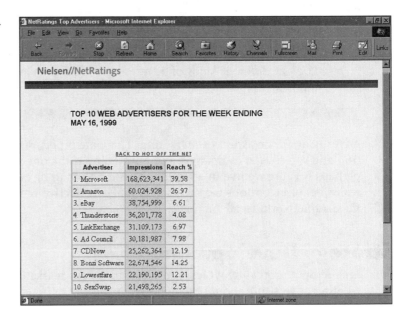

| Advertiser | Impressions | Reach % |
| --- | --- | --- |
| 1. Microsoft | 168,623,341 | 39.58 |
| 2. Amazon | 60,024,928 | 26.97 |
| 3. eBay | 38,754,999 | 6.61 |
| 4. Thunderstone | 36,201,778 | 4.08 |
| 5. LinkExchange | 31,109,173 | 6.97 |
| 6. Ad Council | 30,181,987 | 7.98 |
| 7. CDNow | 25,262,364 | 12.19 |
| 8. Bonzi Software | 22,674,546 | 14.25 |
| 9. Lowestfare | 22,190,195 | 12.21 |
| 10. SexSwap | 21,498,265 | 2.53 |

The Internet is still an advertising-based medium. Look at the statistics. NUA Internet Surveys reported in May 1999 that Internet advertising generated $1.92 billion in 1998, more than double the 1997 total of $906 million, according to the IAB. For the first time, Internet advertising overtook outdoor advertising (billboards) in terms of revenue.

# Integrate, Integrate, Integrate

Consider non-Internet ad channels that have been effective for you and find out whether the same media outlets also have an online package. Check the online media kits. We guarantee that your local newspaper has a Web site, and it probably posts its online rates, well, online.

*Newspapers with Web sites often have rate cards for online advertising.*

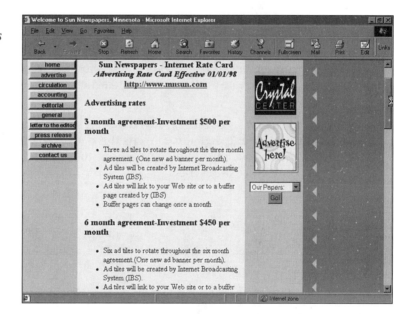

Prices are negotiable in the world of the Internet, especially online ad rates, due to the high percentage of inventory that goes unsold. (More on that subject later.) Only a few targeted outlets such as *The New York Times* can usually get their asking price.

This is a growing trend. More and more Internet companies are expanding their offline marketing component. In a recent study, Internet companies preferred advertising in newspapers and magazines, followed by marketing partnerships, as shown in Table 6.1.

### Table 6.1    Where Internet Companies Advertise

| Medium | Percentage |
| --- | --- |
| Newspapers | 55 |
| Magazines | 54 |
| Marketing partnerships with other sites | 49 |
| Online advertising | 47 |
| Television/Radio | 35 |
| Print catalogs | 35 |
| Sponsorships of third-party sites | 26 |

*Source: The Intermarket Group*

There's another reason to carefully weave your offline media buys with your online ads: Someday you might be able to repurpose the creative material (the ads themselves). Because creative is (usually) one area you have to outsource, wouldn't it be great to be able to create and produce the creative images once, and then use them all over the place?

Infosis (`http://www.infosiscorp.com`) has been granted a patent on a technology that takes print ads and digitally converts them for Web display. Over time, the product should evolve to allow online transactions to be linked to the digitized print ads, building a new source of revenue.

### Online Advertising

Although most online purchases are spurred by offline media, online advertising maintains a strong hold in the marketing mix. Let's look closer. A survey found that 7.6% of online purchases were generated by referrals from AOL. Yahoo! followed, cited by 4.1% of online buyers; Netscape, 3%; Excite, 2.4%; AltaVista, 2.2%; and MSN 1.3%. The survey was conducted between February 17 and March 16, 1999, and was taken from a BizRate.com survey base of more than one million online buyers.

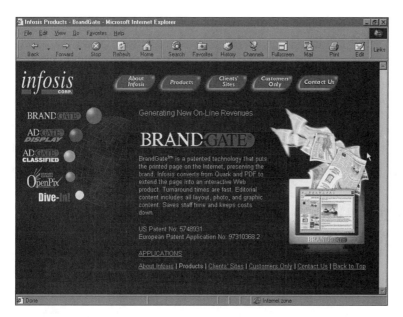

*Infosis Corporation's electronic parallel publishing system incorporates print ads into the online ad strategy.*

# Should I Pick a Partner to Help?

Countless agencies or consultants sell you services based on an area (or areas) of expertise. It can be less expensive for you to retain or hire an external resource to do the things you have neither the time nor the expertise to accomplish. Whether you need one (or more) depends on *what* you need to accomplish as outlined in your strategic plan.

First consider the capabilities of your current consultants, including your advertising or public relations agency or Website development firm.

**Ads That Produce**

Chapter 7, "Ad Creation: What Kind of Internet Ad Should You Use?," provides details on both the various types of Internet ads and some of your production options.

It's unlikely that any one of these companies will have all the answers for both the creation and the execution of a terrific online advertising campaign. But you can realize great savings of time, money, and brainpower when you leverage existing relationships. After all, you've already spent time getting your consultants up-to-speed on your products and services. Identify any shortfalls they might have in the area of online marketing.

Let's look at all the areas of expertise you might need to develop or outsource to create an online advertising campaign:

➤ *Traditional Marketing*

Includes branding, loyalty programs, direct response, and database marketing.

➤ *Strategic Consulting*

Includes research, new business models, Web content, electronic commerce, and communications.

➤ *Internet Marketing Services*

Includes site promotion, online publicity, and affiliate programs.

➤ *Technology*

Includes hosting, networks, computer hardware and software, and applications (such as gathering information from customers who click on your ads or creating digital video for the Internet).

➤ *Creative*

Includes multimedia, video, compelling content, and navigation.

➤ *Media Planning and Buying*

Includes locating the best places to place ads to reach your audience.

Finally, check around for references and talk to an agency's clients. In these days of agencies growing by leaps and bounds, it is a challenge to get a current, strong recommendation for an agency's specific team. But do it.

# Advertising Networks

Scale. Reach. Efficiency. Targeting. An ad network is what it sounds like—it is a company that places your Internet advertisement on several Web sites that are part of their "network." Although there are some variations, most ad networks are extensive networks of sites that share relationships and display ads based on matching ads to specific consumers, and track performance. You can participate in one of these ad networks as an advertiser, as a Web site (called a publisher in ad network lingo), or as both. When you're a publisher, your site becomes part of the network and presents ads from other advertisers. Ad networks can provide you benefits both as a publisher and as an advertiser.

Benefits for advertisers include the following:

➤ An extensive network of categories that target special markets can help focus your marketing effort.

➤ The infrastructure of sales, technology, and software to serve ads, monitor performance, and update results is already in place.

➤ Detailed targeting exceeds anything you can do on your own.

➤ Networks can deliver access to this premium inventory to offer advertisers more opportunities to reach their target audience with mass reach programs and run-of-category buys.

➤ Buys on ad networks can be completely customized to meet your needs.

➤ Sophisticated performance measurement tracks the time of day and other stats to help you refine your placement strategy.

➤ Tracking is done in real-time, so you have maximum flexibility and responsiveness to make changes.

Benefits for publishers include the following:

➤ You can expand your own ad sales efforts. Many networks will represent you on a nonexclusive basis.

➤ An additional ad sales force means more potential ad revenue for your site.

➤ Many ad network companies have extensive lists of advertisers they can bring to you.

Ad networks themselves can target different types of Web sites (and audiences) with ads. Some of them reach broad-based audiences; others focus on people who like the arts, people who read newspapers, children, and so on. Table 6.2 lists a few ad networks and their Web sites.

## Table 6.2    Ad Networks

| Ad Network | Web Site | Target Audience |
| --- | --- | --- |
| 24/7 Media | http://www.247media.com | Various |
| Ad Club | http://www.adclub.net | Various |
| Ad Trends | http://www.knowpower.com | Christian |
| B2B | http://www.b2bworks.com | Business |
| Double Click | http://www.doubleclick.com | Various |
| Flycast | http://www.flycast.com | Various |
| Media News | http://www.medianewsgroup.com | Newspapers |
| Pegasus | http://www.pegasusads.com | Arts |

## *Flycast*

We had a chance to talk with Lyn Chitow Oakes, vice president of marketing at Flycast ad network, to understand more about the ad network game. Flycast works with customers in a very strategic and intimate way to match buyers and sellers in real-time. Ms. Oakes notes that today the focus of the Internet is commerce. As a result, the objective of advertising is to generate responses and leads. All ad networks look at customers, profile them, and watch how profiles change daily.

Flycast's focus is to deliver results based on your business plan, trying to achieve the highest return-on-investment (ROI) and lowest CPM. Reaching more than 900 sites and more than 20 million Web users every month, Flycast has the reach to do this. You know your business better than anyone and no ad network is going to tell you what will work for you. But some things in traditional media just won't work (at least

**103**

not in exactly the same way) online. Flycast media consultants suggest that you forget your preconceived notions of what will and won't work. Using a concept called Zero-Based Media Planning Flycast tracks the results of a campaign and fine-tunes it.

Some ad networks provide the option to partner with local advertisers such as the Yellow Pages. This expands your ability to target geographically. Other ad networks offer risk-free, pay-for-action packages in which you pay only when things work. Be sure to check out those possibilities. Read the fine print. Some ad networks charge sign-up or initial fees. Take time for due diligence before you select your ad network.

## *The Business-to-Business Ad Network*

Online business-to-business advertising spending is projected to reach $2.5 billion by 2002, according to Forrester Research. B2BWorks (http://www.b2bworks.com), an advertising network of business-to-business Web sites across 70 industries, has launched an ad network just for vertical markets. And B2BWorks works just like the consumer-focused networks: measuring ad performance in real-time, serving up targeted ads on-the-fly.

*B2BWorks is an ad network focused on business-to-business marketing.*

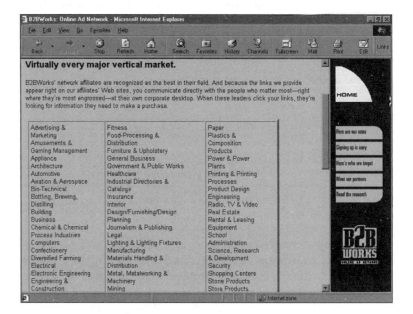

# How Much Is That CPM in the Window?

During many lunchroom conversations, you will hear the debate about what the right price or the best price point for a CPM might be. Recall that CPM, cost per thousand impressions, is the price an advertiser pays to have an ad displayed 1,000 times. When you purchase a larger number of impressions (say 1 million instead of 50,000), the CPM will go down—at least it had better! In traditional media (TV, radio, and print), CPM is also used but is based on the number of readers or viewers.

On the Internet, CPM is an ever-moving target; at press time, it is moving down. But sites rarely publish rate cards except those with the strongest, best-targeted demographics. These publishers can get the CPMs they ask for because they deliver the targeted audience; advertisers are happy to pay. Two things to remember: Everything is negotiable, and forewarned is forearmed. So head over to `http://mediafinder.com` to compare online pricing for advertising to offline pricing.

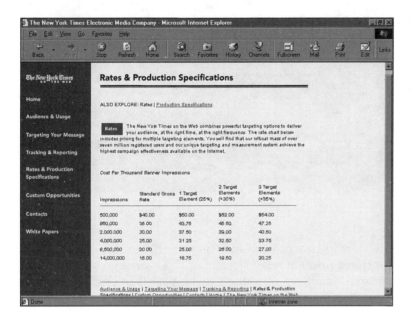

*The New York Times rate card on the Web lists various CPM rates based on how many impressions you purchase.*

# The 800–Pound Gorillas: AOL and Yahoo!

In a discussion about online advertising, we must mention America Online (AOL) and Yahoo!. AOL has more than 16 million customers who subscribe to its online service. That's a lot of viewers for an advertiser. But will your AOL ad work?

AOL's advertisers Web site (`http://mediaspace.aol.com`) notes that a research study by market-research firm ASI shows how banner advertising on America Online generates awareness of brands and increases consumers' intent to purchase products. The ASI Study Results page notes, "AOL's banner ads, in both content and chat areas, resulted in significant increases in recall and persuasion, the two traditional yardsticks that measure advertising effectiveness."

Needless to say, Yahoo! is clearly a leader in Web-site popularity and can provide access to (and charge for) that user base. In fact, with more than 29 million unique visitors each month, Yahoo! constantly is in the top-five list of most-visited Web sites. As Yahoo! goes, so goes the Internet. Indeed, Yahoo! is constantly adding new functions and services on its site—ranging from games to chat to maps to stock quotes— to attract even larger numbers of users. In addition to the huge numbers, Yahoo! can also offer you tremendous reach in the international arenas. If your target market includes non-U.S. audiences, check into Yahoo!.

*A study by ASI indicates that banner ads on AOL are an effective way to reach consumers and encourage them to buy.*

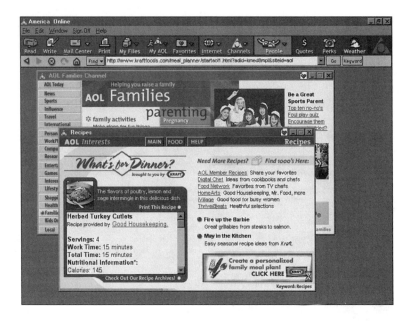

# Ad Auctions

For the world of online advertising, we can use an analogy of the offline marketplace. You can buy products for stated prices at retail stores, but those same goods can be marked down at discount merchandisers. A similar situation exists in online advertising.

In the conventional ad world, advertising impressions are bought on a guaranteed basis determined by a certain price for a certain number of impressions. The site agrees to deliver at least the number of impressions indicated.

Another market—some call it the real-time market—exists because so much of a Web site's inventory of ad space goes unsold. Forrester Research and Jupiter Communications both estimate that, on average, only about 50% of a given site's inventory gets sold in the conventional channels. The remaining inventory either expires unsold or can be made available for purchase in the real-time market. If you want to take advantage of this inventory of ad space, go to Adauction.com (http://www.adauction.com), which offers not only online ads at auction prices, but print-ad auctions as well.

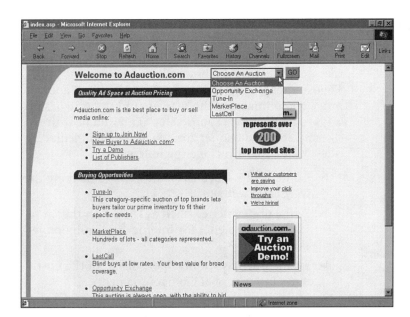

*Adauction.com offers not only online ads at auction but print auctions as well.*

# Ad Placement: Location, Location, Location

It doesn't matter whether you're talking about a restaurant or an online business—location is important. And where your banner ad is placed on a Web page can make a difference. Conventional wisdom says that the top half of the home page (also referred to as *above-the-fold*) is best. Some say that because most people are right-handed, the right side of a page is the best place to get users to click on your ad. But studies by graduate students at the School of Business Administration at the University of Michigan, in cooperation with Athenia Associates, found that banners placed in the lower-right corner (next to the scrollbar) resulted in 228% more click-throughs than banners at the top of a page. Okay, that's just one study.

Just remember to analyze the key components of a good ad before making your decisions: size, quality, compelling call to action, placement, rotation, and number of ads sharing the page. Your trade-off is between proximity to the content that best matches your ad and the price you must pay for the higher probability of a click.

# Other Kinds of Internet Advertising

The whirling dervish we call the online marketing world changes daily, but there are a couple of up-and-coming Internet ad vehicles that might be worth your consideration while you create your online advertising mix.

## Sponsorships

Since the days of Texaco and Milton Berle and George Burns and Carnation Evaporated Milk, sponsors have been stalwarts in the world of advertising.

"Sponsorships are very effective," says Christa Nicholson of the international Web design company iXL. Nicholson drives the Internet Marketing Services practice for one of the largest interactive agencies in the country. Sponsorships are very narrowly focused and targeted. They deliver opportunities to be exclusive, buy frequency, buy fixed placement, and prove commitment to the market. And the varieties of ways to advertise via sponsorship far outnumber the size and shape of banner ads—even the rich media ones. Your choices include the following:

➤ Content sites (such as Neutrogena sponsoring the *Dawson's Creek* site).

➤ E-zine or newsletter (such as Flycast on the *Iconocast* newsletter for Internet marketing professionals).

➤ Events (such as Sprint's sponsorship of the Castle Pines International Golf Tournament).

➤ Games (such as Mapau Online Casino software sponsoring the e-Las Vegas site).

**Shameless Plug**

By the way, we helped developed the Castle Pines International Golf Tournament site to promote the tournament with animated flyovers of each hole and real-time scoring online.

## Interstitials: Better Than Ads?

Traditional television and radio advertising interrupts your favorite program with a message from the sponsor. It's so familiar and has worked so well that it's been ported to the Internet as well. On the Internet, these interruptions are called *interstitials*. Perhaps a better term would be e-mercial because they are like little commercials you have no choice about watching.

Keith Pieper, market strategist for MarketAdviser.com in Boulder, Colorado, has published the quintessential study on interstitial usage, and his findings are very interesting. Interstitials are nearly twice as effective as banners in nearly every category, especially for increasing ad recall and conveying the advertiser's message. Users notice interstitials four times as often as banners. Click rates (how often someone clicks on an ad) for interstitials are on average five times greater than those for banners.

**Interested in Interstitials?**

In Chapter 7, you'll learn even more about interstitial ads, in the section "Interstitial Ads Are in Your Face."

Unicast is a rich media firm that has patented a technology called "superstitials" that creates nearly full-screen pop-up ads that substantially lift user response. Web sites including CBS SportsLine, Women.com, and Excite use this new commercial format.

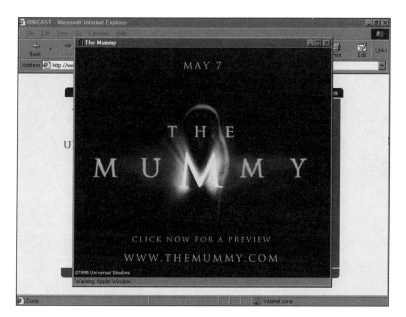

*In a campaign for Universal's movie* The Mummy, *a superstitial ad generated an average clickthrough rate of 22%.*

## There's Always Time for Philanthropy

The Internet Advertising Bureau and The Advertising Council have launched a major online public service effort called the IAB/Ad Council Online PSA Initiative. Members of the IAB will donate 5% of their ad inventory for public service announcements on a space-available basis. This will create an estimated one billion impressions.

NetGravity will donate the ad management services to execute this first-ever online public service initiative. By getting involved with this project, you can donate unused online ad space to worthy causes such as the Coalition for America's Children, Gender Equity in Education, and even Smokey the Bear's Forest Fire Prevention. The Ad Council will greatly appreciate any space you can donate to run PSA ad banners on your Web site. You can go to http://www.adcouncil.org for more information.

---

### The Least You Need to Know

➤ Online ad strategy should complement and be integrated with your offline ad strategy.

➤ Ad networks offer broad-reach, targeted focus and good tracking systems.

➤ Banner ad costs are coming down and are always negotiable.

➤ Sponsorships and interstitials are "banner alternatives" that work effectively.

---

# Ad Creation: What Kind of Internet Ad Should You Use?

## In This Chapter

➤ The different types of banner ads

➤ How interactive advertising works

➤ Rich media advertising: Flash, Java, audio, and video

➤ What the message of your Internet ad is

➤ Who should create your ad

In Colorado, we have a saying about the weather: "If you don't like the weather, wait a minute." And yes, it does change that quickly.

The same might be said about Internet advertising. The types of advertising, the measurements that are created from advertising, and the success rates of different types of advertising seem to change as rapidly as the weather in Colorado. This makes things very difficult for marketing professionals who are familiar with traditional advertising. Television and radio advertising models really haven't changed since these media were created: You pay for a 15-, 30-, or 60-second commercial, and you get some demographic information about the specific channel and pricing is based on CPM (cost-per-thousand). Of course, the content of the ads continues to evolve.

On the Internet, however, the advertisement itself takes on many variations and can achieve many different results, based on your specific marketing goals. This chapter examines the various options that are available to you if you decide to place Internet ads or if you decide to have advertising on your site. It also takes a look at some of the latest technologies that make Internet ads more interactive and multisensory.

# The Basic Banner Has Value

Banner ads represent one of the first efforts for advertising on Web sites. Plus, banner ads play an important role in an advertising plan, depending upon your goals.

Standard banner ads do not move, shake, or speak. They contain information and usually give the viewer the opportunity to click them (called *clickthrough*) to be sent to one of the advertisers' Web pages. Just as newspapers and magazines offer their advertisers a variety of ad sizes (full-page, half-page, quarter-page), banner ads come in a variety of sizes, also.

A combined effort of the Internet Advertising Bureau (http://www.iab.net) and the Coalition for Advertising Supported Information and Entertainment created a proposal for standard banner ad sizes. Standards are important because you need to know that your ads work on any site that accepts advertising. Table 7.1 provides details on these proposed standards; the following figure shows how these ad sizes look on a Web page.

### Table 7.1   Standard Banner Ad Dimensions

| Banner Type | Size (in Pixels) |
| --- | --- |
| Full banner | 486×60 |
| Full banner with vertical navigation bar | 392×72 |
| Half banner | 234×60 |
| Vertical banner | 120×240 |
| Square button | 12×125 |
| Button one | 120×90 |
| Button two | 120×60 |
| Micro button | 88×31 |

The following figure shows a page on the *USA Today* Web site. The top of the page contains both a standard full banner ad (for INVESCO) and a smaller button two ad, for a Visa credit card. The INVESCO banner ad is straightforward. The copy reads:

Make Your IRA Contribution Today

IRA Deadline April 15th

INVESCO Click Here

When you click it, you jump to the home page for the INVESCO Web site (http://www.invesco.com), where you can read articles about IRA contributions. We helped the folks at INVESCO develop their Web site, and we're positive they would like you to click on that banner ad. In fact, they carefully select the sites on which they place their banner ads to target people who would be good potential customers. However, even if you don't click the ad, the impression of seeing INVESCO's name has branding merit.

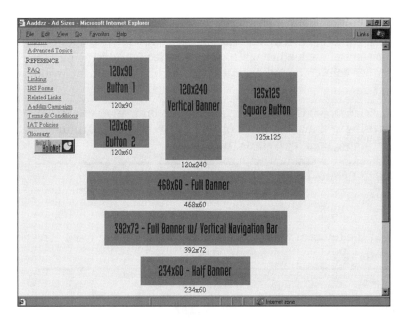

*Standard banner ad sizes on a Web page.*

*INVESCO banner ad at the top of a USA Today Web page.*

Many advertisers feel the only goal of a banner ad is to have the viewer grab his mouse and click. However, standard banner ads are generating relatively low clickthrough rates. I/PRO (http://www.ipro.com) is a company that specializes in traffic verification, analysis, and research. As far back as 1996, I/PRO reported average banner clickthrough rates of only 2.1%. Today it is less than 1%.

Before you gasp and decide never to do any Internet advertising, let's consider the value of impressions. In Chapter 3, "Internet Marketing 101," you learned about branding. You don't always need a clickthrough to achieve effective advertising. Getting people to remember your company or product name has value in the world of advertising.

WebCMO (http://www.webcmo.com) is a Web site that focuses on market research related to Internet advertising and marketing. In one study, WebCMO determined how advertisers would promote their Web sites. The results?

| Technique for Web Site Promotion | Percentage |
|---|---|
| Use search engine submission | 45.5% |
| Use solicited email | 34.6% |
| Use banner advertising in the future | 43.2% |
| Use banner advertising often | 30.9% |

# Animated Banner Ads Offer Action

With relatively low clickthrough rates, advertisers decided it would be important to start attracting attention to the ads. One of the first improvements in banner advertising was the introduction of animated GIFs. GIF is one of the standard image file formats for the Internet (the other popular format is JPEG). I'm sure you've seen animated GIFs. I don't have statistical evidence to prove it, but it seems that about 70% of banner ads now use animated GIFs. These banner ads have text and/or images that move or change as you watch them. There is even an animated GIF artists guild (if you think I'm kidding, go to http://www.agag.com).

The technology behind an animated GIF banner ad is rather simple. It is a GIF file that is composed of two or more individual GIF images, also known as *frames* (as in an animation). Each frame appears on the Web page for a specific length of time and a specific number of cycles (or repetitions).

The time and number of cycles are both determined by the creator of the ad. The changes in the images between frames give the banner ad a sense of motion. And, because no Web browser plug-ins or enhancements are required, everyone can view animated GIF banner ads.

So what can you do with an animated banner ad? Lots. Because you can use any number of frames, you can create a little scene that builds interest. You can use words and/or images to build the sequence. Just remember that the more frames you have, the longer it takes both to load onscreen and for viewers to see the

**Techno Talk**

**Plug-Ins**

A *plug-in* is a software program that works in conjunction with a Web browser to perform a specific task, such as viewing PDF files. Netscape's Web browser, Communicator, uses plug-ins.

complete cycle. If people are viewing your ad on a search engine site, they are probably moving pretty quickly...trying to find a site that meets their needs. They might see your ad for only two or three seconds. That means you should use visuals to attract attention to the ad and get people to click—don't try to tell a huge story. The following group of figures shows frames from a banner ad for Micron PC.

*Frame 1 of a Micron PC animated banner ad.*

*Frame 2 of a Micron PC animated banner ad.*

*Frame 3 of a Micron PC animated banner ad.*

*Frame 4 of a Micron PC animated banner ad.*

# How to Create an Animated Banner Ad

As you just learned, an animated GIF banner ad is a GIF file that has two or more individual GIF images (also known as frames). No plug-ins or enhancements are required for a Web browser to show animated GIFs. However, depending upon a PC's processor speed, the animation might appear to move faster or slower.

Two software programs are required to produce animated GIFs:

➤ **A graphic arts program that creates the individual frames**   Any graphics program can be used, including popular software such as Photoshop, CorelDRAW, and Lightwave 3D. Of course, the individual frames must be saved as GIF files.

➤ **A GIF animator program that you use to assemble the frames you've created, provide the timing (how long each frame appears), and the number of cycles (how many times the animation loops before it stops)**   Popular GIF animator software includes Ulead Gif Animator 3, Microsoft GIF Animator 1.0 (a free supplement to the Microsoft Image Composer tool bundled with Microsoft FrontPage 97), and Andover Advanced Technologies' VideoCraft GIF Animator.

Need some free animated GIFs? Go to the MediaBuilder Web site at http://www.mediabuilder.com. The site has an animated GIF library, and MediaBuilder's image files are in the public domain, which means they are free for use on both personal and commercial Web sites.

**115**

# Embedded HTML Enables Users to Make Choices

An embedded HTML banner ad is (as it suggests) a banner ad embedded in a Web page. HTML code allows the banner ad to accomplish tasks that you can create with HTML. It creates a banner ad with which a viewer can actually interact (as opposed to simply clicking on). Now a viewer can select choices from a pull-down menu, click on check boxes, or even fill in a form. Grey Interactive participated in a study that interviewed 2,400 people; the study suggests that interactivity can increase the click-through rate of an ad by 71%!

Why are these ads so much more popular? One reason might be that the ad empowers the user to make his (or her) own decisions. The user is in control of the information he receives when he clicks the ad. The following examples should give you a sense of the power of embedded HTML. The following figure shows a banner ad that is on the *Gourmet Magazine* site. The ad for CNCurrency.com, a Condé Nast financial magazine Web site, gives you the following choices with a drop-down menu embedded in the ad:

➤ Invest wisely

➤ Start a budget

➤ Save on health insurance

➤ Find the right mortgage

➤ Save for retirement

Great choices, right? There's something for everyone. And when you select one of the choices and click the **GO** button on the ad, you go to a Web page on the CNCurrency site that has that specific information.

*Saving for retirement? Starting a budget? You can decide with this embedded HTML ad for financial services.*

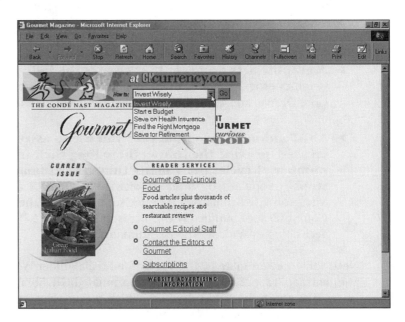

Another thing you can do with embedded HTML is let users type in keywords on the ads themselves, and then click the **GO** button. This initiates a search at your Web site that presents the viewer with a customized page of information that is useful to this specific viewer. In other words, the ad actually serves a purpose, and that purpose can be different for every viewer who uses the ad! Network Solutions, for example, has an embedded HTML ad where you enter a name for a domain address that you might want. When you click the **GO** button, the ad searches the Network Solutions site to see if the domain name is available.

The following figure shows another ad for Career Mosaic (`http://www.careermosaic.com`), a Web site that helps users find jobs. The search field reads, **To find a job enter a keyword above**. If you type `database` and click the **Search** button, the results page is a list of currently available positions that are related to database skills.

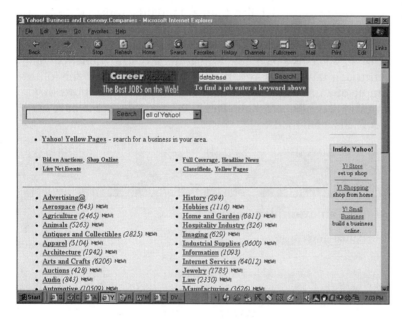

*This HTML embedded banner ad for Career Mosaic enables users to enter keywords, and then creates a results page for the user.*

This type of banner ad moves toward what the Internet does best! First, it creates a one-to-one experience (and marketing opportunity) with each viewer. Second, it uses the database and searching capabilities of computers to create and deliver customized information!

# Interstitial Ads Are in Your Face

Great name, huh? Those of you who are linguists know that an *interstice* is a crevice or crack. From Latin, *inter-* means "between" and *sistere-* is the verb "to set." Therefore, the definition, "to set between," is just what an interstitial ad does. It sets itself between either content or events that a Web user might experience.

Also called *bridge pages*, *jump pages*, *intermercials*, and *pop-up windows*, these ads are closer in concept to traditional radio and television advertising. That's because the viewer really doesn't have a choice except to view the ad, unless they tape the show and fast-forward past the commercials.

For example, you might click on a Web page at a newspaper site to read an article about gardening. But before you get to that page, you have to see an interstitial ad (a full-screen ad) for a garden supply company. The interstitial ad can be static or animated. Usually, these ads are programmed to appear for four or five seconds before the next page appears. Generally, the interstitial advertisement loads, appears, and then disappears between the time that a Web page is requested (when the viewer clicks on a link) and when the requested page is fully loaded. In addition to text, images, and animation, links on the interstitial ad can carry viewers to your Web site.

Because the interstitial ad can be as large as a full-page and capture the viewer for a period of time, the message can be more detailed than a standard banner ad. Because viewers don't really have a choice in the matter, interstitial ads keep the viewers' attention for a longer time. A Grey Interactive study showed that interstitial ads can have a clickthrough rate of 76% versus a 51% rate for banner ads. The interstitial ad can also generate a clickthrough rate that is 44% higher than a banner ad. The following figure shows an example of a full-page interstitial ad for Pappy Productions that loads and runs for about three seconds before the Pappy Productions home page (`http://www.pappyproductions.com`) loads.

*An example of a full-page interstitial ad that holds for a few seconds prior to a new page loading.*

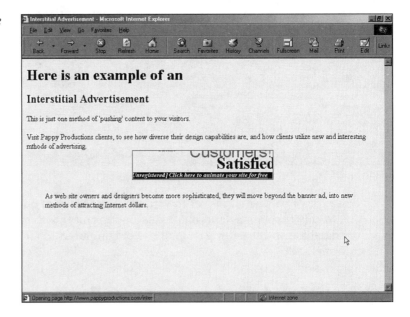

A pop-up interstitial ad appears in its own little window (it pops up). The following figure shows a pop-up interstitial for Intel. After a user clicks a banner ad, a pop-up ad prior to the next page of content appears; this is referred to as a *banner and daughter*.

The pop-up can be less annoying than an interstitial that takes up an entire page. Pop-ups also serve a useful purpose for viewers who have 28.8Kbps modem connections: They provide some interesting content the user can view while they wait for the next Web page to fully load.

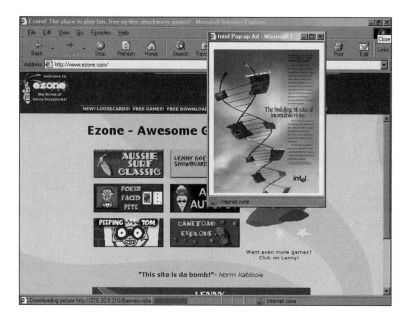

*A pop-up interstitial ad for Intel appears prior to the loading of a Web site.*

Where else can an interstitial prove useful for a viewer? If the viewer clicks on a link to download a file, he or she might have started a process that takes between one and 20 minutes (depending upon the size of the file). An interstitial can provide useful or interesting information during this time.

What are the pros and cons of interstitial advertising? On the pro side: As an advertiser you can be certain that the ad will be viewed (even for a short time) as the most prominent item on screen. Plus, a good interstitial can be unobtrusive, clever, and even informative when it is self-closing. The cons? Some Web users find the intrusive nature of an interstitial or pop-up annoying, and not every Web site offers interstitial advertising as an option.

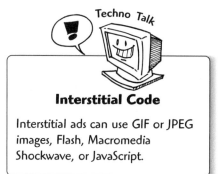

**Techno Talk**

**Interstitial Code**

Interstitial ads can use GIF or JPEG images, Flash, Macromedia Shockwave, or JavaScript.

# Rich Media Ads, Shockwave, and Flash

Rich media. It sounds expensive, doesn't it? Actually, it refers to ads that take advantage of the multimedia aspect of the Internet. Give your ad some pizzazz with animation or sounds, or let the viewer have some fun with the ad as he uses his mouse to interact with it.

Macromedia (`http://www.macromedia.com`) offers two technologies that bring rich media to the Internet:

➤ Shockwave

➤ Flash

Both of these technologies include development software (to create the multimedia) and user viewing software.

So what's the difference between Shockwave and Flash? Flash is designed to create fast-loading Web designs, navigational elements, animation, and advertising. Shockwave is used more frequently to create complex Web applications including online games, and interactive entertainment and training (see Table 7.2).

### Table 7.2 Comparison of Flash and Shockwave Applications

|  | **Flash** | **Shockwave** |
|---|---|---|
| **Authoring Tool** | Macromedia Flash | Macromedia Director 7 |
|  | Macromedia FreeHand | Shockwave Internet Studio |
| **Primary Uses** | Web navigation | Online games |
|  | Animation | Entertainment |
|  | Advertising | Interactive training |

Both Flash and Shockwave player software are free and easy to get, and both ship with Windows 95, 98, MacOS, Internet Explorer CD, America Online, and Netscape Navigator. So there is a very good chance that your audience already has Shockwave installed on their PCs and don't need to do anything special—just enjoy the sites that use it. Indeed, Macromedia notes that more than 40 million Shockwave and 100 million Flash players have been downloaded since 1997. If you want to download the latest Shockwave or Flash players, you can find them at the Macromedia Web site (`http://www.macromedia.com`).

In 1999, King, Brown & Partners, an independent market research firm, conducted a survey to find out how many Web browsers are configured to immediately play Flash, Shockwave, animated GIFs, and Java. Results indicate that 76.8% of Web users can experience Flash content without having to download and install a new player (see Table 7.3) and 51.8% of Web users can experience Shockwave immediately.

### Table 7.3 Percent of Browsers Able to Immediately View Different Ad File Formats

| Technology | Percentage of Users Who Can View Immediately |
| --- | --- |
| Animated GIFs | 99.3% |
| Flash | 76.8% |
| Java | 61.9% |
| Shockwave | 51.8% |

Onsale (`http://www.onsale.com`) is a Web site that enables users to bid for products that range from computer goods to sports and fitness items to travel vacations. They used Macromedia Flash to create a banner (see the following figure) that enables users to point at the name of a computer manufacturer (such as IBM or HP) on the banner ad to view new information about that manufacturer's products appears in the ad. This is also known as a *roll-over*, because when the user takes his or her mouse and rolls over the ad, new information appears.

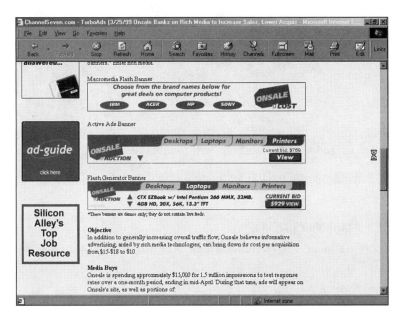

*When your mouse moves over this Macromedia Flash banner ad, new text automatically appears on the ad.*

# Java Jumps

Created by Sun Microsystems, Java is a computer language that can create programs (and just like any software, the programs can run a wide variety of applications). Java programs run over networks (including the Internet), run on any computer, and do not use a tremendous amount of space. When you visit a Web site or view an ad that uses Java, the Java program or application downloads and runs on your PC. So you

**121**

don't have to download Java specifically. If a Web site or ad uses Java, it downloads and runs automatically...you might not even know that Java is being used.

What is a good example of a Java ad? Fry Multimedia used a combination of Java and Enliven/Impulse to create a banner ad campaign for 1-800-Flowers. Enliven/Impulse (part of the At Home Network) is an electronic commerce solution that supports secure credit card transactions within Internet ads. The 1-800-Flowers banner ads provide secure credit card transactions for purchasing Mother's Day flowers. Within the banner itself, users could select an arrangement, specify separate billing and send-to addresses, and include a gift message!

*1-800-Flowers used a Java-enabled banner ad to let people actually place an order for flowers for Mother's Day.*

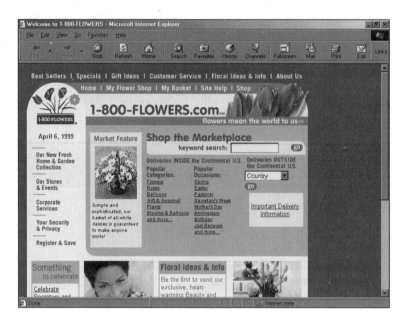

# Audio and Video Advertising

Audio and video are becoming increasingly commonplace on the Internet for two reasons:

➤ First, companies are creating solutions that can deliver audio and video to users even if they have slow Internet access (28.8Kbps or slower). Streaming media plays very quickly even over slower connections because the media is sent continuously in little bits—a *stream*—to the PC.

➤ Second, the number of people with faster Internet access (56Kbps and above) continues to grow.

INTERVU (http://www.intervu.com) is a company that provides Web site owners, content publishers, and advertisers with services for the delivery, or "streaming," of live and on-demand video and audio content over the Internet. INTERVU's services help automate the creation, distribution, and programming of video and audio content.

Several companies have used INTERVU's streaming video technology for Internet advertising. Here are a few examples: Bridgestone has a banner ad that sports a race car driving straight toward the viewer, an FAO Schwarz banner ad features a dancing dinosaur, and a Budweiser banner shows a little video of the now-famous talking lizards.

Real Networks (`http://www.real.com`) is another company that has helped advance the use of audio and video on the Internet. It makes a very popular software program called the RealPlayer, which enables the user to listen to audio and view video that uses streaming. In addition to banner ads with video, many companies use the Real Networks technology to offer live video events as a means of marketing.

Victoria's Secret did a great job with this for a live "Webcast" (sort of like a broadcast but on the Web) of their new fashion lineup. Although many people complained that the video was of less than broadcast quality, it was a wild success. More than two million visitors jumped onto the Web site the day of the event for an opportunity to see beautiful women model sexy clothing in a live event.

*Victoria's Secret gained some two million visitors when they used streaming video to promote a new line of apparel.*

NetRatings, an independent Web traffic measurement service, noted that the event helped Victoria's Secret gain tremendous traffic. They reported: "Until last week, the traffic for this site registered so small on the NetRatings radar screen—less than a half percent reach—that it was not reportable. However, in a single day, Victoria's Secret site traffic tripled, going from 0.7% of home surfers on Feb. 2 1999 to 2.3% of total home surfers on Feb. 3." That's what clever use of the latest Internet technologies for advertising can achieve—not to mention a lot of free publicity!

# Mini-Sites: Marketing and Customer Service

You've probably heard the term *intranet*. Intranets are Web sites created by companies for exclusive use by their employees. Customers and suppliers cannot access an intranet. Employees use intranets to get company news, information about projects, human resources information, job postings, announcements of employee promotions, and other internal information. So intranets are designed to help employees do their job better. If your company makes a product or service designed for business, it is possible that you have useful information that could be added—even tailored—to a company intranet.

For example, perhaps you offer packaging and shipping services for a large company. You could create a mini-site that is a series of Web pages specifically about shipping for this client, including time-of-day for pickups, pricing options, and other useful information. Then, you could offer to let the customer add this mini-site to their intranet. Basically, you get free marketing, and the company gets useful information. Not every product or service is going to be good for this approach, and many companies won't accept any additional information to be added to their intranet (hands-off!), but it offers some interesting possibilities.

# Which Ads Work Best

You've learned about the wide variety of options for advertising. But exactly what type of advertising works best? The end user's access speed is certainly one factor. If you've got a media-rich ad that is designed to work well if the user has a high-speed connection (such as a cable modem or T1 line that provides 1.5Mbps), then you're probably missing some prospective customers who have only 28.8Kbps modems and simply won't wait for your ad to load. We're probably three or four years away from the point where a majority of users have high-speed access.

Advertising research company Ipsos-ASI (http://www.ipsos-asi.com) has done some research about the type of Internet ads consumers find irritating. The results are shown in Table 7.4. Certainly, it is not your goal to irritate your prospective customers. The bottom line is that you must decide which type of advertising works best with the message you are trying to communicate.

### Table 7.4   Types of Internet Ads That Consumers Find Irritating

| Type of Ad | Percentage of Users Who Are Irritated |
| --- | --- |
| Banners | 7% |
| Shared Real Estate (full-page verticals) | 9% |
| Banners with daughters or pop-up windows | 15% |
| Interstitials | 15% |

# The <ALT> Tag

Web users can prevent images from loading as they surf the Web. This, of course, makes pages load a lot faster because there is no waiting for images. Unfortunately, if your ad is an image (which banner ads generally are), they won't be seen.

Even if your potential customer *is* viewing images, if your banner ad takes too long to load on the page, he (or she) might click on a new link. Last but not least, the potential customer might have an older version of a Web browser that does not display the latest banner ad technology (such as a Java ad).

The solution is the **<ALT>** tag. The **<ALT>** tag is an HTML code that is added to a Web page. It tells the user's Web browser what to display if your banner isn't or cannot be viewed. What *can* be displayed is text. For example, here is the alt text for a banner ad that promotes discount tickets at the Expedia Web site:

```
alt="50% off an American Airlines ticket at Expedia.com"
```

So, even in the worst of cases, the viewer would at least see this text instead of a blank image where the banner ad would run. Be sure that sites that use your ads have and run **<ALT>** tags!

# File Sizes: Bigger Isn't Better

In the world of the Internet, size does matter—and bigger isn't better! Smaller files load faster on users' screens. Everyone wants Web pages to load fast, and no one wants to wait for an ad! So, to be sure your ad has a chance to be seen, it must be small in file size to load quickly. Generally, a good size for a banner ad is under 10KB. If you want to check the file size of a banner ad, try this.

When using Microsoft Internet Explorer, perform the following tasks:

1. Right-click the banner ad.
2. Click **Properties**.
3. See the **Size:** attributes line where the file size is displayed.

When using Netscape Navigator, perform the following tasks:

1. Right-click the banner ad.
2. Click **View Image** (the banner opens alone in the browswer).
3. Right-click the ad and choose **View Info**. Read the content length line for the size of the image.

Animated GIFs can be even larger than regular GIFs because two or more frames must load before the animation begins. Again, smaller is better. Try to keep the entire file size for animated GIF banner ads under 25KB.

Media-rich ads can be even worse. Some Java banners exceed 150KB! Users with 28.8Kbps modems won't wait for an ad this big. Fortunately, Java banners can be broken into smaller Java applets that are only 3KB to 5KB and download only as needed by the user.

Procter & Gamble is sponsoring an organization called Future of Advertising Stakeholders (FAST). Like all organizations, this one has subcommittees. There is a narrowband subcommittee that focuses on ads that appear when users have narrowband connections (defined as when a user has a T-1 connection or below). The group is developing a number of recommendations related to advertising on the Internet. One useful recommendation is that ads on narrowband connections should not delay the delivery of content by more than six seconds. When completed, the group's recommendations will be voluntary standards.

### Small File Sizes

If you are having a Webmaster or an advertising agency create your ads, insist that they either keep file sizes small, or better yet, that the ad load in less than five seconds for users who have 28.8Kbps modems. Really, how patient are you? Also, try out the load time of your ad yourself by visiting the Web sites where it appears.

# Effective Ad Content: What Does Your Ad Say?

"The worm lures the fish, not the fisherman and his tackle."
—angler's maxim

What the heck does this mean? Advertising plays an important role in persuading customers to at least consider your products and services. It might not close the deal (that's what the fisherman does), but it will get your customers to move a little closer.

Your Internet advertising should have one of two goals:

➤ Company or product branding
➤ Enticing the viewer to click and go somewhere

From a marketing point of view, you are not using an Internet ad to explain product benefits (your site or pages do that) or provide detailed sales information. If you achieve goal number two, you can lead the prospect to that information.

Similar to a painter, when you create an Internet ad, you have a palette. But your palette contains more than colors of paint. You have text, visuals (pictures, animation and video), and functionality. Each plays a role in attracting the attention of a prospective customer.

Visuals play an important role in attracting people to your ad in the first place. Visuals should be easy to see and load quickly. A lot of the best visuals use only graphic design elements—in other words, no pictures. Then again, pictures can be fun with animated GIFs because you can create a little animation. A frog sticks out its tongue. A deck of cards gets dealt.

Text is equally important because it fills in the details for the ad. Because you don't have a lot of space with banner ads, your message needs to be short and clear. Less is definitely more. Often, I'll drive past a billboard on the highway, and the billboard ad will have a ton of copy. Well, driving at 50MPH, I can't read the ad before I've driven past the billboard. You have a viewer's attention for only about two seconds on most Web pages.

Let's take a look at a few animated GIF banner ads that have several frames of text. Notice that the average frame has fewer than eight words! That's about all the time you'll have before the viewer does something else.

### Service Merchandise—diamonds

➤ April is diamond month.

➤ 25–50% off all diamonds. All Month Long.

### Discover Brokerage—online brokerage

➤ Worried about fly-by-night online brokers?

➤ We're backed by Morgan, Stanley, Dean, Witter & Co.

➤ We're not flying by anywhere.

### Toyota—4 Runner

➤ Image of a newspaper with headline "5-Day Blizzard Hits Chicago"

➤ See, it does pay to own an S.U.V. within city limits.

➤ The 1999 4 Runner.

➤ Toyota every day. Click here.

### Fresh Flower Source/Rainbow Roses—roses

➤ A dozen roses $29.99.

➤ Each bud a different color.

➤ Direct from the grower. Click here.

Finally, functionality. HTML-embedded Flash and Java ads can provide functionality for the viewer. The question is "What functionality do you want to offer?" Is there anything about your product or service that might provide different benefits to different audiences? If so, you could let the viewer click on options that take him to different places on your Web site. Is there any database functionality related to your product or service? If your company is information-based, let viewers search for information right from the ad!

Clever advertising on the Internet engages viewers in several ways. First, use visuals and text to capture the viewer's sense of curiosity or interest. Second, use functionality to make your ad a useful tool. The following list provides ten techniques that can improve the effectiveness of your Internet ads:

1. Create interest based on people's desires. (For example, "Are you hungry?" Not "Try a five-star restaurant.")

2. Sell benefits, not features. (That is, "The X11 vacuum cleaner is the most powerful on the planet." Not "The X11 has a 24-horsepower engine.")

3. Always tell the viewers to "click here" on the ad, or they might not.

4. Translate carefully. International audiences might find that your translation offends them.

5. Be sure the ad loads in less than five seconds with a 28.8Kbps modem (you can do this by keeping the ad file size under 10KB).

6. Be sure that the viewer can read the copy on the ad in less than three seconds. The best way to do this is keep word count to fewer than eight words.

7. Don't have more than four frames with an animated GIF banner ad.

8. If you use media-rich ads, try them on different browsers (particularly Netscape and Internet Explorer), different versions of these browsers (try the 3.0 versions), and different line speeds (28.8Kbps, 56Kbps).

9. Always use the <ALT> tag to provide information for people who can't see the ad.

10. Try two or three different ads and track their effectiveness.

# Build or Buy?

Build or buy? That's always a tough question. If you have a Webmaster or have hired a company to build your Web site, you might already have the resources you need to create effective Internet advertising. A word of caution: Effective advertising requires more than simply using the latest technology. And, on the Internet, effective advertising requires more than simply taking copy or even concepts from your traditional ads and simply "pasting" them onto banner ads.

The Internet is a different medium! It has different rules in terms of the space that you have to work with, the amount of copy you can present, the time that the average viewer spends with your ad, and perhaps most importantly, both how viewers interact with your ad and what actually happens after they click your ad. All these factors really deserve thoughtful consideration before you build and place your ads. If you have marketing staff, get it involved in the process. If you have an advertising agency, get it involved.

Highly effective banner ads can cost between $300 to $2,000 each, depending upon which of the techniques described in this chapter are used. Developing an entire Web advertising strategy and campaign can cost even more.

One technique that is commonly used to test the effectiveness of an advertising campaign is to create and run two or even three different ads (usually no more than three). Then, you can track the effectiveness of the different ads over a short period of time with the intent of running the most effective ad longer. Advertising clickthrough rates can be monitored very closely and you can get detailed reports from the Web sites where you place your ads. Another technique is to have the different ads take the visitor to different pages when they click them—or even list different phone numbers (if you are asking the viewer to call a phone number) for the different ads to facilitate tracking.

---

### The Least You Need to Know

➤ Animated GIF banner ads attract more attention than regular banner ads.

➤ Be sure that all your ads use an <ALT> tag.

➤ Media-rich ads with video and animation should be used only if they add real value to the ad.

➤ The goal of your Internet ads is to get viewers to click on or interact with the ad.

---

# Chapter 8

# The Role Search Engines and Directories Play

## In This Chapter

➤ Why search engines and directories are important to your online success

➤ How search engines and directories locate sites and provide results pages to users

➤ How to register your site with popular search engines

➤ How to effectively design and maintain your site so it can be found by your customers

So far, you have learned the unique aspects of the Internet and developed a powerful marketing plan. Your site is chock full of compelling messages that move the visitor to answer your call to action. But nobody ever visits. This is probably the most frustrating part of expanding your business to the Internet: How do you drive visitors to your site? This chapter introduces search engines and directories as critical partners that can help deliver customers to your doorstep.

## Field of Dreams Marketing? Absolutely NOT!

Don't listen to those people (even if they look like Kevin Costner) who say, "If you build it, they will come." They won't. Driving traffic is one of your greatest challenges because your site is not like a billboard, not even like a print ad in a magazine. It is hidden under a rock until you put it in front of people.

Search engines and directories are two of the best avenues to deliver prospective customers to your site. In Chapter 3, "Internet Marketing 101," you learned that 57% of your site visitors arrive from a search engine.

You've heard the names and you've watched the stock prices take off: America Online, Yahoo!, Netscape, Lycos, and so on. But this collection of companies can help you earn an impressive return on your investment just as they do for their shareholders—IF you know how to present your site properly.

# How Visitors Find Your Site

First, let's come to some common ground with our definitions. Search engines and directories are different—they return different results and behave differently. But the lines are blurring.

## Search Engines

Also called *spiders* or *crawlers*, search engines automatically visit Web pages, catalog the information, and index the content. These are best suited for searches for general topics or areas of interest as opposed to searches for specific companies. Searches return a list of sites when the words embedded in the sites best match up with the user's request.

*The Lycos search engine scours through indexed Web pages to match Web sites with the search query* **caribbean cruise**.

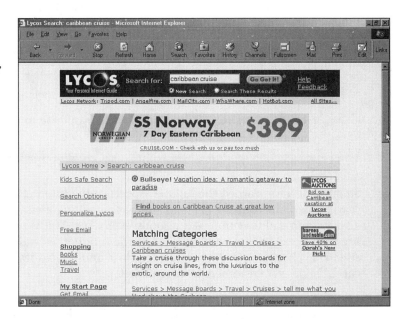

## Directories

Much like the Yellow Pages, directories assign every Web site to a category. Because humans choose categories for each site, often these results can be more valuable than those received from a search engine. Sites pass searches when the assigned category recommended by the site publisher and/or the directory's human catalogers best match up with the user's request.

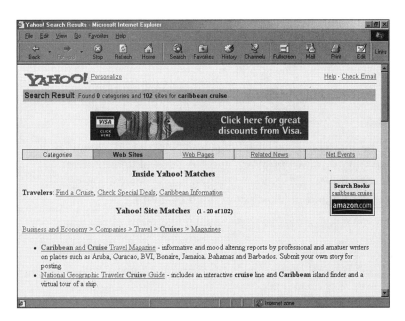

*The Yahoo! directory returns results of sites that match the user's query for **caribbean cruise**.*

## Metasearchers

As the name suggests, these Web sites submit your queries to several different search engines at once. Using MetaCrawler (`http://www.metacrawler.com`) or SavvySearch (`http://www.savvysearch.com`) delivers a broad variety of search results. Metasearcher engines also return search results based on keyword matches.

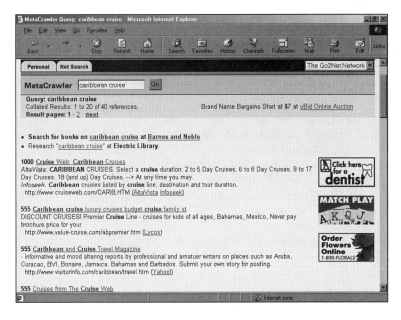

*MetaCrawler metasearch engine returns search results found across a variety of search engines for the keywords **caribbean cruise**.*

**Portals**

Some search engines and directories are rebranded by other portals or destination sites. For example, LookSmart powers AltaVista and HotBot. Ask Jeeves drives results for AltaVista. Excite drives AOL NetFind and Netscape Search. Infoseek is rebranded by Disney's go.com and by search.com, used by CNET.

There is nothing magic or scientific about how users tap into the power of search engines and directories. Just think through how YOU might look for answers to your Internet questions.

# The Major Players: Each Has a Different Game Plan

Table 8.1 provides descriptions of the most popular search engine Web sites. At any point in time, these heavy hitters joust for position, audience, and preferential status with advertisers. Business models have changed for each of these companies since their inception; no doubt, the strategies and competitive pressures will continue to make this a slippery playing field.

### Table 8.1   Popular Search Engines and What Each Does Best

| Engine | Address and Description |
| --- | --- |
| AltaVista | http://www.altavista.com<br>Based on indexed pages, one of the largest search engines on the Web. Recently redesigned with new features such as Photo Finder to search for graphic images. Parent company, Compaq, looks to expand AltaVista into more of a portal with the acquisition of Zip2, which will allow AltaVista to create local portal sites. |
| LookSmart | www.looksmart.com<br>Newest challenge to Yahoo! with human-compiled directory. Supplements search results with AltaVista. Also drives AltaVista and HotBot. |

| Engine | Address and Description |
|--------|------------------------|
| Excite | `www.excite.com`<br>Medium-sized index. Offers broad range of services including Newstracker, a news search service. |
| Yahoo! | `http://www.yahoo.com`<br>The most popular search service, delivering twice as many users as its closest competitor. Largest human-compiled directory. Supplements listings with matches from Inktomi. |
| Lycos | `http://www.lycos.com`<br>Popular but smaller search engine with impressive focus on community building with Lycos Community Guides. |
| Infoseek | `http://www.infoseek.com`<br>Employs search algorithm that combines index and human-compiled directory. Combined with Disney and Starwave to create the Go portal site (`http://www.go.com`). |
| HotBot | `http://www.hotbot.com`<br>Part of the Lycos network, HotBot is a large index powered by the Inktomi engine; the directory is powered by LookSmart. |
| Webcrawler | `http://webcrawler.com`<br>Similar to Excite with small index; good for general searches. |
| Snap | `http://www.snap.com`<br>Human-compiled directory chasing the industry leader, Yahoo!. Backed by CNET and NBC. |
| Google | `http://www.google.com`<br>Evolved from Stanford University project that returns sites based on the number of relevant links to them. |
| Ask Jeeves | `http://www.askjeeves.com`<br>Natural language engine that matches users' "everyday words" to Web pages. Also powers AltaVista. |

# Search Engine Behavior

Companies such as Yahoo! and Lycos are in the business of attracting huge audiences to garner revenue from advertising, sponsorships, and additional services. To that end, their primary objective is to bring visitors back time and again because their engines returned the best matches and the most relevant links to sites that were right on the money.

Seems reasonable, right? Well, here's where it starts to get muddy. Because of these compelling reasons to provide good hits, search engines are constantly refining and improving their search algorithms—the calculations that their computers make to deliver results pages with useful information. One leapfrogs the rest with collaborative filtering. From back in the pack, another engine adds another factor to the equation by referring to directory listings, too. This is good news for users: It means that finding what you want continues to get easier, but is bad news for Web sites because it

**135**

becomes increasingly complicated to keep your sites properly designed and indexed so engines present you in the highest possible ranking to your potential customers. Let's take a quick look at the long-standing factors that engines check to find sites their users are looking for.

### Collaborative Filtering

Collaborative filtering, an information filtering technique, is a descendant of the family of agents, robots, spiders, and crawlers. Users supply ratings that constitute their profile; ratings are compared to those of other users, and similarities are measured. Predictions are computed as a weighted average of the opinions of other users with similar likes and dislikes. These predictions are used to make recommendations to an individual user based upon the correlation between the user's own personal profile and the profiles of other users who have similar tastes.

## There's a Reason They're Called KEYwords

Keywords might be the biggest reason a prospective customer finds your site. When deciding what keywords to embed in your site, think through the words that most accurately and uniquely define your business, products, and competitive advantages.

There are three places where you should use your keywords:

➤ In your Web site's pages

➤ For search engine registration

➤ For directory listings

Let's talk about using the keywords in your site. First, be sure the text of each page accurately describes your page. Search engines actually "look at" the copy on every page of your site. Next, ask your Webmaster to be sure the keywords are included in each of the following HTML tags on your site/pages:

➤ **The <TITLE> Tag**   Make your title as descriptive as possible using your key-words, but remember, this tag is going to be used by the search engines as the title of your site. Be as specific as you can. For example, if you sell lawn equip-ment, then list mowers, weed whackers, hoses, furniture, and so on (up to 60 characters) in your page's title.

➤ **<META> Tags**   <META> tags are hidden descriptions of your Web pages that simply describe the page's content and help point search engines to the right places. These descriptors are especially important if your site contains frames or many graphics.

## Meta Tags

<META> tags are used as part of your HTML code. Some "spiders" use the information contained within <META> tags to index your page. In most cases, a spider grabs only the first few words, sentences, or paragraphs, and use those words as the keywords for your Web site. <META> tags, on the other hand, tell the spider what information to use.

When your page is properly constructed, you can actually control how these robots display your Web page in their search engine. With <META> tags, you can have the robot display your page description the way you want it displayed and help people find your page by providing keywords that describe your page.

Following is an example of how to properly include the <META> tags. These <META> tags MUST be located between your <HEAD></HEAD> HTML tags, and before any JavaScript or FRAMESET tags.

```
<HTML>
<HEAD>
<TITLE>Your Title</TITLE>
<META Name="description" Content="This is where you
would put your description.">
<META Name="keywords" Content="keyword1 keyword2 this
is a keyword phrase this is another keyword phrase put
your most important keywords first. </HEAD>
<BODY>
Your viewable Web page content here...
</BODY>
</HTML>
```

Let's look at each <META> tag separately:

➤ The <META> tag keyword attribute is the most obvious place to enter your keywords. You can use up to 1,000 characters (includes letters, spaces, and commas) but the best advice is to be sure to use words that describe what actually appears on that page.

### Keyword Spamming

Your site might be excluded from a search if an engine detects you've "loaded" your keywords. "Loading" means repeating keywords more than five to seven times and is commonly treated as search engine spamming, and might result in being banned by some.

### Tag Treatment

Tags are treated differently by almost every search engine. HotBot and Infoseek give preference to pages with keywords in their <META> tags. But Lycos and Excite don't.

### Caution

Because of the nature of their construction, framed sites cannot always be interpreted by search engines. Please consider this before choosing to build a frame-based site.

➤ The <META> tag description attribute is used by some search engines to give you the opportunity to write your own description of what your site is about. Be sure you use several of your keywords in your description.

➤ **<ALT> Tags**  Use the <ALT> tag for all of your images because the tag tells most browsers to display a text description for your image as it prepares your page layout for viewing. That means the text goes ahead and loads so your viewers can read and scan worthwhile information while the images load. This way, your viewers will be happier and less likely to abandon the site.

## The Danger of Frames

During the creative process to design the navigation and content of your Web site, no doubt you discovered the importance of usability and easy navigation. Visitors leave quickly if the site makes it hard for them to get around or find the information they want.

To address that conundrum, many creative Web site developers argue very effectively for frame-based sites. Framed sites simply divide the content of a page into chunks, each with its own scrollbar, to help the visitor find his way around the site.

## Must We Say It? Content Is King!

There is no doubt that content is king, but the content we mean here is the kind that search engines can see—and that's only textual content, no graphics. So update the HTML words on each page when your business changes or you add a new product or hire a new Rainmaker. Some search engines boost your ranking if your site content, <META> tags, or other keywords are refreshed on a regular basis. Just as important, of course, it's more likely that visitors will come back to your site if they can expect to find new stuff there.

As described in the next section, your site might rank higher depending on which sites link to yours; so keep those links updated, and correct all broken links.

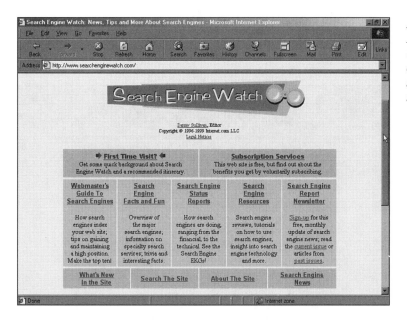

*Danny Sullivan's Search Engine Watch is an excellent resource to help you earn and keep your Website ranking high in search engine results.*

For more details about specific behavior of specific search engines, visit
`http://www.searchenginewatch.com/webmasters/features.html`.

# A Popularity Contest? New Trends in Search Results

With the exponential growth in the number of Web sites coming to the Web , and the large numbers of "dead" sites that are not cleaned off the Net by their owners, it is clear that search engines need new methods to find sites that meet users' criteria. Most of these new algorithms are not without controversy. Let's look at a few of them.

## Popularity As a New Ranking Factor

The Direct Hit Popularity Engine returns sites that draw the most clicks from previous users who entered the same search query. The new technology analyzes past user preferences on several of the major Web search engines and maintains databases that determine which sites users select most often from traditional search results lists. HotBot and LookSmart have announced alliances with this company. Newcomer Google.com ranks sites based on the popularity of which sites link to you.

## Win-Place-Show: The Pay-for-Placement Game

Borrowing a page from the Yellow Pages, GoTo.com from Idealab ranks Web sites based on each's willingness to pay for a high ranking. A GoTo advertiser submits the list of keywords that best describe his site and assigns a bid price to each. GoTo.com charges the site when a user query matches the keyword. The higher the price bid for each keyword, the higher the site ranks in the search results.

*A search for children's books on GoTo.com returns the Amazon.com Web site that is willing to pay $.19 for a user to click through to their site.*

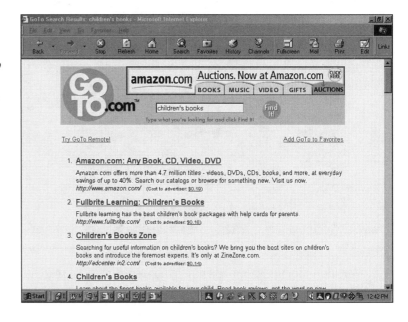

*Shop121 pays GoTo.com one penny for a user to click through to their site when searching for desk chairs.*

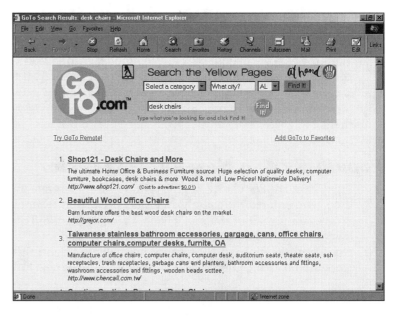

GoTo's entry fee is minimal: A $25 deposit account is debited every time a user clicks through to a site and quantity discounts can be negotiated.

Because the advertiser's success is driven by the growth of GoTo's audience of searchers, its strategy includes a backup to populate the listings on the GoTo database. Unpaid listings appear below the paid listings on the search results pages and are provided by Inktomi.

## The Human Touch

Some folks claim that real live people can still outperform the mighty computer. The Mining Company (http://www.miningcompany.com) and Suite101 (http://www.suite101.com) are search engines where human beings analyze and propose the answers. In fact, The Mining Company recruits guides to provide content and links, essentially creating category experts.

## Natural Language

Probably one of the greatest ideas for us everyday Joes, Ask Jeeves (http://www.askjeeves.com) is a search engine that answers your everyday questions—in your own language. Natural language questions are run through a database of question templates and return uncannily relevant results.

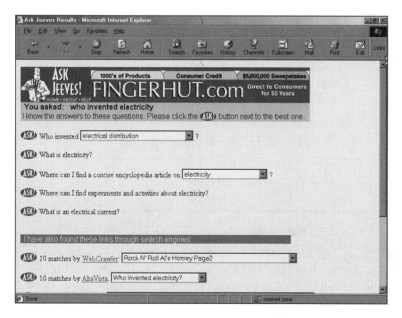

*The search engine, Ask Jeeves, evaluates a search for information about who invented electricity.*

# Register Your Site: Tips and Techniques

This is where the rubber meets the road. You want to register your Web site with the search engines to ensure that your site is in their databases, and that when your potential customers use the search engine to look for products and services that you offer, they find your site. The registration process requires a significant investment in a combination of time and money—and not just in the beginning when you launch your site. It is crucial that you continually update your site and your site registration for a number of reasons:

➤ You need to reflect changes to your business, such as adding a new product line or offering special discounts.

➤ Some search engines move your site up on a hit list if your site gets regular updates to deliver more updated content to its users.

➤ As seen in the last section, search engines continually change the way they direct traffic to your site.

Just as with a physical workout regimen or when you're studying for an exam, there's just no way around it: You've got to do the work. The good news is that you have a wide range of choices, from do-it-yourself registration with each search engine to comprehensive consulting services. Check out the more common Web-based services that offer a kind of "blast registration" with numerous search engines, directories, awards sites, appropriate newsgroups, classified ad listings, "what's new" sites, and so on. Table 8.2 provides a list of six Web sites that (for a fee) will help you register your site at multiple search engines and directories.

### Table 8.3   Web Sites That Offer Registration Services to Get Your Site Listed at Search Engines and Directories

| Company/Product | Address |
| --- | --- |
| Register-It! | http://www.registerit.com |
| SubmitIt | http://www.submitit.com |
| Signpost | http://signpost.merseyworld.com |
| Postmaster | http://www.netcreations.com |
| The Web Hitman | http://www.webthemes.com |
| FirstPlace Software | http://www.webposition.com |

These services range from free-of-charge to approximately $30–$60 one-time fees.

Beware! There's no such thing as a free lunch! If a submission service guarantees results or makes promises that are too good to be true, they probably are. And many of these services cast themselves as Web-site promotion services, which enables them to charge more for services beyond search engine and directory registration. Plus, your site's success might depend greatly upon the accuracy and thoughtfulness with which you register with each search engine and directory. Because virtually every search engine sets out different criteria, we strongly urge you to consider your decision in this area.

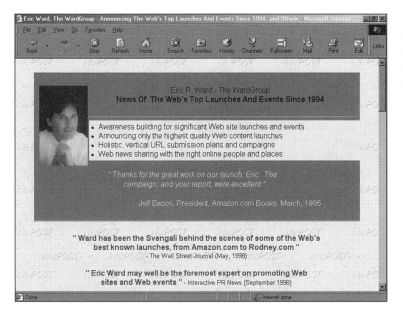

*Several consultants offer high value-added packages; Eric Ward promotes his service, NetPost, that some consider one of the best in the industry.*

# Hello? Directory Assistance: Yahoo!

There's no denying it—Yahoo! is one of the most popular sites on the Internet and has been the long-standing market leader of directories. In fact, the Yahoo! directory format has been so successful, even search engine-only sites such as AltaVista have expanded their format to include directory listings. Even though newcomers LookSmart and Snap have begun to mount a challenge, Yahoo! remains the unquestioned champion.

Based on February, 1999 rankings released by Media Metrix Inc., Yahoo! edged Microsoft for the second most-visited site on the Internet with 31.075 million users compared to 30.866 million for Microsoft. America Online's combined Web and proprietary networks held on to the top spot with 38.1 million.

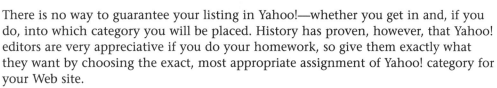

**Fees**

Many Web site developers include substantial site registration services in their fees. And they already know the content of your site and your business goals—both of which are important to picking good keywords. Before you pay a separate service to register, talk with your Web developer.

There is no way to guarantee your listing in Yahoo!—whether you get in and, if you do, into which category you will be placed. History has proven, however, that Yahoo! editors are very appreciative if you do your homework, so give them exactly what they want by choosing the exact, most appropriate assignment of Yahoo! category for your Web site.

Yahoo!'s exact instructions (go to `http://docs.yahoo.com/info/suggest/`
`appropriate.html`) are provided as follows to help you pick your category. This is
so vital that we have reprinted these instructions. A tutorial is also available at
`http://howto.yahoo.com/chapters/10/1.html`. What's appropriate? Consider the
following pointers as you navigate Yahoo! looking for the right category for your site:

➤ **Get Specific**   Yahoo! is made up of 14 main subject headings, or top-level categories: Arts and Humanities, Business and Economy, Computers and Internet,
Education, Entertainment, Government, Health, News and Media, Recreation
and Sports, Reference, Regional, Science, Social Science, and Society and Culture.
Every site listed by Yahoo! is contained somewhere within these 14 major categories, available from the top page of the directory. Each one of these categories
is made up of subcategories, all organizing information from the general to the
specific. New subcategories are created all the time by Yahoo! Surfers as the
directory grows.

When you suggest your site, get as specific as possible. Dig deep into the directory, looking for the appropriate subcategory. You can't submit your site to a
top-level category. If you suggest a link in a top level, or very broad category,
you will almost certainly receive an error message asking you to try again. Look
at the place you've chosen. Are there any sites listed there? Or does it simply
break down into appropriate sub-categories? Dig deeper.

➤ **Commercial or Noncommercial?**   Yahoo! always distinguishes between
commercial and noncommercial sites. If you're suggesting a site that is in any
way commercial—it sells something, promotes goods and services, or promotes a
company that sells goods and services—then the site belongs somewhere in the
Business and Economy section of Yahoo! That "somewhere" is more than likely
within Business and Economy: Companies.

Yes, commercial categories do appear in Yahoo! in related or equivalent noncommercial areas. (For example, in Arts: Architecture there is a cross-reference
from Business and Economy: Companies: Architecture called Companies@.)
Yahoo! Surfers create these links to make navigation between commercial and
noncommercial categories easier for everyone. Even so, when suggesting a commercial site to Yahoo!, be sure you've chosen a subcategory within Business and
Economy. Unless…

➤ **Regionally Specific?**   Yahoo! always distinguishes between regional and
nonregional sites. Ask yourself, "Is my site specific to a particular place? Am I
a local business? Is this a local history? Are we a local sports club?" If your sug-
gested site is of particular interest or relevance to a specific geographic region,
then place it in the Regional hierarchy.

Regional sites and categories in Yahoo! are often cross-referenced to appropriate
areas (under other main subject headings) in the directory. For example, a
genealogy conference in Denver appears in the Denver: Events category and
is also linked to the category for genealogy conferences, located elsewhere in
Yahoo!. Again, this is cross-referencing done by Yahoo! Surfers, but there is
a place on the Add URL form for you to suggest other suitable categories.

If your site is both regionally specific and commercial, then place it in the appropriate Business and Economy category. In other words, let Yahoo! know that it is a commercial site; it'll take care of the regional placement.

➤ **Personal?**   All personal home pages live in the Society and Culture: People: Personal Home Pages category. Is your page personal? Is it about you? Visit the category and suggest your listing from there. If a personal page has sufficient content about a specific topic, a Yahoo! Surfer can decide to link the site into another, related category. Again, there's a place on the submission form for you to suggest other suitable categories.

➤ **Look Familiar?**   Armed with the preceding knowledge, browse and search your way through Yahoo! looking for the appropriate category in which to suggest your site. Look for categories that list similar sites. Are you suggesting a music magazine? A real-estate company in Siberia? An Urkel fan page? A quick guide for beginner investors? If you are suggesting a business site, look for the competition. When you make your way to a category—actually, subcategory— ask yourself, "Does this look familiar?" Yes? Good. Suggest your site. And, remember, it is free. You pay us nothing.

Thanks, Yahoo!, we couldn't have said it better ourselves.

So you've identified the category to which your site belongs. From that category in Yahoo!, click on the "Suggest a Site" link in the bottom-left corner of each Yahoo! page. Now the easy part: filling out the forms. There are only four steps:

1.  Enter information about your site and its URL.

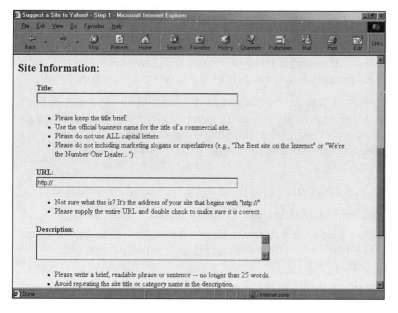

*Yahoo! offers an easy-to-use submission process. Here you put in your site title and the URL.*

2. Enter whether you want to suggest another category that better fits your site.

3. Fill out company and contact data.

*Yahoo! also requests some information about you and your company for its database.*

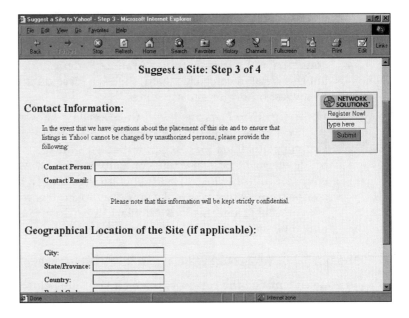

4. Enter any time-sensitive information about the site.

Due to the tremendous growth in companies that want Yahoo! to list their site, the average time between submitting a site and listing has ballooned to many months. But Yahoo! won't even review your request for submission until the entire site is launched and operational—and that can create a terrible delay between when you launch your site and when potential customers find it in a Yahoo! directory listing.

To alleviate the crushing delays, Yahoo! has introduced Yahoo! Business Express. For $199, Yahoo! guarantees a yes or no answer within seven business days as to whether it will list your site. That doesn't mean your site will be listed in seven days; it just means you will know whether you can count on the Yahoo! listing in your marketing mix.

To qualify, store owners must meet and agree to accept a number of conditions:

➤ The site must be located in the U.S. and offer e-commerce transactions.

➤ The site must operate 24 hours a day, seven days a week, and all links must be operational (Hint: Meeting these criteria is a great idea, whether you use Yahoo!'s service or not).

➤ The site should support multiple browser versions.

# Design an Effective Site to Maximize Search Hits

Let's review what you can do to take full advantage of every opportunity that search engines provide. (It just so happens that these suggestions also make for effective Web-site maintenance.)

## *A Site Checklist*

➤ Think like a customer

    Always

➤ Keywords are crucial

    Be creative
    Be specific, strategic, and focused
    Include any rare or unique product or service you offer
    Track your competitors' keywords
    Update your site whenever your business changes
    Place the most important keyword in page titles, <ALT> tags, and so on
    Repeat (without spamming) the very most important keywords that describe your products and your business
    Use <META> tags

➤ Content counts

    Keep a balance between text and graphics
    Keep a balance between the needs of visitors and advertisers
    Update time-critical material (such as press releases)
    Update product information
    Check all links coming to and going from your site
    Monitor content constantly

➤ Be careful with frames

    Be sure you know which engines ignore frames before designing your site
    Check with your Webmaster

➤ Dynamic versus static pages

    Consider an engine's ability to find content created in a dynamic, database-driven site (check with your Webmaster)

# Other Good Places to Get Listed

In addition to search engines and directories, there are a number of places you should consider to obtain a listing your site. Many of these sites do not charge for a listing; they merely provide a service to *their* members. Check with each group for its particular procedures.

➤ **Business organizations** Examples include the Better Business Bureau, Chambers of Commerce, and the Economic Development Council.

➤ **Trade organizations** You or your customers might belong to organizations such as the Teamsters, Small Business Association, or the American Medical Association.

*The American Seed Trade Association site offers a members list, a newsletter, and many resources on agribusiness.*

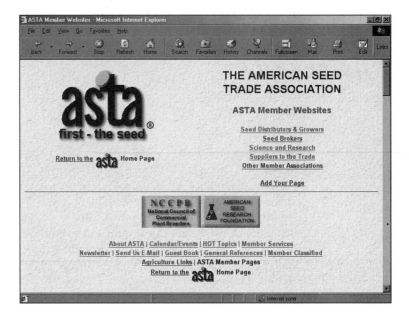

➤ **Affinity groups** Groups that might attract your customers include fan clubs, hobbyist groups, and lobby organizations such as the National Rifle Association or Classic Car Club.

➤ **Charity and nonprofit organizations** These are groups to which you might already donate money or contribute time, including colleges, religious organizations, and philanthropies such as the Migraine Foundation or your own alma mater.

➤ **Online malls, online communities, and community guides** These might serve a local audience or provide value to your target customers.

---

### The Least You Need to Know

➤ Search engines and directories are one of the most important tools your prospective customers use to find your products and services.

➤ Getting a high position in search engine results is dependent on many algorithms and conditions that vary from engine to engine and directory to directory and change all the time. You should constantly monitor these algorithms and make changes to your site's search engine and directory listings.

➤ There are many tips and tricks you can employ on your site itself (such as <META> tags) to increase the odds that your site will meet search queries.

# Part 3

# Making Your Action Plan Work

*Having a good plan is half the battle. The other half is implementation, which is the focus of the chapters in this section. The Internet is unique in its capability to provide a wealth of information about the success of marketing initiatives. You will learn all about the various statistics you can gather from both your Web site and your online advertising. Perhaps more important, you'll learn how to translate those statistics into "plain English" to make appropriate adjustments to your marketing efforts. In addition to online advertising, there are three significant tools every online marketer must consider. One is the use of email for marketing. The second is the use of Internet newsgroups. And the third is the use of your company's Web site. We will take a close look at each of these tools and how you can take advantage of them.*

# Chapter 9

# How to Measure the Effectiveness of Your Internet Strategy

## In This Chapter

➤ How statistics can provide information about the effectiveness of your Web site and Internet advertising

➤ How you can use statistics to change and enhance your Internet strategy

➤ Which companies and software programs provide the statistics you need

➤ See how Web sites are being rated, and how you can benefit from the ratings information

➤ How you can measure the return-on-investment from Internet advertising

How do you measure successful marketing? That's a good question, and there is more than one "right" answer. One way to measure success is to look at a specific marketing effort and statistically calculate the impact—for example, a direct mail campaign where you send out 20,000 letters to a target audience and ask the reader to call a specific phone number to receive more information. If you get 400 calls, you achieve a 2% success rate (which is typical for direct mail campaigns). It is a little bit more difficult to quickly measure the effectiveness of branding campaigns, although you hope that brand awareness increases over a period of time. Marketing can clearly help facilitate the sales process by producing qualified lead generation, but there are usually other variables involved in closing a sale.

The Internet is a little different. First, online buying is largely driven by online marketing from initial interest through an online purchase. So marketing plays a direct role in the sales process, and the impact of marketing can be carefully measured. Indeed, the Internet offers a unique opportunity to gather and analyze the effectiveness of your marketing efforts.

On the Internet, you can closely track how people click into and through Web sites—even to the point-of-sale. You can find out exactly how many people click your advertising, which ads they click, the number of people who visit your Web site, where they go, and what they do when they visit your site. This chapter describes the type of statistical information that you can get about the usage patterns of your target market. It also talks about how you can analyze this information to make future marketing decisions and to evaluate the success of your marketing. You'll learn about Web sites that can help you measure usage patterns and provide easy-to-read reports, as well as some of the efforts by Internet ratings companies.

# The Big Picture: Measure Against Goals

Let's be honest. You don't want to pore over pages and pages of statistics that are difficult to understand. You want information that helps you analyze the effectiveness of your Internet advertising and your Web site. You want information that helps you tailor your Internet efforts to more effectively reach your target market. From a marketing point-of-view, tracking and analysis (and tracking terminology) focuses on two areas:

➤ **Your Web site**   Tracking and analyzing visitors and visitor usage patterns on the site

➤ **Your Internet advertising**   Tracking and analyzing the use and effectiveness of Internet advertising

You can obtain a wealth of information about both of these areas (and we'll talk more about exactly what you can learn shortly).

Tracking can help you find out how people use your Web site and how effective your Internet advertising is. In fact, there is so much information available that it becomes easy to focus on only two pieces of statistical information related to the Web site and advertising.

➤ How many visitors are coming to my Web site?

➤ What is the clickthrough rate of my advertising?

These certainly are useful statistics, but they don't tell the whole story, which is "Are you accomplishing your goals?" I recommend that before you jump into the statistical analysis of your site and advertising, you step back and ask some questions that connect goals to the statistics. Here are a few examples:

➤ **Branding**   Will a customer change his (or her) perception of my company or product brand based on the frequency of his visit, the length of a visit, and the content he views?

➤ **Target audience**   Based on surveys and visitor profiling, am I attracting the type of customer I want to my Web site?

➤ **Site content**   Can the information about the volume of use of various pages on my site provide insight that can improve the site design?

Do users find what they are looking for or visit the pages and information that you want them to?

➤ **Sales**   How many visits does it take before the average visitor makes a purchase? Does my Internet advertising bring visitors directly (or indirectly) to the point of sale?

# What You Need to Know

Now that you've created a framework for using statistics, let's take a look at the type of information you can get about your site and advertising. Table 9.1 defines terminology for statistics that might be available for your Internet site and/or advertising. Indeed, the quantity of statistics can be overwhelming. Here is a list of the top ten report subjects:

1. **Number of unique site visitors**   How many different people came to your site over a week? A month?

2. **Impressions/page views for each page of the site**   Which pages on your site have been the most popular over a period of a week or month?

3. **Search phrases**   What are the most popular keyword searches that visitors are using to find your site?

4. **Most common site entry point**   Through which page(s) on your site are people most frequently entering the site?

5. **Most common site exit point**   From which page(s) on your site are people most frequently leaving the site?

6. **Most requested page(s)**   Which are the most popular pages?

7. **Top referring sites**   Which other sites are getting people to visit your site?

8. **Busiest day of week and time of day**   Statistics on the traffic volume by day and time of day.

9. **Ad clickthrough rate**   Which ads are getting the most visitors to your site?

10. **Ad referring sites**   When people click your ads, from which sites are they coming?

## Table 9.1   Definitions of Statistical Reporting Terms

### I. Web Site Measurement Terminology

| | |
|---|---|
| Visitor (or user) | An individual who visits your Web site. |
| Hit | A hit represents the individual files that are requested from a Web server when a visitor views pages on your site. Hits include HTML, image, and other files. (If your home page has 50 different pictures on it, one visitor would generate 50 hits at the time he loads your home page on his Web browser.) Hits are generally not a good indication of the success of a Web site because they don't really tell you about individual users who come to your site. |

*continues*

**153**

## Table 9.1  Definitions of Statistical Reporting Terms (Continued)

### I. Web Site Measurement Terminology

| | |
|---|---|
| Impressions (or page views) | The number of HTML pages that are requested from a server. One visitor could create multiple page views. Impressions or page views are important because they can tell you which areas of your site are most popular. |
| Visit | The series of Web pages that a visitor requests at your site. |
| Online session | The series of visits made by a visitor to a series of Web sites. |
| Unidentified visitor | A visitor to your site who has not provided any personal information. |
| Identified visitor | A visitor from whom you've been able to collect and store a personal profile (this could include the visitor's age, income, and interests). The identified visitor usually has a user ID and password that he (or she) uses to access a portion of your site. His behavior or usage patters can be tracked through multiple visits to your site. |
| Personal profile | A file created from a survey that a visitor voluntarily fills out. Generally includes email address, some demographic information (age, sex, location), and psychographic information (what the user likes to do). |
| Exposure (ad or page) | The total number of times that all visitors view an ad or page over a period of time without regard to visitor duplication (one person could see the ad or page multiple times). |
| Reach (ad or page) | The total number of individual visitors exposed to an ad or page over a period of time. Site reach is the total number of individual visitors that come to your Web site over a period of time. |
| Visit duration | This is the total length of time a visitor spends at your Web site during one visit. |
| Raw visit depth | The total number of Web pages that a visitor sees during a single visit to your Web site (in other words, the visitor might go back to your home page 10 different times and each time would count). |
| Visit depth | The total number of *unique* Web pages a visitor is exposed to during a single visit to the site (this eliminates duplicate page views). |
| Top pages accessed | This is a list of the most popular Web pages on your site based on all visits (see *impressions*). |

**I. Web Site Measurement Terminology**

| | |
|---|---|
| Top files downloaded | This is a list of the most popular files that visitors download from your site (these could be screen savers, software programs, PDF files, or audio or video files). |

**II. Advertising Measurement Terminology**

| | |
|---|---|
| Clickthrough | When a Web user clicks one of your ads and jumps to a predetermined page. |
| Ad clickthrough rate | The percentage of times that Web users who see a specific ad click it. |
| Ad clickthrough reach | Total number of individual Web users who click an initial ad and then see an additional ad in a time period. |
| Ad effective frequency | The number of exposures to a single ad that are required to prompt a Web user to click the ad. |
| Ad duration | The length of time a Web user views an ad. |
| Return on investment | The ability to track online advertising to know when a user clicks a specific ad, and then moves through the online sales process to actually make a purchase. |

# Use Measurement to Improve Your Internet Strategy

The definitions in the previous section should provide some meaning to the statistics that you can receive. Statistics by themselves are rather meaningless. You need to take the numbers and A) understand what they mean, and then B) evolve your Internet strategy based on your understanding. What you don't want to do is simply say, "Well, enough people are coming to our Web site," or "We need to get more people to our Web site." You need to dig into the statistics (known as *data mining* in the database world) to find meaningful patterns that can help you improve your site and your advertising. In addition to answering your big-picture questions about goals, you can ask a few specific questions related to your Web site and Internet advertising. These can include the following:

**Your Web Site**

1. How many people are actually visiting your Web site?

2. Geographically, from where are your site visitors coming?

3. If visitors are clicking into your site, from what companies and/or Internet services are these people coming?

4. Which pages and/or sections of your site are the most popular/get the best reach?

5. On average, how long do viewers stay at your site?

### Your Internet Advertising

1. How many people are clicking on specific ads?

2. If you're running the same ad on multiple sites, which site is producing a better clickthrough rate?

3. What do people do after they click your ad?

4. Do some ads work better for closing an online sale?

5. What days of the week and what time of day produces the best ad results?

Let's take a look at a few examples that illustrate how statistical information can affect your Internet strategy:

➤ This seems somewhat obvious, but if month after month you are not increasing the number of unique site visitors to your Web site, things aren't working. You'll need to modify your online and offline marketing strategies to get more visitors.

➤ The impressions or page views of various pages on your site can be quite telling. For example, if a lot of people are visiting customer service areas, it suggests that both your site has valuable customer service information and that your customers really do need customer service. If your most popular page is a game, contest, free download (such as a screensaver), or one of your product information pages, then take advantage of this knowledge to use this page(s) for marketing messages.

*This report furnished by NetTracker software shows which pages on a site are most popular and how long visitors stayed on the page.*

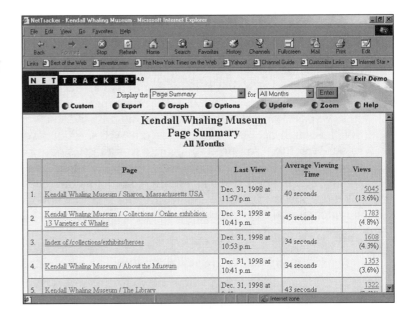

➤ Information about search phrases that people use to get to your site can help you with additional marketing efforts as you can use these words in your advertising and branding messages.

➤ Learn where people are leaving your site. Are they leaving where you want them to (after they make a purchase or submit a query for additional product information)? If they are leaving in droves at a page from which you don't think they should be leaving, there might be some confusing information or choices on that page.

➤ When you know which Web sites are the biggest referring sites (those that get people to your site), you can decide whether you want to do additional (or any) advertising with those sites.

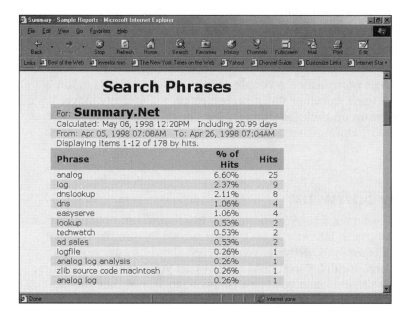

*This report created by Summary.Net software shows the keyword search terms used at the search engines to find your site.*

➤ Time of day/week information can also be useful. Are people coming to your site during the daytime (when they are probably at work) or during the evenings and weekends on their "free" time? You can use this information to enhance your offline marketing efforts, such as selecting radio advertising that targets these time periods.

➤ Clearly, you want to get information about the clickthrough rates of different ads (and the sites that deliver those clicks). You can use this information to determine which ads and sites for placement are the most effective, increasing your efforts in those areas that provide success.

These are a few examples of the type of analysis and actions that you can take based upon site and ad statistics.

## Who Tracks the Stats?

You've got a lot of great questions ready for your review of the statistics about your site and ads. But where do you get these statistics? Well, like everything else with the

Internet, there is not one single answer. Here are a few different places where you might be able to gather useful data. The next few sections take a closer look at each option.

➤ **Your company Webmaster**   Your Webmaster could use one of the site-analysis software programs. These programs run on the Web server (where your site is), and track site usage.

➤ **The company that hosts your Web site**   Most Web site hosting companies offer some type of site analysis reporting. See whether you can request to have 24-hour online access to these reports.

➤ **A company or online Web site service that provides tracking and analysis services**   These companies offer a variety of services for the generation of site statistics.

➤ **A Web site ratings company**   A couple of large companies are randomly surveying Web site users to gather statistical information about site usage. Your site might not show up on their radar screen, but the information about the most popular sites is helpful when considering where you want your own ad placement.

## Web Site Tracking Software

If you run your own Web server, your Webmaster can install and use site-analysis software to track site and ad usage. Likewise, if your site is hosted by another company, that company can use site analysis software. Your interest should focus on getting easy-to-understand reports. Ideally, you should request that you have access to these reports via a secure Web site (one that you use a password to access) that you can access 24 hours a day, and that the reports on your site be updated every day.

WebTrends offers one of the popular site analysis software programs. It provides a wealth of data, ranging from site usage to page views to ad clickthrough rates. The following figure shows an online report generated by WebTrends that shows general site usage statistics including page views and user sessions. The next figure shows a graphical representation of ad views or exposures from different ads over a period of one week. Table 9.2 provides a list of six popular site analysis software programs.

### Table 9.2   Site Analysis Software

| Company | Software | Site |
|---|---|---|
| Access Watch | Access Watch | www.accesswatch.com |
| MarketWave | Hitlist | www.marketwave.com |
| Net.genesis | Net.analysis | www.netgen.com |
| Sane Solutions | NetTracker | www.sane.com |
| Summary | Summary.Net | www.summary.net |
| WebTrends | WebTrends Enterprise | www.webtrends.com |

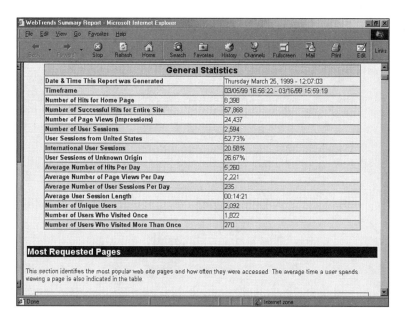

*An example of an online report that shows site usage patterns.*

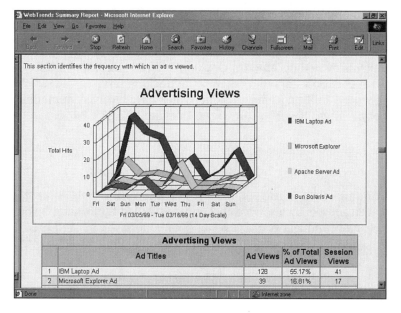

*Graphic representation of the success of ads over a period of time.*

# Web Site Tracking Services

You can also outsource your Web site and advertising traffic measurement service. I/PRO (http://www.ipro.com) offers a service called NetLine, which continuously measures your Web site traffic. NetLine automatically delivers daily, weekly, and monthly reports (see the following figure). Information includes audience profiles and site traffic. You can also order custom reports to analyze traffic on specific banners, taglines, pages, or content areas of your site.

*I/PRO offers an outsource solution that measures your Web site and advertising.*

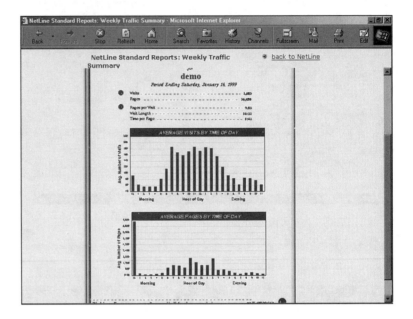

Owned by Netscape (which is owned by America Online), AtWeb is a company that provides a variety of useful site tools, including a Web site tracking service. The services have been used by several million Web site owners, and have received numerous awards, including Yahoo! Internet Life's 50 Most Useful Sites, and CNET's Editor's Choice Award.

AtWeb is the largest Web site maintenance and promotion service on the Web, with millions of customers ranging from small businesses to large corporations.

For as little as $4.99 per month (that's right, less than $5), you can have Web site analysis for one URL or Web address by a service appropriately called "Hitometer." The service tracks usage on your site and lets you access statistical reports via its Web site.

The information you can get includes statistics about the following:

➤ Domains (country and type) from which people access your site

➤ The top referring pages (pages that people come from)

➤ The browsers that people use to access your site

➤ Visitors by month, day, and hour

➤ The top search engines that are used to find your site

➤ The keywords that people are using to access your site

The following figure shows some of the reporting functions of Hitometer. To learn more about the Web analysis service, go to http://www.hitometer.com.

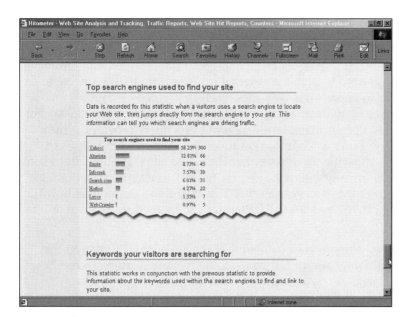

*Search engines that find your site and keywords that people use are two reports provided by Hitometer.*

## The Ratings Game

In the world of advertising and measurement, there is always room for third-party analysis of audience behavior. Why? Quite simply, advertisers (including yourself) want to know what television or radio programs people are watching and listening to—and now you want to know which Web sites people are visiting. Sure, you could go to every Web site owner, ask how many visitors they have, and request a demographic profile. But an independent third-party might be a better resource.

Nielsen Media Research is well known for its television ratings service. With Nielsen, families across the United States keep daily diaries of the television programs they watch; this information becomes the basis of television program and network ratings. Now, Nielsen is working with NetRatings, a California-based company that provides technology for collecting and reporting data collected from survey groups (their Internet site is at `http://www.nielsen-netratings.com`).

For the Internet, Nielsen and NetRatings initially equipped 9,000 consumers with software that carefully tracks their online experience—every mouse click, every site they visit, the ads that are clicked, the purchases that are made, and so on. Then,

### Ad Networks

Chapter 4, "Marketing in Cyberspace: Unique Aspects of Internet Marketing," describes the services of ad networks. These companies take your Internet ads and both place and serve the ads to Web sites. They also offer ad tracking services that tell you how well your ads are doing.

combined with demographic data on these 9,000 users, Nielsen creates market research reports. These reports and the online services can help you make your Internet marketing more effective.

For example, suppose you need to plan a banner ad campaign that targets women. Clearly, you would want to know what Web sites reach this audience. The Nielsen/NetRatings service offers customized queries such as: Females, ages 35–40, college education, above $40,000 annual salary. The result of a query provides a list of target sites by what Nielsen calls a "composition index." A composition index of 100 indicates that visitors to a specific site meet either the expected or average Internet gender proportions based on your query. A site that has a composition index of 138 has 38% more women than the average Web site. This is just one example of how the statistical information gathered by Nielsen/NetRatings can be used to enhance online marketing.

Other queries could tell you where your competitors are advertising, show you the creative content of their banner ads, or tell you whom your site is reaching and how your audience compares to that of your competitors.

*Nielsen/NetRatings uses their statistical data to offer customized reports that can enhance Internet marketing efforts.*

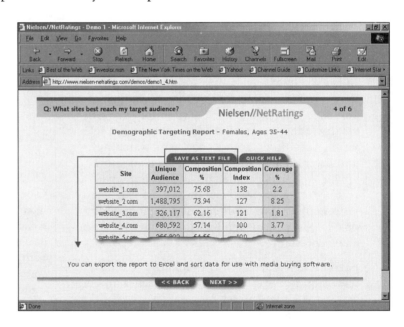

Another big player in the Internet ratings game is New York-based Media Metrix. This company has measured Internet users since 1996, surveying approximately 40,000 users. Table 9.3 shows a comparison of the ratings and unique visitors for the top 10 Web sites from research by Nielsen and Media Metrix. The tallies of audience size were conducted one month apart. Although the measurement is close in terms of the top 10 sites, the number of unique visitors is not particularly close. It shows the difficulty of acquiring a completely accurate statistical sampling for large audience sizes.

Nevertheless, as the industry continues to grow, comprehensive ratings, consumer behavior, and demographic reports play an increasingly important role in determining where ad dollars are spent.

**Table 9.3    Comparison of Ratings of Top 10 Web Sites by Nielsen and Media Metrix**

| Rank | Nielsen | Unique Visitors Millions | Media Metrix | Unique Visitors Millions |
|------|---------|--------------------------|--------------|--------------------------|
| 1 | America Online (Web sites) | 26.3 | America Online (proprietary and Web) | 37.9 |
| 2 | Yahoo! | 24.5 | Microsoft | 30.1 |
| 3 | Microsoft Network/ Hotmail/MSNBC | 20.8 | Yahoo! | 29.5 |
| 4 | Lycos | 18.8 | Lycos | 28.5 |
| 5 | Go Network | 15.8 | Go Network | 22.7 |
| 6 | GeoCities | 13.2 | GeoCities | 19.3 |
| 7 | Excite | 12.2 | Excite | 18.2 |
| 8 | Netscape | 11.5 | Netscape | 18.0 |
| 9 | Blue Mountain Arts | 9.6 | Time Warner Online | 12.2 |
| 10 | Time Warner Online | 9.2 | AltaVista | 11.2 |

# A Click Is a Click, Maybe

Is your Internet advertising working? One measure of ad effectiveness is clickthrough rate. As we've learned, this is the percentage of people who click a specific ad. Certainly, if someone clicks on your advertising and you bring the visitor to another page of information, the ad has achieved some level of success. Nevertheless, wouldn't you like to know whether your ad actually made people purchase your product, download a software program, or fill out a registration form? Known as "return-on-investment" (or ROI) measurement, several companies track not only clickthrough rates, but also exactly what happens after the click. In other words, it seeks to determine what activity the advertising campaign creates.

The advantage of this type of detailed tracking is that if you find that an ad campaign is not creating the desired response, you can quickly change it. Unfortunately, not every ad agency or Web measurement company offers ROI tracking. You need to ask your advertising agency or the company that places your ads whether they offer this service. The following steps provide an example of how it is possible to create return-on-investment measurements.

1. A banner ad is presented on a Web site.

2. A user clicks on the ad and the user is "identified" with a code stored in a cookie on the user's Web browser.

**Cookies**

A cookie is a very small file that is used for identification and tracking. For example, many sites that have you sign in with a user ID and password offer an option where a cookie is placed on your computer, eliminating the need for the sign-in process (your ID and password are stored on your hard drive, and automatically presented to the Web site).

3. The user goes to the link that is connected to the ad.

4. An ad tracking company posts a small, pixel-sized image on certain pages of the site that the advertiser needs to track. An example would be a page that starts a software download, or a page where a purchase is made.

5. As the user clicks on one of these key pages, the user's identification information (stored on the cookie) goes to a central server that tracks the pixel-sized image and the consumer's action. The cookie doesn't know exactly who the user is. For example, it wouldn't know that John Smith printed the 10% off coupon. It is tracking the flow of clicks only to see whether the ad creates a specific action.

6. Results logged at a central server are compared to investment in the advertising. This creates a return-on-investment report.

# Who's Linking to Your Site?

Wouldn't it be nice to have a list of other Web sites that have links to your site? (Please say yes.) Such a list could help you with ad placement strategy—there must be some reason they think your site is important! The standard way to check which sites contain links to yours is through an analysis of your Web server's referer log file. (It might also be available in one of the reports that you have asked to receive.)

The AltaVista search engine (owned by Compaq Computer) offers a fast method that also enables you to quickly view these "link from" sites. The following figure shows that this technique brings up 522 pages that have links to the Diner's Club home page. Here's how you do it:

1. Go to the AltaVista home page (http://www.altavista.com).

2. Enter a search query such as this one in the form: link:http://www.mycompany.com. (where *www.mycompany.com* is your company's Web address).

3. Click the **Search** button.

4. The search returns a list of Web pages that have links to your site. You can click the links to these sites to see what they are all about.

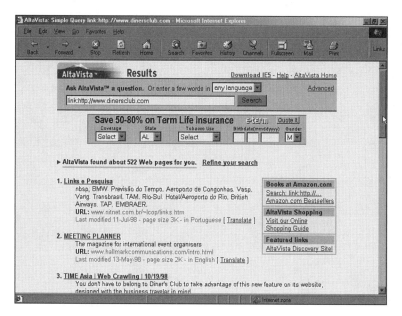

*You can use AltaVista to perform a search of other sites that link to yours.*

---

### The Least You Need to Know

➤ Get and review a statistical report about your Web site and advertising at least once a month.

➤ Learn where your Web site visitors are coming from (geographically and which Web sites).

➤ Find out which pages on your Web site are most popular and use this to your marketing advantage.

➤ Use statistics to discover which of your Internet advertising campaigns is most effective.

# Chapter 10

# How to Use (but Not Abuse) Email Marketing

## In This Chapter

➤ How email marketing fits into your entire Internet marketing strategy

➤ The process of creating, delivering, responding to, and managing email

➤ How to collect or purchase useful email marketing lists

➤ Spam versus unsolicited email

➤ How opt-in email campaigns can deliver prospects to your Web site

➤ Create email messages that attract attention and serve your customers needs

October 1969. The Rolling Stones song "Honky Tonk Woman" is one of the top five songs in the U.S. *Life Magazine* has a cover appropriately called "Revolution"—What are the causes? How does it start? Can it happen here?" And at UCLA, computer science professor Leonard Kleinrock starts a different kind of revolution as he sends the first email message to a colleague at Stanford University. The computer crashes.

Today, email is more abundant than postal mail. How abundant? Try five million emails every minute. Or, 293 billion email messages every day! That's quite a bit more than the 293 million pieces of first-class mail that are distributed daily. Email has become a daily ritual for people of all ages in all countries.

In fact, it's almost "uncool" to not have an email address. The applications are as diverse as the uses—business, romance, family, politics, and, of course, marketing. In this chapter, we take a look at the benefits of using email for a variety of marketing efforts. We examine the differences between unsolicited emails, spam (junk email), and opt-in email (where the recipient actually wants the message).

# Email Is Hot! Here's Why

Email can be the most powerful Internet marketing communications tool you have. First, don't think of email marketing as simply a variation on junk mail. You know, where you send thousands of unsuspecting Netizens (Internet users) an unsolicited offer to buy your products. That's spam—and we'll learn more about that shortly. Email can be used much more effectively and more subtly. And email is NOT a stand-alone tool. Email should be an integrated part of your entire Internet strategy. For example, your Web site has links for users to send your company email. You collect email addresses from customers and prospects at your Web site. Your business cards and brochures have email addresses. Email quickly becomes an important aspect of marketing communication.

From the end users' perspective, email is one-to-one communication. You're sending a message directly to the user's PC (or the user is sending you one). Email is all about creating and maintaining relationships. It's about providing timely and useful information to the recipient—your customer or prospect.

And, most importantly, it is a two-way street. There is outbound *and* inbound email. Unfortunately, it's easy to think about email as only a one-way communication vehicle. You create a message, click **Send**, and you're done. Wrong. The minute you send something out, there's a chance that you will get something back.

Indeed, the goal of *outbound* email frequently is to get a response. Certainly that's the goal of most direct mail campaigns that are sent via the postal service. The company that mails a new credit card offer wants readers to sign up. A special deal on refinancing. A new magazine subscription offer. A discount coupon book from local merchants. These are all examples of direct mail campaigns that hope the person that receives the message will DO SOMETHING (remember the call to action).

One of the reasons you use email for marketing purposes is because it's relatively easy (and inexpensive) to reach a large audience. Well, it's just as easy for the prospective customer to send a response back. It's not very typical that a paper-based direct mail piece causes a recipient to send a reply (the recipient usually just throws it away if he doesn't want it, right?). Not so with email. The reader can, and often does, send an email message BACK to you or your company. *Inbound* email can take even more work to process than the outgoing email, depending upon what the person writes (or wants). An inbound response could ask for more information, or there could be a question about pricing, product specifications, delivery issues, company background, investment opportunities, and on and on.

No, don't say, "Oh goodness, this is going to be a lot of work." If you have a Web site, you have already created (or should have) an avenue for two-way communications. Remember the "contact us" button on your home page? Your customers and prospective customers are going to send you email, even if you don't solicit it with email of your own. The trick is learning how to manage both the outgoing and incoming mail.

# Who Reads the Mail? Statistics About Email Usage

Email has a variety of applications and is relatively inexpensive to use. But does it work? Apparently, email is habit-forming. According to Pew Research Center, the percentage of Internet users who check their email on a daily basis has grown from 50% in 1996 to more than 59% today.

Email is also more likely to gain an immediate response from a user. According to Jupiter Communications, 80% of customers who reply to initial messages respond within four hours to an email message. Also, 15% of the public reads all of its email messages, which is much higher than direct mail rates. The downside? Approximately 16% of users delete all email messages that aren't from friends, family, or colleagues.

# How Can You Use Email?

Email is versatile. You can use email to support or enhance any of the different aspects of marketing and customer communication—advertising, customer service and support, and branding. Four areas stand out:

➤ Ongoing communication

➤ Service information

➤ Customer service functions

➤ Direct marketing

## *Ongoing Communication with Email*

Many companies use email as a cost-effective means to create and distribute electronic newsletters. Keeping regular contact with both existing and prospective customers is an excellent way to maintain a relationship, as well as heighten brand awareness. The focus of a newsletter is information—information that the person receiving the newsletter wants to have.

Tap into the interests and hobbies users have that relate to your products and services. For example, if you sell outdoor clothing and camping gear, your email newsletter should have articles about places to go hiking, tips on cooking outdoors, and suggestions for products that make the wilderness experience more fun.

People in every industry have an interest in what's happening in that industry. Satisfy their curiosity. For example, Medscape (`http://www.medscape.com`) is a subscription Web site where workers in the medical industry find a variety of useful information services. Medscape has a free email newsletter that offers useful tidbits about upcoming medical conferences and treatment practices. The newsletter also (wisely) contains links that bring the reader back to the Medscape Web site, where members are immediately brought to specific articles with more in-depth information, and nonmembers are brought to a page where they can join.

*Medscape uses email to deliver an informative newsletter.*

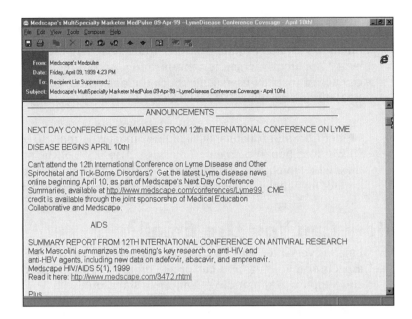

*The Medscape newsletter brings readers back to the Medscape Web site.*

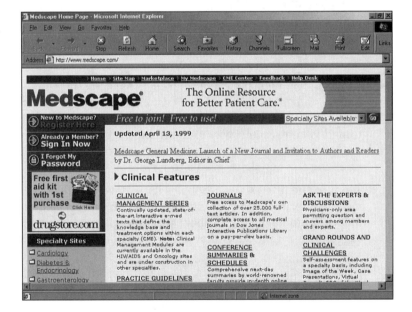

What else can you do with a newsletter? Use it to tell your readers about new products and services. Use it to tell readers about significant changes in your company. Use it to deliver press release information. Use it to enhance sales by offering special Internet-only pricing discounts. For example, sports retailer REI ran a contest for a bicycle helmet (see the next figure) as partial incentive for site visitors to sign up for their email newsletter called *Gearmail*. REI's Web site touted, "Sign up for Gearmail today...and you'll be the first to hear about new online products, sales, special events, and more...plus, you can enter to win in our latest sweepstakes!"

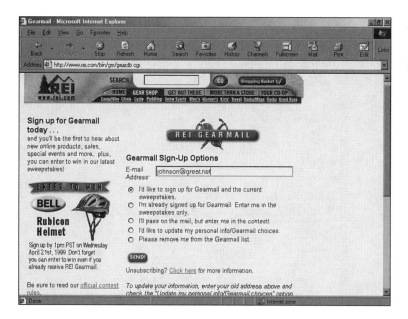

*REI offers Web site visitors an opportunity to sign up for* Gearmail, *an email newsletter.*

## Service Information with Email

Someone buys a product from your Web site. Now is the time to use email to send them a confirmation notice. Let him know his order was received, and you're thrilled that he is a customer. Send another email when the product ships. Keeping customers informed about the status of their orders is a valuable service (for the customer) that gives you an opportunity to maintain and improve the relationship. When you think about it, you could use email for these services even if the customer makes a purchase at your "real-world" store. Simply collect their email address at checkout and tell them that the reason you want it is to keep them informed about their order (or about new products and pricing—the newsletter thing).

The next figure shows an example of an email that Amazon.com sends to the customer after he makes a purchase. The email also notes: "As an Amazon.com customer, you'll occasionally receive email updates about important functionality changes to the Web site, new Amazon.com services, and special offers we believe would be beneficial to you. We hope you'll find these updates interesting and informative. But if you'd rather not receive them, please visit your Amazon.com Subscriptions page."

Service information sent via email is usually sent automatically. In other words, you don't have a person sitting at a PC write a "Thank you, your order has been received" email message. The computer system that hosts your Web site is programmed to send these messages based on certain triggers, such as an order being placed. These email messages are known as *triggered* or *dynamic emails* and there is little human interaction.

**171**

They are different from a direct marketing email campaign or email newsletter that is a scheduled event that occurs at a predetermined time.

*Amazon.com automatically sends customers an order confirmation email with a review of the order price.*

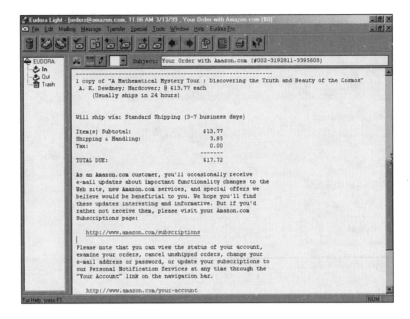

## Customer Service with Email

Customer service is a little different from service information. Customer service is any type of customer inquiry that requires immediate response—the same type of issues that arise via telephone, such as questions about invoices or billing, how a product works, whether a certain repair is under warranty, and so on.

Every business has a variety of questions that come into "customer service." Hopefully, these calls are either answered by an in-house or outsourced customer service representative, or they are routed to the appropriate department or individual for response. On the telephone, interactive voice response systems (IVRs) bring callers through a series of "push 1, 2 or 3" options to try to either solve the problem or route the question.

The Internet is similar. You need to be sure that the email question gets to a person who can answer it—and answer in a timely fashion. Most people who submit email questions to a company expect to have an answer within 24 hours. This 24-hour rule can create a challenge within organizations. You need to ensure that emails are a) routed correctly and b) answered in a timely fashion.

One way to achieve this goal is to have a Web page that enables users to select the department to which they think their question should go. The Web site can then route the question to that department or individual. For example, the General Motors Web site has a contact page on which you can submit a question or suggestion to departments that range from community affairs to sales to investor relations.

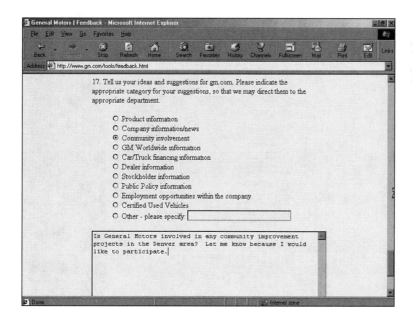

*The General Motors Web site has a contact page in which you can submit a question or suggestion to various departments.*

At the Web site for the online florist 1-800-FLOWERS (`http://www.1800flowers.com`), the company promotes customer service and customer interaction. This is their guarantee:

> At 1-800-FLOWERS we guarantee that your floral arrangement will stay fresh for seven days. We further guarantee your 100% satisfaction on all floral and gift items. If you are not completely satisfied, contact us by taking advantage of any of these convenient methods:
>
> **1.** Call us toll free at 1-800-468-1141.
>
> **2.** Connect to a live customer service associate utilizing our 1-800-FLOWERS online customer service live feature and "chat" with us online.
>
> **3.** Complete our Customer Service Inquiry Form and an associate will contact you within 12 hours.

All three choices offer fast responses.

John Vaeth, Jr., Director of Consumer Affairs at Kodak, told me that there are at least three goals for consumer affairs via the Kodak Web site:

➤ Enhance loyalty of customers through quality service.

➤ Leverage the information they receive from customers for product development.

➤ Move toward a self-service environment.

*1-800-FLOWERS lets you use an email form to inquire about an order or make changes.*

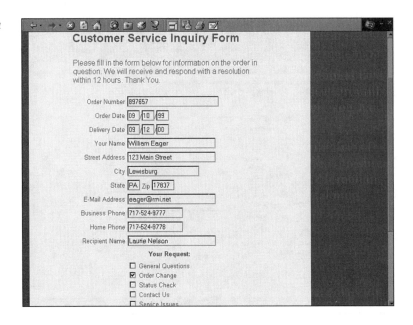

To this end, the Web site offers 24-hour-a-day service. It includes frequently asked questions and information on many of Kodak's 55,000 products, and visitors can email product questions directly to the consumer affairs department. Kodak receives hundreds of comments and questions every day, and uses online surveys to "get inside the customer's head."

*The Kodak Web site provides a variety of customer service functions, including the ability to email questions about products.*

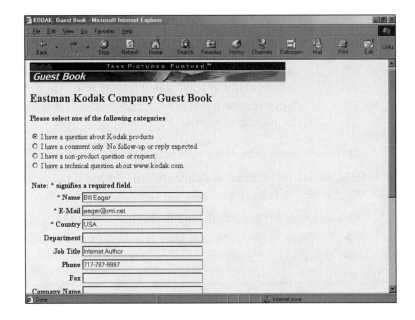

# Direct Marketing with Email

Here we go: the online equivalent of direct mail, only better. The cost for creating and delivering email marketing efforts can be significantly less than direct mail. A successful campaign can bring in results or inquiries as high as 25%, compared to the average of 1% or 2% response from direct mail. One of the great aspects of successful email marketing is that the reader who finds your message to be of interest can easily forward the message on to friends who might also find it of interest. Rarely with direct mail will anyone ever put the letter in a new envelope, address it to a friend, put on a stamp, and send it out again!

Even so, email marketing campaigns need serious thought to be successful. What exactly are the procedures and costs involved in email marketing? There are four steps:

1. Produce the message
2. Obtain the recipient list
3. Deliver the message
4. Manage email responses (both from email marketing and your Web site)

The next sections of this chapter provide useful information and suggestions on these four areas.

# Produce the Perfect Email Message

Perfection really relates to the goal you have. What is your message? Is it an offer to sell? Is it an enticement to visit your Web site? Is it an offer for membership?

First determine the nature of your message and the type of response you desire. Then, create the message. Here are seven tips for creating effective email marketing messages.

➤ Always provide a `From:` address to which the recipient can reply.

➤ Have a `Subject:` line that is straightforward and to the point.

➤ Capture your reader in the first couple of sentences.

➤ Give the content of your message a tone of information as opposed to sales.

➤ Always include a link(s) to your Web site.

➤ Always include a "signature file" with your company's full name, address, and phone number (you do want them to contact you, right?).

➤ If you are running an unsolicited email marketing effort, give the recipient an opportunity to decline any future marketing efforts.

Marketing-based email is a little like an ad that someone will give a chance. The first opportunity to capture attention is with your `Subject:` line. I recommend being honest and avoiding hyperbole—and stay away from those misleading subjects that make the reader think they might know who you are. How many times have you received junk email with `Subject:` lines such as

Low investment, high profits

Right person can earn $6K per week

Enjoy the good life, work at home

What you've been waiting for

These vague `Subject:` lines might work a couple of times, but users quickly learn which `Subject:` lines are pure garbage. If you sell swimwear, tell the reader that Fred's swimwear site has new designs and reasonable prices. Here's an example of a straightforward email message soliciting contributions.

**Subject:** Join a winning team—be a hero and help Doug Flutie fight autism!

**Partial message:**

The Doug Flutie, Jr. Foundation for Autism

To make a donation or find out more information, please visit `http://dougflutie.clickzchallenge.com/beyond/main.html`. Even if you are unable to make a donation at this time, just adding your email address to the Foundation's database will help.

Just as a good ad must capture the audience's attention in a few seconds, you have only a few sentences to capture and keep your audience with the content of your email message. This is especially true with unsolicited email. If the reader doesn't like what he reads immediately, he won't continue to read the message. Remember, that **Delete** key is easy to reach.

There is a theory in the direct mail business that it is okay to enclose a lot of information in the envelope. You start with a teaser that gets the reader interested. Then, when you have their interest, you flesh out all of the details of your offer, proposition, or call-to-action. The theory is that the reader who is really interested wants as much information as he or she can get.

Email is a little different. An email message that goes on for ten pages is a little boring; who likes to sit at their PC scrolling down? It's much better to provide the details in the message that readers understand—what you offer—and then have a link(s) that bring them to your Web site where they can learn more.

Here is an example of an unsolicited email that is quick and to the point. If the reader is interested in the concept, he or she can learn more by clicking on the link to the Web site.

**Subject:** Do you have any ideas?

**Message:**

Are you working on an invention?

...a new product idea?

...an add-on to an existing product?

Patent Services available

Request Inventor's Information now

at our convenient Web form...

```
http://206.100.120.21/inv2
```

## *Your Signature File*

A signature file is the text that appears at the end of an email message (like a signature). Almost every email software program enables you to create a signature file that you can automatically attach to every email message you send. At the very least, this file should contain your company name, address, and phone number. The following figure shows the signature file for software company Blue Squirrel. The company's physical address, URL, phone and fax numbers, and email address are all parts of its signature. Note that also provided is one Web address where people can subscribe to their email newsletter and a second address where users can unsubscribe.

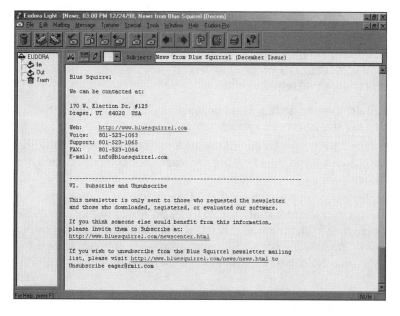

*The signature file for the Blue Squirrel software company provides everything the reader needs to contact the company.*

## *Media-Rich Email and Attachments*

Any email software that supports HTML mail (that is, email that incorporates HTML codes, the same codes that create Web pages) enables users to view email that includes colored text, a variety of fonts, and even images in the body of the message. Microsoft's Outlook Express, Netscape's Messenger email, and Eudora Pro all read media-rich messages. Unfortunately, not every email program can do this, so it is generally wise to not send media-rich emails to a broad group of people.

**177**

*Media-rich email can include a variety of fonts, colors, and images. Unfortunately, not every email program is able to display them.*

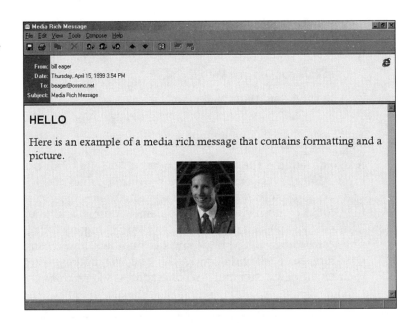

You can also attach files to your email messages, such as a Microsoft Excel spreadsheet that shows calculations, or a JPEG or GIF picture file that shows a product. However, I have three words of caution about attachments:

➤ People are a little afraid to open attachments because of all of the viruses that have been sent out over the Internet as attachments.

➤ Files that are large take a long time to download, and members of your audience might not like to use their online time waiting for what they consider to be an advertisement to download.

➤ If you send an attachment, it needs to be in a file format that everyone can open. For example, not every user has Microsoft Excel on his or her PC, and so won't be able to open your attachment. For multimedia purposes, you can usually send a JPEG or GIF picture file because most users have a program to open them—such as a Web browser (be sure the file is less than 20KB).

## Obtain or Create an Opt-In Recipient List

To whom are you mailing? Obviously, not everyone who has an email address. You want to target your campaign. One way to get a list of email addresses that help you reach your target market is to gather email addresses at your Web site. You can do this when people register at your site (assuming you have a registration process), purchase a product, or sign up to receive your email newsletter. If you reach a large audience (such as more than 1,000 people), you should ask several pertinent questions when you collect a user's email address so that you can target your email campaigns in the future. The first question, of course, is: "Do you mind whether we occasionally send you follow-up emails with useful information?" Let the users tell you that it's okay to send them mail in the future.

When users tell you (or an email list-gathering company) that it's okay to send them email, it is known as *opt-in*. There are two ways to create an opt-in situation:

➤ **Explicitly**   The user actually clicks on a button or check box on a Web page, saying it's okay.

➤ **Implicitly**   A customer might anticipate but does not formally agree to the email (as is the case with a confirmation email after a sale on your Web site, or a "thank you" email with password confirmation after a visitor registers).

Gather some basic information from Web site visitors when you collect your opt-in database; this should include the following:

➤ First name

➤ Last name

➤ Email address

➤ Mailing address

➤ Phone number

Other relevant questions during the opt-in process help you categorize visitors. For example, if your business supplies a medical service for doctors, have a series of check boxes where the doctors mark their specialties. Why? Because after you get 50,000 email addresses, you are probably going to want to send a specific email campaign to only the 10,000 urologists or 7,000 oncologists. The more information you gather during a registration process, the easier it is to custom-tailor future email campaigns. Remember, as with all survey and data collection, ask only the questions that you intend to use. The following figure shows a Web site that lets you register for a variety of email newsletters, based on your selection of subject matter.

Most marketing and sales people know the process that moves a potential customer toward a sale. First, you have suspects: people who might or might not have any interest in your product or service. Then, you have prospects: people who, because of their interests, might become customers. Next you have leads: people who are very likely to become customers if you can convince them of the superiority of your products and services. Finally, you have customers and return customers. This process is also known as the *sales funnel*, illustrated by an inverted triangle in which suspects enter at the top, and sales and marketing efforts help filter out the customers at the bottom.

Opt-in should be an important part of your email marketing strategy—whether you use your own list or purchase one. That's because when people opt-in and answer questions that segment their interests, your email message goes to qualified prospects. Your Web site can then help turn the prospect into a lead (especially if you capture the prospect's name, address, and phone number at your site).

*Decide what topic areas are of interest to you for future email newsletters.*

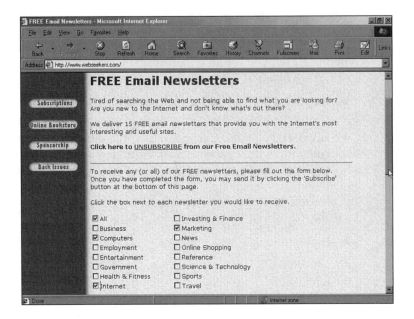

## Email List Vendors

There are several Internet-based companies that manage and rent targeted email lists. They also have services available for the distribution of your message. Here is an overview of four companies that offer these services. Each of these services does claim to work only with opt-in mailing lists.

### Company: Postmaster/Netcreations

http://www.postmasterdirect.com

➤ 100% opt-in mailing lists

➤ 9,000 lists with 2 million names

➤ 20 to 25 cents per name for list rental and distribution

➤ Minimum order $400

➤ Offers services to help you create and mail your own list

### Company: BulletMail

http://www.bulletmail.com

➤ Email your message to 2,500 people for only $350, including professional email-ing of your message by BulletMail (order more emails at $.14/email)

➤ Email your message to an entire email list and save 28%—just $.10/email includes emailing of your message by BulletMail

➤ Your email message can be up to 55 lines long

### Company: HTMail

http://www.htmail.com/customer.html

➤ $14.95 per 100 names mailed

➤ Prices include forename and surname of recipient for tracking actual response, mailing carried out by HTMail

➤ Includes report on who read your email and responded

### Company: Targit

http://www.targ-it.com

➤ More than 3 million opt-in, email addresses

➤ Hundreds of topical lists

➤ Minimum order is 1,000 pieces

➤ Member of the Electronic Direct Marketers Association

# Email Management Companies

The companies mentioned in the previous section focus on delivering your email message to a target audience you select from a variety of opt-in email lists. Sometimes you might want or need a company to completely handle all aspects of your email. Services ranging from message creation and delivery to full email management of responses and inquiries derived from email campaigns and your Web site are available. Large companies can have hundreds, even thousands, of messages that come in and need to be handled.

Boulder, Colorado-based Message Media (http://www.messagemedia.com) provides comprehensive email services. As is claimed on the Web site, Message Media "provides a seamless solution for relationship-based, transactive communications using Internet email. Termed *e-messaging,* this personalized sales and service channel enhances customer loyalty while cutting the cost of interacting with large numbers of customers." One of the big advantages of outsourcing email services is that email services for large companies and organizations require a different set of technologies. In other words, you can't really use a PC-based email program to distribute messages to and monitor the reactions of thousands of customers. Even bandwidth becomes a consideration with large email volume.

Brigade Solutions (http://www.brigadesolutions.com) is another company that provides a range of Internet-based customer support services. Using the Internet, Brigade's staff answers incoming email for your company. The staff is trained to understand support issues specific to your company or products.

# Spam, Spam, Spam

It is impossible to have a chapter about email marketing without mentioning spam. *Spam* refers to junk email that is sent to thousands, even hundreds of thousands of email users without regard to their interest in the material or consent to receive it. Spam is, in fact, an attempt to use the Internet to do marketing. However, most spam campaigns are for products and services of a dubious nature.

Spam presents many problems for Internet users and the marketing community. For one thing, people who spam emails usually don't pay for their efforts. It's similar to getting a direct mail letter with postage due. Indeed, if you get a spam email, you are paying for both the Internet connectivity and your time to read/delete the Spam message. The reason that spam campaigns are bad for the marketing community is because most of the recipients do not want or have interest in the spam messages, and all email campaigns begin to get a bad name...especially as the quantity of spam messages increases.

Lorrie Faith Cranor of AT&T Labs-Research and Brian LaMacchia of Microsoft produced a report that analyzed several aspects of spam. Of particular interest are the topics that spam messages advertise. As part of this study, Cranor and LaMacchia reviewed some 400 messages sent to certain AT&T and Lucent addresses and identified by email administrators as spam. Table 10.1 identifies the areas.

### Table 10.1   An Analysis of Spam Content

| Subject | Percent of messages |
| --- | --- |
| Money-making opportunities | 35% |
| Adult entertainment, singles services, and sexually oriented products and services | 11% |
| Direct email marketing products and services | 10% |
| Informational and how-to guides | 9% |
| Internet services, computer hardware and software, and office products and services | 7% |
| Other products and services | 25% |
| Noncommercial or suspected to have been solicited | 3% |

What gives spam a particularly bad name is the number of scams perpetuated by spam that attempt to cheat people. The Federal Trade Commission released a list of 12 of the most common types of spam scams. Their list was created from a sample of some 250,000 junk email messages that consumers forwarded to the FTC mailbox set up to collect spam (uce@ftc.gov).

Bernstein said the 12 most common types of spam scams include

**Business Opportunity Scams** Most of these scams promise a lot of income for a small investment of time and money. Some are actually old-fashioned pyramid schemes camouflaged to look like something else. "Consumers should be careful of money-making schemes that sound too good to be true," said Bernstein. "They usually are."

**Making Money by Sending Bulk Emailings** These schemes claim that you can make money sending your own solicitations via bulk email. They offer to sell you lists of email addresses or software to enable you to make the mailings. What they don't mention is that the lists are of poor quality; sending bulk email violates the terms of service of most Internet service providers; virtually no legitimate businesses engage in bulk emailings; and several states have laws regulating the sending of bulk email.

**Check This Out**

**The FTC Press Release on Spam Scams**

"The Dirty Dozen list of junk email is a tipoff to a ripoff," said Jodie Bernstein, Director of the FTC's Bureau of Consumer Protection. "Spam is a problem for practically everyone with a computer. It's annoying, it slows down the email system, and a lot of it is fraudulent. We have an email box where consumers can send unwanted, unsolicited email. We're receiving more than 1,000 complaints a day."

**Chain Letters** These electronic versions of the old-fashioned chain letters usually arrive with claims such as, "You are about to make $50,000 in less than 90 days!" "But you don't," said Bernstein, "and these electronic chain letters are every bit as illegal as the old-fashioned paper versions."

**Work-at-Home Schemes** These email messages offer you the chance to earn money in the comfort of your own home. Two popular versions pitch envelope stuffing and craft assembly. But nobody really pays you for stuffing envelopes, and craft assembly promoters usually refuse to buy the crafts claiming the work does not meet their "quality standards."

**Health and Diet Scams** These offer "scientific breakthroughs," "miraculous cures," "exclusive products," "secret formulas," and "ancient ingredients." Some come with testimonials from "cured" consumers or endorsements from "famous medical experts" no one's ever heard of. "These bogus cure-alls are just electronic snake oil," said Bernstein.

**Easy Money** Offers such as "Learn how to make $4,000 in one day," or "Make unlimited profits exchanging money on world currency markets," appeal to the desire to get rich quick. "If making money were that easy, we'd all be millionaires," Bernstein said.

**Get Something Free**  The lure of valuable, free items—such as computers or long-distance phone cards—convinces consumers to pay membership fees to sign up with these scams. After they pay the fee, consumers learn that they don't qualify for the "free" gift until they recruit other "members." "These scams are just lowdown, high-tech pyramid schemes," Bernstein said.

**Investment Opportunities**  These scams might tout outrageously high rates of return with no risk. Glib, resourceful promoters suggest they have high-level financial connections; that they're privy to inside information; or that they guarantee the investment. To close the deal, they might serve up phony statistics, misrepresent the significance of a current event, or stress the unique quality of their offering. But they are not unique. They're just like the other scams.

**Cable Descrambler Kits**  For a small initial investment, you can buy a cable descrambler kit so you can receive cable without paying the subscription fees. "There are two small problems with these schemes," Bernstein said. "The kits usually don't work and stealing cable service is illegal."

**Guaranteed Loans or Credit, on Easy Terms**  Some scams offer home-equity loans, even if you don't have any equity in your home. Others offer guaranteed, unsecured credit cards, regardless of your credit history. The "loans" turn out to be lists of lending institutions and the credit cards never arrive.

**Credit Repair Scams**  These scams target consumers with poor credit records. For an up-front fee, they offer to clear up a bad credit record—for a fee—or give you a completely clean credit slate by showing you how to get an Employer Identification Number. "No one can erase a bad credit record if it's accurate, and using an Employer Identification Number to set up a new credit identity is against the law," Bernstein said.

**Vacation Prize Promotions**  Like their snail-mail counterparts, these email "Prize Promotions" tell consumers they've been selected to receive a "luxury" vacation at a bargain-basement price. But the accommodations aren't deluxe and upgrades are expensive.

## The Law on Spam

Both United States federal government and individual states are creating laws related to the use of the Internet for spam. One pertinent effort is Senate Bill S759.IS, the Inbox Privacy Act introduced to the Senate in 1999 by Senators Frank Murkowski (R-AK), Robert Torricelli (D-NJ), Conrad Burns (R-MT), and Harry Reid (D-NV). As stated in a press release, "the Inbox Privacy Act would require email marketers to honestly identify themselves, honor consumer remove requests, and allow Internet domain owners to set up electronic "stop signs" to give domain owners the ability to block unwanted solicitations. In order to allow the Internet consumer to have the ultimate choice, unsolicited emails could be sent to those who still want to receive such solicitations. Internet service providers, state attorneys general, and the Federal Trade Commission would have the authority to seek up to $50,000 per day in damages."

Now you don't want to spam the Senate, but comments on this bill can be emailed to spamfree@murkowski.senate.gov.

## Political Spam

You probably wouldn't think of spam as an element of a political campaign, but it can be. When NATO forces were bombing Belgrade, the Belgrade Academic Association for Equal Rights in the World sent email messages to thousands of Internet users. The message specifically decried the bombing. "In the last nine days, NATO barbarians have bombed our schools, hospitals, bridges, killed our people but that was not enough for them now they have started to destroy our cultural monuments which represent the core of existence of our nation."

Certainly, war is a terrible, terrible thing. What is interesting is that the Internet is now viewed (correctly) as a system that can reach a global audience. It presents an opportunity for any organization to effectively communicate a viewpoint that might not have been otherwise heard on the normal information channels of television and radio. Whether or not you believe in the cause or message of political spam, I am certain that we will see more of it.

## Unsolicited Email Versus Spam

Direct marketing organizations make a point of clarifying the difference between unsolicited email (also called UCE) and spam. From the recipient's point of view, neither UCE nor spam is mail that was requested (such as opt-in mailings). But there are significant differences between the two, which are highlighted in Table 10.2.

### Table 10.2    Differences Between UCE and Spam

| UCE | SPAM |
|---|---|
| Legitimate content. | Frequently scams. |
| Honors request to remove from future mailings. | Usually not removed from list. |
| Sender uses valid FROM: field. | Mail sent anonymously. |
| Senders pay for transmission and use their own ISPs. | Rarely pays, and abuses networks. |

The Direct Email Advertisers Association (http://www.deaa.org) offers a few ways to know whether a message you receive is spam.

➤ If you reply to a message and the sender's email address is nondeliverable, then it is spam.

➤ If the content of the message seems unacceptable, or is possibly a scam, then it is spam.

**185**

➤ If the message does not identify itself as UCE or an advertisement in the header of the letter, it is spam.

➤ If the message does not contain a company name, address, or phone number, it is spam.

# Managing Incoming Email to a Web Site

If you decide to handle incoming messages yourself (as opposed to outsourcing to an email management service company), you need to set up some procedures and guidelines. Let's start with your Web site. There are two ways to set up incoming email requests:

➤ **Direct all incoming email to the department that is best suited to answer it**  You can have several different `mailto:` links (these are links on Web pages that send mail to a specific person) on your customer service page. This might expedite your incoming email, but it doesn't do a very good job of tracking.

➤ **Send all incoming email to a central customer service desk**  This individual/department then performs the following:

1. Logs the request/suggestion.
2. Stores a copy of the request/suggestion in a database for future reference and analysis.
3. Answers the request if possible.
4. Forwards the request on to other departments if necessary.
5. Ensures that he or she receive a copy of the response that is sent back to the recipient.

For tracking purposes, you want to save the following information about the email:

➤ The name of the person who submits an email

➤ The individual's email address

➤ The nature of the request/problem/suggestion (you could place these into different categories such as "Billing Questions" or "Product Defects")

➤ The day and time of day of the request

➤ The day and time of day of the response

➤ A copy of the response

➤ Whether a telephone call back was involved

Why all this work? Well, over time you want to know whether your Web site is having a positive impact on business procedures (are customers happier? do you get fewer telephone inquiries?). Tracking is the only way. Plus, you create a valuable list of email addresses that you can use for future communications.

Another option is nonhuman interaction. An email autoresponder (also sometimes called a "mail reflector" or "mailbot") is a software program that receives incoming email and automatically sends back a "canned" response. So suppose you have a link on your Web site labeled `prices@yourcompany.com`. If the user sends an email to this address, the autoresponder automatically sends a message with detailed product pricing information back to the person. You could also have a `productbenefits@ yourcompany.com` link; any type of prepackaged material that would be appropriate to email to someone can be sent by an autoresponder without human intervention. The more advanced autoresponder software programs can even "read" the subject lines of someone's request to determine which canned response would be best.

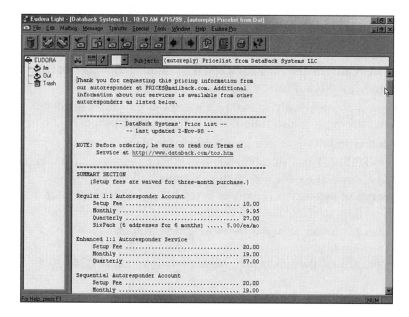

*An autoresponder automatically sends a "canned" message, such as this one about pricing, to a user's inquiry.*

How do you get an autoresponder? Your Internet service provider or the company that hosts your Web site should offer this service. There are also companies that provide autoresponder services (Table 10.2). Here are a few:

## Table 10.2 Companies That Offer Autoresponse Services

| Company | Web Site |
|---|---|
| Databack | `http://www.databack.com` |
| Netbox | `http://www.netbox.com` |
| Net Space | `http://www.netspace1.com` |
| Your Domain Host | `http://www.`*yourdomainhost*`.com` |

Autoresponders are pretty straightforward in terms of functionality. A message comes in; then a message goes out. A little creativity can make the autoresponder a bit more powerful. For example, if a message comes in, an initial response message is sent immediately; it might be something such as, "Here is the product information you requested." Then, after, say, 24 hours, a follow-up response is sent (again automatically). This one could say, "Any Questions?" and have the phone number for the sales manager. So the autoresponder begins a little dialog with the customer.

One step up from the autoresponder is an email management system that has more functionality. These are systems either for large companies or companies that get lots of email that needs to be managed. Sometimes referred to as Automatic Email Distribution Systems, they sort, route, track, and follow up on email. GTE, for example, has a product called inResponse. Here's how it works:

1. A customer visits the Web site and submits an inquiry via email.

2. GTE inResponse system assigns the message a tracking number and automatically sends the customer a "thank you" email.

3. The customer's email is automatically routed to a specific department or customer service representative. It is also time-stamped for tracking purposes.

4. Data from the customer inquiry is stored in a "knowledge base" (a database) for future searching and company decision making.

5. The individual who receives the customer inquiry responds to the customer (there might be a series of prewritten responses based upon different types of inquiries).

6. The customer receives his or her personal response to the inquiry.

There are several other companies that offer email management systems. Table 10.3 provides a list.

### Table 10.3   Email Management Systems

| Company | Web Site |
|---|---|
| Brightware | http://www.brightware.com |
| Dialog Software | http://www.dialogsoft.com |
| GTE | http://www.gte.com/inresponse |
| MCS | http://www.mcsdallas.com |
| Mustang Software | http://www.mustang.com |

## Managing Responses to Email Campaigns

You've created an email campaign. Your message is perfect. You've rented an opt-in mailing list and hired a company for distribution. The Send button is pushed. What now?

In some ways, dealing with responses to an email marketing campaign can be easier than incoming mail from your Web site. That's because you usually have a message that focuses on achieving a specific goal. You send out an offer with a 10% discount coupon for a specific product. You are inviting people to come to the page on your Web site that promotes a new service. It is easier to track the responses. In fact, if you are going to include your phone number, you might want to mention in the email message that people should refer to "offer 117," for example, so the operator knows that the call refers to a specific email campaign and can forward appropriately.

The only challenge is your ability to respond quickly, or your Web server's ability to handle the load of requests. For example, let's say you send out a campaign to 100,000 email addresses asking people to click on a link that brings them to a "buy" page on your site. If 10% (10,000 people) try the link within one hour, your site might not be able to handle the load and people will get error messages. Or think about this: If 10,000 people tried to call your switchboard, would they all get through? One way to deal with potential overload is to stagger the campaign and send out 20,000 messages a day over a period of five days. Remember, what you don't want to do is turn an interesting and valuable offer to prospective customers into a situation that offers bad customer service.

## The Least You Need to Know

➤ Set up a system to quickly handle incoming email from customers and prospects.

➤ You can use email for direct marketing, service information, customer service, and ongoing customer interaction.

➤ Create and use a signature on email messages, providing useful information such as your company phone number to readers.

➤ Use opt-in email lists to ensure that people want to receive your email marketing messages.

# Chapter 11

# Marketing with Newsgroups

---

## In This Chapter

➤ How newsgroups can enhance your marketing efforts

➤ Use DejaNews and Microsoft Outlook Express to access and participate in newsgroups

➤ How to find the best newsgroups for marketing and/or research

➤ How to create successful newsgroup messages

---

Using *newsgroups* is a popular method for exchanging ideas on a variety of topics via the Internet. You can find a topic in which you have an interest (or that is useful for your customers), and then either read the ongoing discussion of other people from around the world or join in the discussion yourself. Because these discussions take place with messages, they are not in real time as is a chat session. In some ways, newsgroups are better than chats because the information is stored and you can find what you're looking for.

For marketing purposes, newsgroups serve two very important functions. One is that you can use a newsgroup as a research tool. Learn about your competition. Find out what people might be saying about your company. Second, they can be a marketing vehicle, a tool that you use to answer questions Internet users might be asking, respond to online complaints, or offer newsgroup-friendly marketing messages. In this chapter, you learn about newsgroups: how to locate useful newsgroups, how to participate in newsgroups, and how to craft messages that work.

# Introduction to Newsgroups

Officially, newsgroups are known as *Usenet* (users network) newsgroups. Technically, Usenet uses the Internet to distribute messages (also called *articles*) on specific subjects. Newsgroups are categorized by subject and the articles are added to specific newsgroups. For example, the newsgroup `rec.outdoors.fishing` contains articles about—guess what—fishing!

Are newsgroups popular? You bet! There are more than 24,000 different newsgroups. And it's estimated that every day as many as **one million** new messages (known as *articles*) are added to newsgroups. In fact, there are so many messages that most Internet service providers save only two or three weeks' worth of messages on their computers. It is a combination of the global reach of newsgroups and the volume of usage that makes newsgroups an important aspect of online marketing.

*Newsgroups have a global reach, and people talk about subjects in which they have personal interests, such as this message in the* `alt.support.diabetes` *newsgroup.*

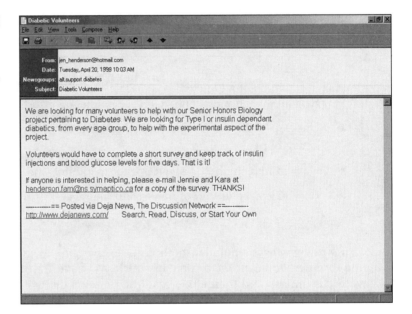

If you only read other people's newsgroup messages without writing and posting your own, you are what is known as a *lurker*—and there is nothing wrong with being a lurker if you find what you want. If you want to participate, however, you can send a message back to the newsgroup (in which case the entire world can read your message). This is referred to as *posting* your message or article. You can also send a reply message to only the author of a message—perhaps someone who has a question, complaint, or idea about your company.

There are some common terms used in the world of newsgroups which might be helpful:

➤ **Article**   This is the message that you or another person adds to a newsgroup.

➤ **Binary**   A file that is attached to an article. Frequently pictures.

➤ **Flame**   A nasty or inflammatory article that someone posts to a newsgroup.

➤ **FAQ (short for Frequently Asked Questions)**   A list of common questions and answers about a newsgroup.

➤ **Lurker**   Someone who reads messages but does not post any.

➤ **Newbie**   A person who is just learning how to use newsgroups.

➤ **Newsgroup**   A specific topic that has articles.

➤ **Post**   To send your message to a newsgroup.

➤ **Shout**   To type in ALL CAPITAL LETTERS.

➤ **Spam**   To send the same message to many newsgroups (also to send an email to many people, usually selling something).

➤ **Subject**   The subject of a newsgroup article.

➤ **Subscribe**   Join a newsgroup to quickly view articles.

➤ **Thread**   An ongoing discussion between people related to one original message.

➤ **Usenet**   The complete name for newsgroups—Usenet Newsgroups.

### Privacy and Security

Sometimes it's easy to forget that newsgroups and message boards are public places. Whatever you say can be seen by literally millions of people. For privacy and security, it's usually wise not to put your personal address or phone number on a message or a company phone number that you don't want other subscribers to call.

Following are a few newsgroups that offer tips and information to help you get started:

➤ `news.newusers.questions`   A newsgroup that answers new users' questions.

➤ `news.announce.newusers`   New users can find useful tips and information.

➤ `news.answers`   This newsgroup lists Frequently Asked Questions for newsgroups.

### First-Time User?

If you are new to newsgroups and want to try posting without getting embarrassed, you can use `alt.testing`, a newsgroup designed specifically for first-time users. All of the messages posted say something like "just a test." It's a good way to see how quickly your message is added to the group.

## Newsgroup Names

Newsgroups are categorized to make it a little easier to find what you're looking for. A hierarchy is used in an effort to organize topics. There are eight main categories at the top of this hierarchy (see Table 11.1). Then, each of these top-level categories is broken down into subcategories. One example of the main categories is that of alt, representing "alternative" (which translates into lots of different topics). You can find the newsgroups name `alt.music.tapes`, which is a newsgroup for people who like music and specifically tapes. Another example, `alt.tv.xena`, translates to alternative, television, *Xena* (a popular television show).

### Table 11.1   Newsgroup Top-Level Categories

| Newsgroup Top Level | Topics |
| --- | --- |
| Alt | Alternative—hundreds of different topics |
| Comp | Computer-related |
| Misc | Miscellaneous topics |
| News | News |
| Rec | Recreational, sports, hobbies |
| Sci | Science-related |
| Soc | Social and societal topics |
| Talk | Area for talk and discussion |

## Are They Talking About You? Newsgroup Research

What type of research can you do with newsgroups? Well, here are three suggestions:

➤ You can conduct competitive intelligence to find out whether your competition uses newsgroups.

➤ You can find out whether the Internet community is "talking" about your company or products (and learn what they are saying).

➤ You can locate newsgroups in which to participate.

There are two types of searches that you can conduct:

➤ One is to search for newsgroups that have names that relate to your topic. For example, say your company makes canoes. You could search for newsgroups devoted to "boats." You will find the following newsgroups:

    rec.boats

    rec.boats.building

    rec.boats.cruising

    rec.boats.marketplace

    rec.boats.paddle

    rec.sport.waterski

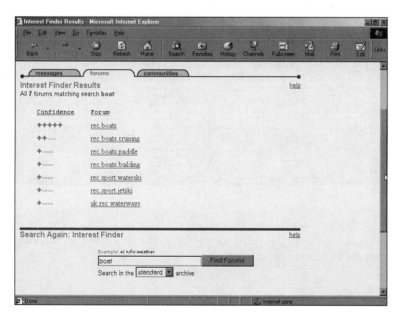

*Search for newsgroups that pertain to your products and services.*

Each of these newsgroups has articles about boats. Obviously, if you manufacture canoes, rec.boats.paddle is of more interest than rec.boats.cruising. You could also expand your search for newsgroups that relate to the outdoors, camping, fishing, and other activities that relate to boating.

➤ The second type of search you can do is for any articles (in all forums) about boats. It is very likely that people might post their boat messages to another newsgroup—possibly one about camping. Indeed, a quick search finds messages in both `alt.fishing` and `rec.outdoors.camping`.

Additional newsgroup marketing research includes searches for articles about either your company or your competition. The following figure shows that a search for "coleman canoe" locates 70 messages. Some of these might be inquiries by people who are investigating the purchase of a Coleman canoe, suggestions about product improvement, or questions about use and repair. You can use this information as a source of ideas for your company, or you can respond directly to individuals who post articles.

*A search for "coleman canoe" finds 70 current messages. Use newsgroups to learn what customers are saying about your products.*

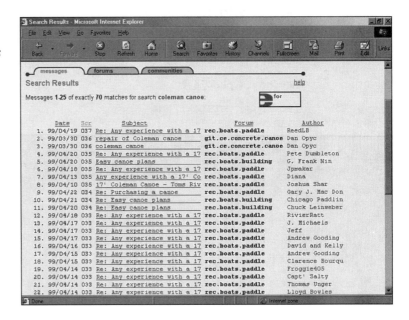

When you locate newsgroups that you feel reach a target market, write down the name of the newsgroup because you might want to regularly monitor the messages in this group or even participate in the discussions.

# Use Deja.com for Newsgroups

DejaNews (`http://www.deja.com`) is the only Web site that lets you read, search, participate, and subscribe to all of the Usenet newsgroups. You must register to post and reply to messages and to have a personalized page where you can subscribe to newsgroups, but it's available to you at no charge. DejaNews offers advantages over the traditional approach of using Outlook Express or Netscape Messenger to read newsgroup messages (the obvious advantage being an easy-to-use Web interface for searching and viewing messages). You can search through *all* the newsgroups simultaneously to find messages about specific topics, which you cannot do with Outlook Express or Netscape Communicator.

# Using Outlook Express for Newsgroups

Outlook Express is Microsoft's newsgroup/email software that is included with standard or full installations of Internet Explorer 4.0, Windows 98, and Office 97 and 2000. If you don't already have it, you can download Internet Explorer from the Microsoft Web site (http://www.microsoft.com). You launch Outlook Express for newsgroups from Internet Explorer by clicking on the **Mail** button on the toolbar and then choosing **Read News**.

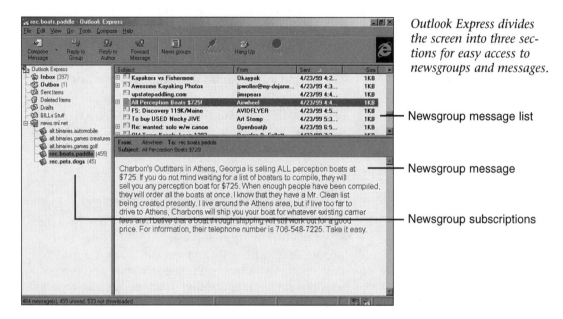

*Outlook Express divides the screen into three sections for easy access to newsgroups and messages.*

— Newsgroup message list

— Newsgroup message

— Newsgroup subscriptions

The upcoming subsections offer instruction for performing tasks relating to using Outlook Express to participate in newsgroups.

## Search and Subscribe to Newsgroups

There are two ways to use newsgroups:

➤ You can simply search for a newsgroup, and then retrieve current articles.

➤ You can subscribe to specific newsgroups. It costs nothing to subscribe; you simply use Outlook Express to do this.

The advantage to subscribing is that it saves you time. You quickly go to the newsgroup(s) to which you subscribe and receive current articles, so you eliminate the task of always finding the newsgroup. And, if you find that you don't like the articles on a newsgroup, you can always unsubscribe (see the earlier section titled "Unsubscribe to

**Check This Out**

### Subscribe Versus Go To

When you subscribe to a newsgroup, Outlook Express keeps that newsgroup listed in the Newsgroup subscription list for easy access. If, however, you just want to try a newsgroup, instead of clicking **Subscribe** in the Newsgroup display window, simply click the **Go To** button.

a Newsgroup"). To search and subscribe to newsgroups in Outlook Express, perform the following steps:

1. Launch Outlook Express (from within Internet Explorer, click the **Mail** button on the toolbar and then choose **Read News**).

2. Click the **News groups** button on the toolbar.

3. If this is your first time with the newsgroups, click **Reset List** to get the most current list of newsgroups.

4. In the **Display Newsgroups Which Contain** field, type a subject about which you would like to find a newsgroup (for example "pets" or "medicine").

5. Click the name of the newsgroup(s) you want to view.

6. Click **Subscribe**.

**Check This Out**

### Plus Sign

If there is a plus sign to the left of the subject, it means that several other people have already joined in a discussion about the topic. Click the plus sign to see all the messages related to the current subject.

## Read a Newsgroup Message

Messages are the "guts" of newsgroups. They contain all of the information and sometimes pictures that people share with one another. Outlook's main window enables you to simultaneously view newsgroups, message subjects, and individual messages. To read a newsgroup message, perform the following steps:

1. At the Outlook Express main window, double-click the name of the news server (for example, `news.rmi.net`). This opens a list of the newsgroups to which you have subscribed (see previous section).

2. Click any specific newsgroup.

3. The current messages for this newsgroup appear in the upper-right window.

4. Click once on any message to read the message in the window at the bottom of the screen, or double-click the message to open it in a new "read message" window.

## Save a Newsgroup Message

To save a newsgroup message, perform the following steps:

1. Highlight the message (see previous section) you want to save.

2. Choose **File**, and then **Save As**.

**198**

3. Type a filename, choose the directory in which you want to place this file, and click **Save** (the file is saved as a text file).

## Reply to a Message

You can reply to the messages you read either to the entire newsgroup or to the author of the message in which you're interested. To reply to the entire newsgroup, perform the following steps:

1. Highlight the message you want to reply to (see "Read a Newsgroup Message").

2. Click the **Reply to Group** button on the toolbar.

3. Type your message.

4. Click **Post** to post your message to the newsgroup.

### Sorting Messages

On top of the message window are headers showing the message subject, whom the message is from, and the date the message was sent. Click any of these to change the way the messages are sorted and displayed.

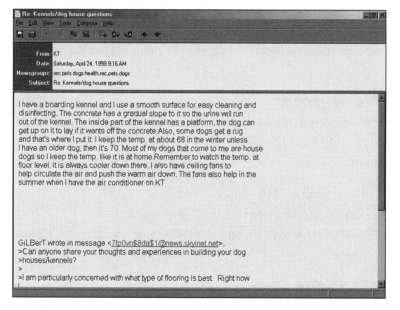

*You can open a newsgroup message in its own window.*

To reply to only the author of a message, perform the following steps:

1. Highlight the message to which you want to reply (see "Read a Newsgroup Message").

2. Click the **Reply to Author** button on the toolbar.

### Check This Out

**Posting Delay**

When you post a message to a newsgroup, it might not appear for several hours, possibly even a day, as your message is routed to all the newsgroup servers on the Internet.

**3.** Type your message.

**4.** Click **Send** to send the message.

## Post a New Article

By posting an article (or message) to a newsgroup, you are participating in a global discussion. It is your chance to let other people read what you think. You might even be pleasantly surprised at the responses people have to your information both on the newsgroup and in emails you receive. To post an article, perform the following steps:

**1.** Choose the newsgroup to which you want to post by clicking the name of the newsgroup in Outlook Express (the newsgroups to which you've subscribed are listed under the name of the news server).

**2.** Click the **Compose Message** button on the toolbar.

**3.** Type your subject and the message (the address is already filled in).

**4.** Click **Send**. Your message is now on its way to the newsgroup. It usually takes several hours before your message shows up on every news server in the world.

### Unsubscribe to a Newsgroup

If you've subscribed to a newsgroup but no longer find it useful, then you might want to unsubscribe. To do so, perform the following steps:

**1.** Choose the newsgroup to which you want to unsubscribe by clicking the name of the newsgroup in Outlook Express (the newsgroups to which you've subscribed are listed under the name of the news server).

**2.** Choose **Tools**, then **Unsubscribe from This Newsgroup**.

**3.** Outlook Express asks you whether you are sure you want to unsubscribe; click **Yes**.

## Yahoo! Message Boards

Yahoo! is one of the most popular Web sites on the Net. Yahoo! started as a search engine and directory in which you could find other Web sites. Today, the site offers much more, including its own message boards. The message boards on Yahoo! are similar to newsgroups—except that only members of Yahoo! are participants.

Yahoo! creates these message boards when it feels there is a subject that merits enough interest. Users can also submit requests for Yahoo! to begin new message boards.

The upcoming subsections offer detailed instruction for participation in Yahoo! message boards. If your company is publicly traded, there is probably a Yahoo! message board where people are "talking" about your company.

## Access Yahoo! Message Boards

To get to the Yahoo! message boards, perform the following steps:

1. Go to http://messages.yahoo.com.
2. Click a link to one of the message board categories (like Health).
3. Click a link to a subcategory (such as Medicine).
4. If necessary, click another subcategory, until you arrive at a list of messages.

**Boards for Companies**

If you want to request a board for a publicly traded company and its stock, you should know that Yahoo! adds boards only for stocks that are traded on the NASDAQ, American, or New York Stock Exchanges.

## Search Yahoo! Message Boards

You can also perform searches with Yahoo! message boards. To do so, perform the following steps:

1. At the message board home page (http://messages.yahoo.com), type a keyword (such as pets).

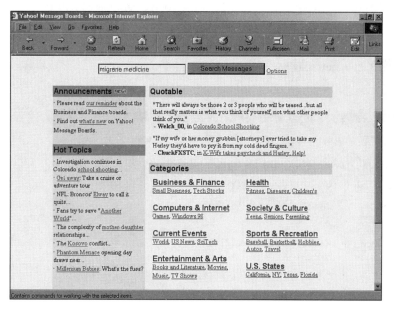

*At the Yahoo! message boards, search for messages by keyword or category.*

2. Click **Search Messages**.

3. You receive a list of both message boards and messages; click a message board link to go to the board, or click a message to view the message.

*Check This Out*

### Stock and Public Company Message Boards

The Yahoo! message boards about public companies are extremely popular and easy to access. In the keyword field, type a stock symbol (for example, WLA for Warner Lambert) and search for the Warner Lambert message board. For very large companies, there might be thousands of messages. Investors sometimes add very negative messages about companies if they feel that the stock is not performing as they would like. Be careful not to start an online war of words or disclose any nonpublic information on these boards. Also, Yahoo! warns: "Reading information from message boards is no substitute for independent research, and it's a bad idea to trade or make any investment decisions based on message boards."

## Read a Yahoo! Message Board Message

To read a message you've located (see either of previous two sections), perform the following steps:

1. Click a link to any message (see either of previous two sections).

2. The message opens in a new page.

## Reply to a Yahoo! Message Board Message

To reply to a message you've located, perform the following steps:

1. Open the message to which you want to reply.

2. Click the **Reply** icon at the top of the message.

3. On the Compose Message page, type a subject.

4. Type your message.

5. Click **Post Message** (or Preview before Posting).

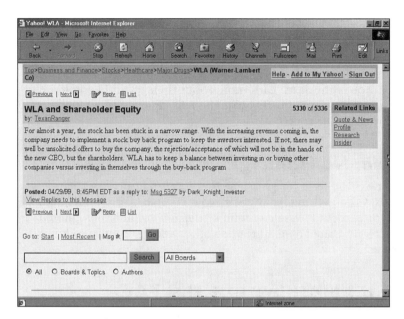

*Yahoo! has an easy-to-use Web interface on its message boards. Many publicly traded companies have message boards on Yahoo!*

# Rules of the Road: Participate Without Offending People

You've found newsgroups that really hit your target market. You know how to participate using DejaNews or Outlook Express. What should you say? How often should you say it? The last thing you want to do is accidentally annoy prospective customers. Like electronic mail, there are some "rules" for successful participation in newsgroups.

## Rule Number One: No Spam!

Don't spam newsgroups. You could, for example, create a marketing message about your company's great new fly swatter, and then post this article to all 25,000+ newsgroups. It wouldn't take long before YOUR mailbox would be full of hate mail. People subscribe to newsgroups because they want to find information that is useful, therefore related to the topic of the newsgroup. Now if you post a message about fly swatters to `alt.insects.destroy` (I don't think this exists), you're in fine shape. So, post your messages only to appropriate newsgroups. And DON'T send the same message day after day. People get sick of it.

## Rule Number Two: Avoid Blatant Commercialism

Don't be blatantly commercial. Most newsgroups are designed to be resources of information and discussion, not bulletin boards for sales pitches. There might be some exceptions, and after you view some of the messages in a newsgroup you get a feel for what is acceptable newsgroup behavior. Generally, it is better to create an "infomercial" type message. Provide some useful information that relates to the people who read a specific newsgroup. There's nothing wrong with submitting a message to the `rec.boats.paddle` newsgroup that informs readers of a new Web site (or Web site feature) that helps canoe enthusiasts learn more about their sport. In some ways, newsgroups are similar to opt-in email lists because the participants want to receive useful information about a specific topic.

## Rule Number Three: No Flaming!

Don't *flame* people. Flame is the term for an article that has inflammatory rhetoric. If you read an article that says something nasty about your company or product, don't start an online war of words about it. Use common sense. You could either ignore the message entirely, or discreetly write an email to the author asking them to call you if they have any further suggestions.

# Only the FAQs and Nothing but the FAQs

Because new people are constantly joining, participating in, and leaving newsgroups, it is common that the same issues and questions arise again and again. As a result, most newsgroups have created a FAQ document, which is a list of frequently asked questions (with answers). Often, the newsgroup FAQ list also provides an introduction to the newsgroup and mentions any specific rules or codes of conduct for the group. Here, for example, is a brief overview of the `rec.arts.animation` newsgroup:

> "`rec.arts.animation` is a relatively high-volume newsgroup which is intended to discuss animation of any kind. No subjects are taboo, but discussion tends to focus on cartoons of all sorts—how they are made, how good they are, how BAD they are :-), and any other toon-related issues."

The FAQ list then jumps into the Q&A with questions such as: "Q: Are there any magazines, and so on, dealing with animation? A. A list follows, which is surely not all-inclusive...

This is mentioned because it is worth spending a few minutes reading the FAQ for a newsgroup before you participate. To obtain the FAQ for a newsgroup, go to the Internet FAQ Archives Web site at `http://www.faqs.org/faqs`, as shown in the following figure. You can search this database of the FAQs for newsgroups either by keyword or by newsgroup category.

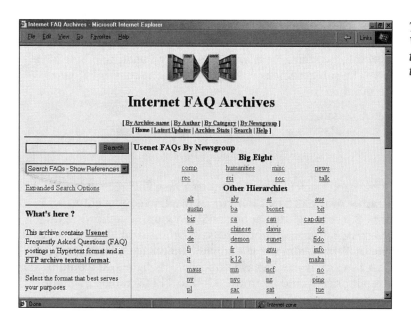

*The Internet FAQ Archives Web site provides access to the FAQ's pages for thousands of newsgroups.*

# Make Your Message Work

If you follow the rules mentioned earlier, you won't get in trouble. But you still need to create a message that succeeds. Here are a few tips:

➤ Make the subject of your message clear. Don't be misleading. People hate it when you waste their time. We advise keeping the subject line to fewer than 40 characters because most email programs display only the first 40 characters of subject lines. Here are a few examples for subjects that would work well on the rec.boats.paddle newsgroup:

> ➤ Try our new kayak Web site
>
> ➤ XYZ company—list of great canoe trips
>
> ➤ Would like advice/input from paddlers
>
> ➤ Ten tips for purchasing a new canoe
>
> ➤ December 10% discount on wooden paddles

➤ AVOID USING A LOT OF UPPERCASE WORDS (also known as *shouting*). It's not easy to read words typed in all uppercase.

➤ The message itself should be relatively short. Two, three, or four paragraphs are all that most people have time to read.

➤ You can include links to your Web site or a Web page in the message. Just type the entire URL—such as http://www.*yourcompany*.com. This gives the readers quick access to your site...usually by clicking the link in the message itself!

Here is a message I found in the `rec.boats.paddle` newsgroup. It is a good example of an effective message. The company is looking for input on a new product concept for a portable global positioning system. Clearly, people who go boating might have an interest in the product. The subject line is straightforward, the message itself is short, and it is easy to respond to.

Subject: GPS Market Research

Message:

Early Adopters,

We are seeking initial market reaction and input to a new GPS receiver product concept. The key feature of the product is a virtual display (equivalent to a 17" monitor viewed from 2 feet away) that supports SVGA graphics, allowing the viewing of standard color raster maps and charts, in bright sunlight. The product must be held about 1 inch from the eye to view the image. The maps would be loaded on a PCMCIA card. It would have onboard GPS. The unit would run Windows CE. The retail price would be in the $500 to $1,000 range. What do you think? Thanks in advance.

Author

Email address

How often should you post articles to newsgroups? It would be inappropriate to send the same message to the same newsgroup again and again. But if you have something new and worthwhile for the group, go ahead and participate.

Some companies monitor newsgroups simply as a marketing and public relations technique for damage control. If a dissatisfied customer starts to use the Internet to say bad or untrue things about your company or product, you might consider using the newsgroup to set the record straight in a polite and honest fashion—just don't get into an online flame war.

---

### The Least You Need to Know

➤ Regularly read newsgroups about your industry or company to learn what people might be saying about your products and services.

➤ Read the FAQs for newsgroups you participate in to find out what the topics and rules of the newsgroup are.

➤ Avoid being blatantly commercial in your newsgroup articles.

➤ Use newsgroup articles to invite readers to visit your Web site.

# Chapter 12

# Your Web Site Is a Marketing Tool

---

### In This Chapter

➤ Learn the design and content components of a powerful Web site

➤ Discover how your Web site can be a cost-savings communications tool

➤ Identify how many specific areas of your site can make a significant economic impact on your business

➤ Learn how your Web site can enhance your relationship with business partners

---

In this chapter, we will examine the four C's of a good Web site:

➤ Content
➤ Commerce
➤ Community
➤ Communication

We will investigate design principles that will make your site more effective, and we will focus on the elements and functionality of a Web site that enhance marketing, serve customers, and provide bottom-line benefits.

## Design a Showcase of a Site

Some of you might not have a designer's eye when it comes to look and feel, layout, and ease of use. These are words used by ad agencies, Web designers, and others to describe the artsy features of a Web site. But the artsy parts of your site have true, bottom-line effects. Think of the site design as the packaging of the content and commerce capabilities of your site. Gateway used to deliver PCs in plain boxes, but now the cowhide brand of a Gateway PC is immediately apparent to all—even without the name of the company visible.

The packaging must be not only attractive and memorable, but also easy to open. Web designers call this *usability* and often attain it through focus groups in which Web users try a site and market researchers monitor their actions to determine whether the site is effective. Perhaps you've struggled with a heavy-duty plastic bag that requires a sharp knife to open. We want to ensure that your Web site opens easily. Consider these guidelines for site design:

➤ *Easy Navigation*

Use the two-click rule: Make everything a visitor wants to see available within two clicks of the home or start page.

### What Visitors Want

Visitors to your neck of the Net want to know three things: where they *are*, where they can *go*, and how they can *get back* to where they came from.

➤ *Graphics That Load Quickly*

High-speed Internet access looms in the future. In the meantime, most of your customers have to get by with less than lightning speeds. Today, the ordinary Internet user has a modem speed of 28.8Kbps. Be sure to minimize the download times of graphics to address this modem speed. Be sure that your home page and other pages load in less than one minute at 28.8Kbps. Technically, that translates into a page that has less than 100KB of graphics.

Present text the user can read while graphics download, and be sure that your quality-control process includes testing your site with slower modems. Far too often, we find that Web development companies create sites that load quickly on their computers (they have the latest computers and high-speed Internet access) but very slowly on most customers' computers. If you really want to have a bells-and-whistles site, consider having a home page that enables the user to choose to enter either your "regular site" or the "high-speed site," with a warning that the high-speed version of your site requires a certain speed modem (56Kbps or faster).

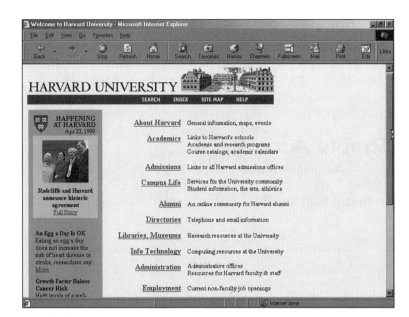

*The Harvard University home page. Good site design helps users get where they need to go with two clicks of their mouse.*

### ➤ Help Your Customers Connect

Incredible as it sounds, many Web sites make it difficult to actually find the phone number or address of a company. This is ridiculous. Your business card has this information; why not your Web site? We recommend including basic address, phone, and fax numbers on your home page. The information can be at the bottom of the home page—just have it on the home page!

### ➤ Capture Interest Quickly

Just as with other forms of communication, you have only a few seconds to pique someone's interest, grab their attention, and give them a reason to stay at your site. Put the best offers, the most compelling copy, and the headline that stops them in their tracks *right up front*.

### ➤ Less Is More

Web-site design has come a long way since the early days. Trends, patterns, and preferred styles are as common on the Web as they are in home construction and men's ties. Many styles are effective, including the common magazine format found on many news sites. But clutter is distracting, so keep animation to a minimum and increase the effectiveness of that animation. Don't have too many scrolling marquees (where the text moves across the screen). Direct your site visitor to the most important information.

### ➤ Have Links, but Not Too Many

As with the Less Is More principle, populate your site with links to other sites that are relevant and well-maintained. Nothing is worse than a huge list of links whose relevance to your business and your customer is marginal. Include a regular link check with your site's quality-control efforts to eliminate all broken links.

**209**

➤ *Consistency Across All Media*

Finally, make the look and feel of the site match your company's personality and culture. If your company is a down-to-earth group that sells organic fruits and vegetables, you probably don't want to use Hollywood glitz or Silicon Valley flash.

# What Your Site Should Accomplish

We've talked about how to overlay your business goals with the opportunities of the Internet. Successful companies launch the digital components of their business by tying together specific goals with the four C's of the Internet:

➤ Content

➤ Commerce

➤ Community

➤ Communication

Together, the four C's drive traffic and determine the degree of stickiness your site has. *Stickiness* means exactly what it sounds like: how long visitors feel compelled to stay (glued) to your site or want to return because of great content, easy commerce, a sense of community, and useful communication. Although there are no standards of stickiness yet, it is a useful marketing target. The following sections in this chapter provide ideas and suggestions that can help you develop useful content, commerce, community, and communication on your site.

## Content That Supports Your Goals

The content of your site defines your message. Like any other marketing channel, your Web site must clearly express your key marketing message and convey it in a compelling way. Don't get distracted with ancillary messages and don't distract your visitor, either. Remember, less is more. Your Web site should help you achieve your business goals, whether they are related to sales, customer service, or investor relations.

Content can be many things and can tie into the other three C's. In fact, *comm-tent* is a term that describes the combination of commerce and community with content. Here are a few categories of content you should consider developing for your site:

➤ Company overview (history, current developments)

➤ Company contact information (phone numbers, addresses, maps, offices)

➤ Investor relations (public companies can post financial information, current stock prices)

➤ Articles, white papers, and product literature

➤ Product information (detailed features, benefits, product specifications)

➤ Company and/or industry news (includes press releases)

➤ Ordering information (or e-commerce for online ordering)

➤ Customer support materials (frequently asked questions, inquiries)

If your site grows to the point that you have more than about 50 pages (which isn't hard to do), consider adding a site map. This can be a simple page that provides an index to the sections and pages on your site. A step beyond a site map is a search feature in which every page (and the text) of your site is stored in a database and users can use keywords to search your site to find exactly the content they are looking for.

For example, CIGNA is an international provider of health care, employee benefits, insurance, and financial services. Indeed, CIGNA helps 21,000 companies provide valuable benefits for their employees. To describe all these services, CIGNA has a public Web site with hundreds if not thousands of pages. To help users navigate through this wealth of information, the company offers both a site map (see the following figure) and a keyword search function.

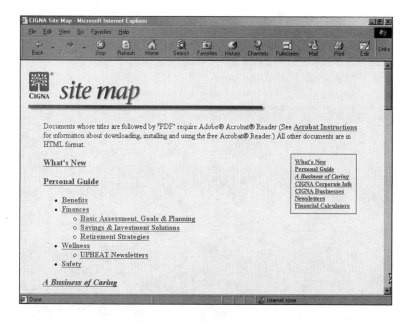

*The CIGNA Web site includes a site map to help users find what they are looking for.*

## Shorten the Sales Cycle

You can't pick up a newspaper or listen to a newscast today without hearing about electronic commerce (also known as e-commerce). But what *is* e-commerce? E-commerce is much more than simply selling widgets online. E-commerce encompasses anything that affects the financial performance of your company: the creation of new sales, enhancement of productivity, reduction of costs, increases in the lifetime value of a customer, and so on. These quantitative results don't have to be measured in billions of dollars; there are smaller but equally important ways to affect your business.

Let's look at a few generally accepted reasons why people buy online:

➤ Immediacy of the purchase

➤ Comprehensive inventory

➤ Anonymity

➤ It is cool

Because we focus more on marketing than sales in this book, let's consider the sales-support aspect of marketing online. Of course, there are many ways to add value, including using the Web to shorten the sales cycle and move the customer one step closer to saying yes.

For example, buying a home can be an intimidating process. A prospective buyer has to open his wallet and show his balance sheet to perfect strangers who can approve or decline a homeowner's loan. From a lender's perspective, many people *think* they can afford a house, but few have a good grasp of exactly *how much* house they can afford.

This uncertainty from both sides of a mortgage transaction makes the Internet a terrific vehicle to shorten the sales cycle. A mortgage company can offer an online form that prequalifies potential buyers and filters the list of suspects down to prospects. This is also faster and more convenient for the buyer.

*The GetSmart Mortgage Finder service prequalifies potential borrowers online.*

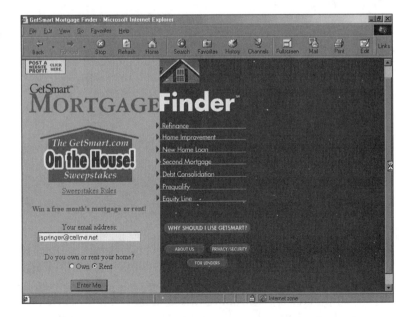

Think about the steps any prospective customer takes to reach a purchase decision. Anywhere along the continuum, you can apply an Internet application to speed things along. For example, many times, a customer with loyalty to a brand name needs help finding retail outlets where he can purchase products. Providing this information online shortens the sales cycle.

## Image Maps and Searchable Databases

If you have a large number of retail outlets, regional offices, or distributors, consider having a Web page with the information or, better yet, a searchable database where users can enter their zip code to find a nearby location.

Alternatively, you might provide an *image map* (a clickable image on a Web page). When the user clicks on a specific area of an image map (suppose he clicks on Ohio on a map that has the United States), he receives a new Web page with information about that topic (dealers in Ohio). Image maps can be used to help visitors locate specific offices or retail outlets.

Image maps do not have to be literal maps. You could, for example, have a drawing of a tree and the branches could each be clickable to bring the visitor to new pages.

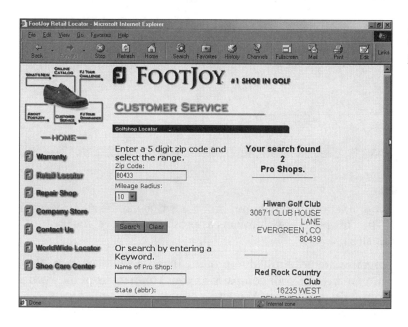

*FootJoy helps golfers find retailers that sell their products.*

If there are not specific distribution channels for products, customers have even more difficulty finding what they need. In the case of Mattel Hot Wheels, more than 15 million boys, ages 3 to 10, are avid collectors, owning an average of 27 cars each.

In addition, there are more than 41 million men who grew up playing with Hot Wheels cars as boys. On its Web site, Mattel helps customers locate the cars they want to add to their collection.

Word-of-mouth marketing is a tried-and-true way for many kinds of businesses to grow their customer base. The economics of these businesses are often not able to cost-justify conventional marketing expenses because their targeted customers are heterogeneous. Consider summer camps. It must be excruciating for parents to investigate the tremendous number of camps available. An innovative service, the Camp Channel, has built a database of camps from around the world that offer academic, sports, outdoors, and various programs for children. Parents can tune in to the Camp Channel at `www.campchannel.com`, submit their search criteria, and review a list of summer retreats for their kids.

*The Camp Channel offers an interactive way to select a summer camp.*

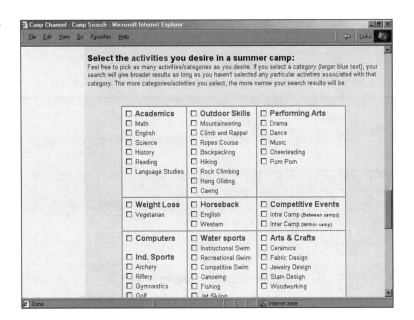

### Cut Marketing Costs

You can develop product marketing materials and brochures that can be either viewed online or downloaded. The cost per piece plummets as prospects retrieve your brochure from your Web site.

Of course, marketing programs are not limited to product literature. Indeed, marketing crosses various functional areas of your company. If your company is public, you market your company to the financial press. You also promote your company, its experts, and your products within the industry and trade press and with future employees. You can use your site to minimize marketing costs in all of these areas.

### Reduce Recruitment Expenses

Let your Web site tell prospective employees all about your company before you invite them in for an interview. You can devote a section of your Web site to job opportunities; here you can describe current positions, overview the corporate culture, describe international operations and employee benefits, and even allow online résumé submission.

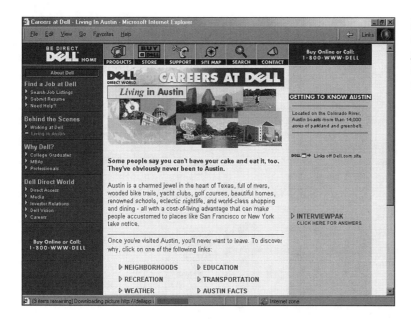

*Dell Computers features an entire community guide to showcase Austin, home of corporate headquarters.*

### Lower Expenses to Communicate with Stakeholders

In addition to new customers, other groups need information from your company. Investors, media representatives, and potential partners need product and company information. Even if only 10%–25% of these constituents are PC-savvy and interested in supplementing their communications with online capabilities, you can still enjoy a significant reduction in overall expenses by providing this information via the Web.

## Lock In Customers with Entertainment and Communication

Your products and services are terrific. Customer support is outstanding. Pricing offers a good value. But there is more you can do to nurture customer relationships and build loyalty, and there are many ways to do this; just keep in mind some common elements of human behavior.

Beyond the useful product information and the value proposition, customers want to enjoy themselves. With its capability to offer multimedia and interactive games, the Web is a great medium for entertainment. Consider developing a diversion that is related to your company: a theme, a tag line, or a community image. You succeed if the entertainment value of your Web site keeps visitors from leaving the site.

For example, Coca-Cola's Web site creates an irreverent spoof on a museum that places Coke and its place in history on a time-honored pedestal. Visitors can buy merchandise and memorabilia, including some delightful diner counter items such as toothpick and napkin dispensers.

*Coke offers e-cards for collecting, sharing, and trading.*

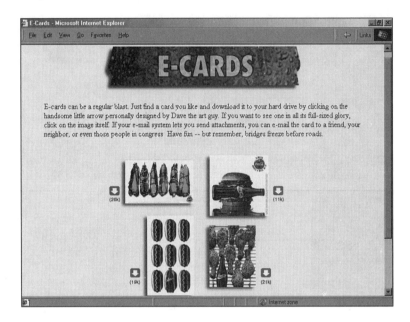

Whether the topic is the movies, politics, the latest hot stock tip, or the current state of baseball, everybody has an opinion. Asking for feedback from your customers is one of the best ways to get information about improving products, competitors' challenges, R&D opportunities, and the general state of the customer's relationship with your firm.

**Check This Out**

**Managing Customer Inquiries**

In Chapter 10, "How to Use (but Not Abuse) Email Marketing," we discuss how you can use technology to effectively manage customer inquiries.

## *Manage Customer Service Costs*

The Internet can (and should) raise expectations about the quality of customer support that is available with online business. Higher levels of service, such as faster response times for customer inquiries, can enhance customer loyalty.

Just as with the cost savings you achieve when prospects look at electronic brochures instead of printed brochures, you can attain cost savings when customers use your Web site to get information instead of calling your company. Not that you want to avoid phone calls—but if the Web can more effectively deliver the information to your customers or prospects, you should take advantage of it.

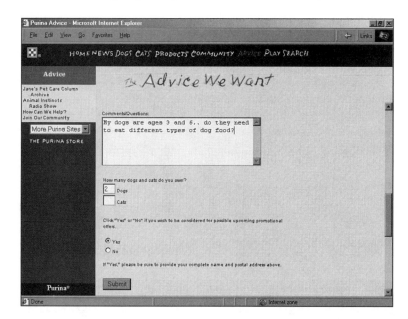

*Ralston Purina asks for customers' advice about their products as well as the Web site. Throughout the site, Ralston Purina creates a community of visitors by sharing common questions and helpful answers for the family of Purina customers.*

Web pages of Frequently Asked Questions (also known as FAQs) can offer answers to typical questions. Online manuals, training, how-tos, and interactive documentation can all assist a customer who is looking for information. For example, we had the opportunity to work with satellite television pioneer Echostar (http://www.dishnetwork.com, shown in the following figure) in the design of a Web site that includes online instructions for installation of a home satellite system for The Dish Network. You can use Adobe PDF files, audio clips, and video clips to enhance online instruction.

Online forms and surveys offer several advantages. First, there are the convenience and speed with which the user can fill in information and get it to your company. Second, you can design Web-based forms in such a way that the information (or data) the users submit can be easily compiled into your existing computer databases without any need for rekeying of the information. Using your Web site to save time and enhance workflow really pays off. Chubb Insurance, for example, lets customers file claims online in addition to gaining access to all policy information.

### Support Your Partners

Increasingly, businesses create partnerships, alliances, joint-ventures, or new distribution channels to remain competitive. These other companies and the individuals who work for them are as important as your customers. So use the Web to help the people who help you.

*Echostar's Dish Network Web site features helpful information on satellite dish installation.*

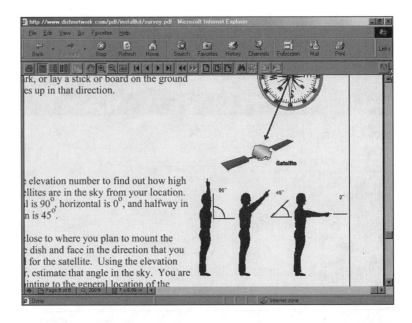

*Chubb Insurance lets customers file claims online and access all personal and policy information.*

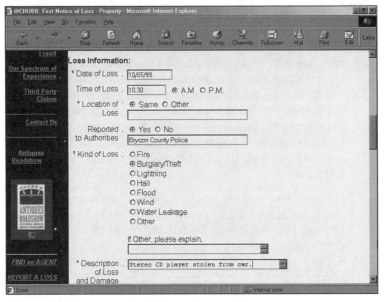

Update your Web site with new price lists, product specification changes, and new terms and conditions for your reseller agreements. Identify when and where you offer training or certification courses. Promote your resellers and VARs on your site as valuable participants in your success. If you feel uncomfortable letting your customers have access to the same information you share with distributors or partners, you can create a secure, password-protected area of the site. For example, the Hi-Tech

Forwarder Network, which helps companies ship products around the world, has a secure site that allows its network of companies to get bids on shipments as well as order supplies.

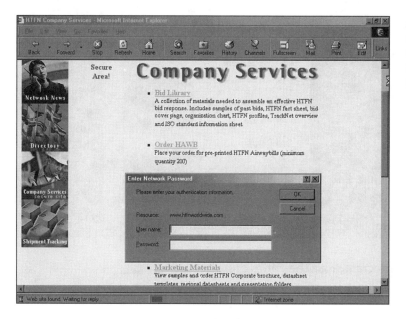

*A password-protected extranet can provide access to information you want only your suppliers or distributors to have.*

As another example, consider the way presidential hopefuls use Web sites to recruit and organize volunteers, solicit donations, and discuss issues. These sites represent a solid melding of the marketing concepts we've discussed, including customer service, education, feedback, and information dissemination (even though they aren't commercial sites in the conventional e-commerce sense).

## *Keep 'Em Coming Back for More*

The practice of creating customer loyalty is as old as marketing itself. You want to do more than conduct one commercial transaction; you want to create a relationship that will last for years. Since AT&T broke new ground in long distance with its *Opportunity Calling* program and MCI answered with its *Friends & Family* program, successful frequency-marketing programs have used these key components:

**Techno Talk**

**Intranets and Extranets**

The term *intranet* refers to a Web site that is designed only for employees of a company. It might have human-resource information, internal news, company policies, and procedures. An *extranet* is a Web site that provides information (and secure access) to partners, suppliers, and distributors.

➤ The offer of a real (and perceived) value

➤ Communication with customers

*Thousands of supporters have registered with Senator Bill Bradley's site.*

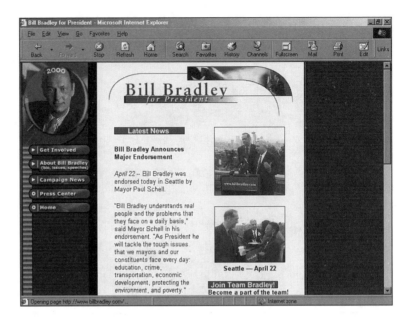

➤ Support for the program from the entire organization

➤ A well-maintained database of customer information

Here are a few specific ways to achieve success in building customer loyalty:

➤ Create a sense of community in which visitors contribute and return to participate. For example, E!Online wants visitors to review their favorite movies. Just like at the coffeehouse across the street from the multiplex, conversations get started, opinions start flying, and, pretty soon, Oscars have been awarded.

➤ Ask for customers' feedback; let them know that their opinions count. Remember New York City Mayor Ed Koch asking his constituents, "How am I doing?" The Big Apple kept Mayor Koch around for most of the 1980s.

➤ Save time for your customers. Beyond information, your site can help customers solve problems. Perhaps they can't find their user manual—offer how-to tips online. Go beyond email inquiries by either having customer service agents call customers back within an hour of an inquiry or creating "real-time" online chat with customer service representatives.

➤ Keep it light. Don't be afraid to introduce humor into your site. Principles of marketing should guide your hand, but business does not necessarily lose credibility when you bring a smile to a customer's face.

**Check This Out**

**Virtual Communities**

Chapter 15, "The Value of a Virtual Community," provides an in-depth look at the benefits of virtual communities.

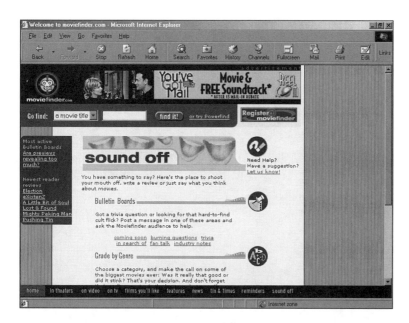

*Movie fans get to pretend to be movie reviewers online with E!Online.*

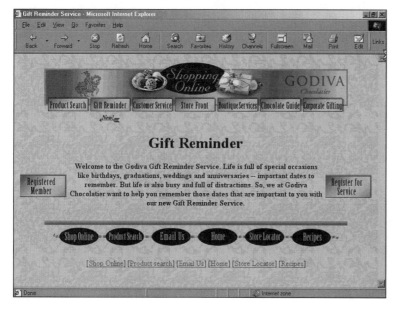

*Godiva Chocolatier's Gift Reminder Service ensures that you don't forget that special occasion.*

*The Home Depot gives a leg-up to do-it-yourselfers with the how-to section of its site.*

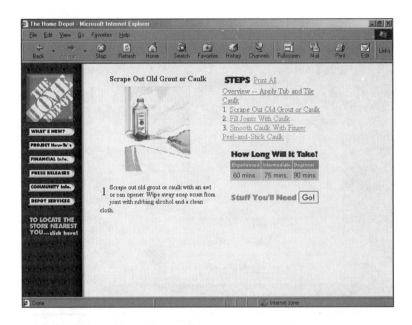

*Dilbert adds fun and games in his Brain Teaser section.*

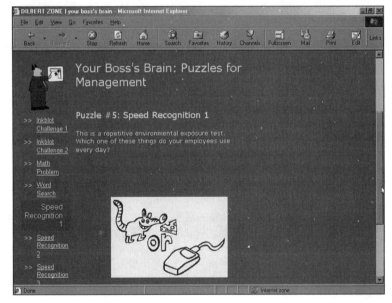

➤ Reward your best customers. Retailers have long sought to retain good customers with incentives. Loehmann's sends coupons to customers with discounts that are in proportion to the amount of money spent by the customer over the preceding season.

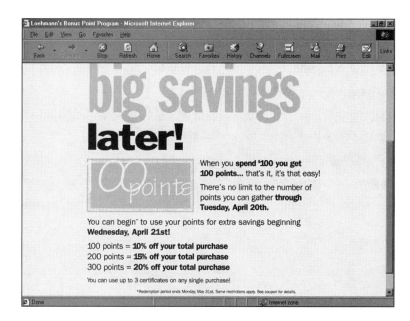

*Loehmann's awards bonus points and special awards to members of its Insider Club.*

As an "interactive" medium, the Internet has requirements for success. You need to create a well-designed home page, constantly update information, provide complete data, and offer immediate response to inquiries.

Don't forget where customers land in your site when they click on one of your banner ads or a link from another site. Be sure that the best of your content rises to the top and is immediately apparent, and that your Web-site visitors do not have to work hard to find what they need or what you want to show them.

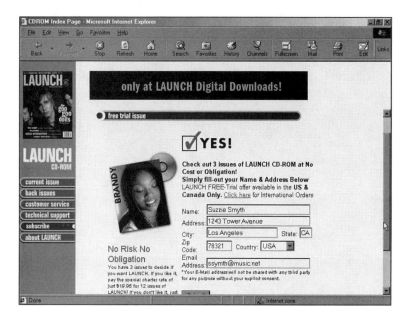

*Launch, a new music site, immediately drops the visitor into a free-trial offer form from a banner ad.*

**223**

**The Least You Need to Know**

➤ Site design should have a consistent look-and-feel and be easy to navigate.

➤ Site content should be relevant and to-the-point.

➤ Communicate with stakeholders by delivering valuable information, answers, assistance, and by soliciting their feedback and suggestions.

➤ Create loyalty and a sense of community.

# Part 4

# Fine-Tuning: More Tactics for Success

*Are you interested in saving some money? Would you like to cost-effectively reach each and every one of your customers or prospects? Of course, you would. The chapters in this section offer great suggestions that will enhance your online marketing without stretching your budget too thin. You'll learn about the ways you can cross-promote your Web site with other sites that reach your target market. You'll learn how to use electronic coupons to get new customers and retain existing customers. We'll show you how the Internet can be used to reach a target market of "one." That's right, when you gather information from your customers, you can use it to tailor information and increase the opportunities for future sales. We also give step-by-step instructions on how you can create a virtual community where your own Web users will communicate with one another, and simultaneously enhance your online marketing.*

# Chapter 13

# Money-Saving Marketing Tips

> **In This Chapter**
>
> ➤ Different types of affiliate marketing programs that can increase your online sales
>
> ➤ Loyalty and affinity marketing tactics such as coupons and customer loyalty programs on the Web
>
> ➤ How to generate online publicity and press coverage

This chapter focuses on ways to effectively promote your online business without spending big bucks. In fact, time and a little brainpower can buy a lot of marketing muscle for very little money. The following text provides examples of companies and products that can help you get the most for your money.

Before you decide to spend pretax dollars or time, sweat, and brainpower on marketing, try to quantify your options, including the costs of taking your and your team's time to launch marketing attacks. You should weigh the free versus paid-for marketing tactics and the returns you earn on both methods.

## Affiliate Programs: It Works for Amazon.com

Affiliate marketing programs are based on *contextual selling*, which is a fancy way of saying that firms that sell complementary products to the same customer can benefit from sharing those customers with one another within their network. Sales commissions, fees, or some sort of compensation is paid to affiliates who sell one another's products. A variation on this theme is to think of affiliates as additional sales channels for you and your products.

Amazon.com started this ball rolling by offering a 15% commission to affiliates on book sales. The way it works is when an Amazon.com customer arrives at Amazon.com by clicking on a link that is on an affiliate's Web site and then buys a book, the affiliate receives the commission. The cost? Only a link from your Web site to Amazon's site.

For example, Big Nest Aviary is a small aviary located on a 115-acre cattle ranch near Shiner, Texas. They use the Amazon.com affiliate program to promote and sell—you guessed it—bird books.

*When you "purchase" a bird book at the Big Nest Aviary site, you jump to Amazon.com to make the purchase.*

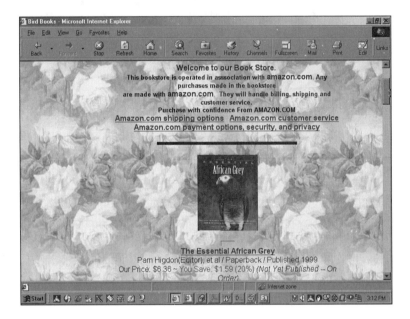

Just as Amazon.com realizes additional sales and revenues by having affiliates (companies with Web sites) send traffic and business to their site, you can use affiliates to realize new prospects and customers. GartnerGroup analyst Roy Satterthwaite says the affiliate model is very valuable. Beyond CPM [cost per thousand advertising models], beyond tenancy agreements, affiliate models represent a win-win for both affiliates and merchants, and are increasingly easy to implement.

Internet research firm Jupiter Communications noted in a December 1998 report that only 16% of surveyed sites had such programs in place. But with sites drawing as much as 20% of their overall revenue from affiliate programs, more and more online merchants are interested in setting up programs.

# When Content and Commerce Become Logical Partners

For small and medium-sized businesses, affiliate programs can be a nice two-way street. In other words, you can become an affiliate by adding links to your site to earn commissions on other companies' products. And you can pay other sites (your affiliates) commissions when your products sell because they bring you customers. Essentially, an affiliate program is another sales channel, but without the fixed costs of traditional sales. It is truly a performance-based system; you pay the commission only when a purchase is made.

The Web is ideal for affiliate programs because Web users enjoy leaping from one site to another. Say, for example, you have a Web site that sells sports equipment. It would be natural to have an affiliate relationship with a Web site that sells dietary supplements for athletes or a sports magazine.

Another benefit is the increased reach the program generates. More traffic to your site means a better chance of selling something to your visitors. And more leads translate into more sales. These programs really level the playing field and enable the little guys to act like the bigger guys.

There's probably no easier way to add valuable content to your site than to do so with information from affiliates. Web visitors have begun to expect these alliances. Because customers trust your decision to affiliate, programs create loyalty.

A well-maintained affiliate program can generate a significant percent of your online business. With a sales channel such as this, don't underestimate the importance of the need to staff this function. This is a common mistake. You need to communicate with your affiliates. Clearly, they want to know on a monthly basis how much traffic and sales they brought to your site and what their commission is. If an affiliate never receives a report or a commission, they won't want to stick around. Finally, remember to focus on the sales generated through your affiliate network, not the number of affiliates that you have[el]quality is better than quantity.

Art.com is a business (and Web site) that sells both unframed and framed prints online. Art.com provides a selection of more than 125,000 posters, representing thousands of artists. It offers the delivery of unframed prints within two weeks and framed prints within three. You might say that affiliate programs are a keystone for the success of this company; its affiliate program produces some 20% of company revenues! There are more than 2,800 affiliates, and approximately 350 new prospective affiliates apply every week. Art.com is selective in terms of who it accepts as an affiliate; 85% of sites that apply are accepted. An affiliate can be dropped from the program if sales fall below a certain level. Art.com pays affiliates 15% of sales.

Affiliate companies have products and services that relate to one another. Zing.com (`http://www.zing.com`) is an affiliate of Art.com. It offers a utility program that enables Web users to listen to audio, read jokes, and view images from various channels, including Art.com, as Web pages download.

**Downsides**

A couple of possible downsides to affiliate links: A visitor might bypass your site altogether and go directly to the merchant's site, or the visitor might be overwhelmed with links on your site.

*Art.com promotes its affiliate program on its Web site.*

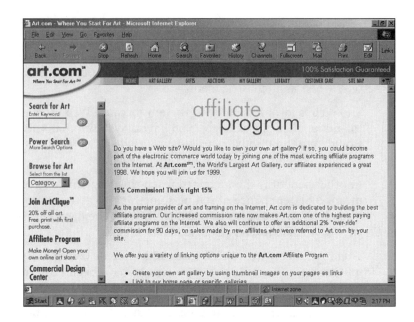

# How to Take Advantage of Affiliate Programs

Overall, keep a few common threads in mind, including a strong contextual focus, a delicate balance of links on your site that don't overwhelm the visitor, and a way to return to your site after linking out. Affiliate programs of all sorts are a great way to drive traffic. There are three ways to do it:

➤ **Affiliate Networks**  Join an affiliate network and let the third party manage it for you.

➤ **Advertising Cross-Promotion Networks**  You can swap ads and links with services that help Web sites with cross-promotion.

➤ **Do It Yourself**  Create your own affiliate program and trade ads and links on a site-by-site basis.

The following sections provide some insights into each of these methods.

## How to Research Affiliate Networks

Shopping for an affiliate program is a multistep process that is very manageable. Do not be intimidated by the fact that there are many affiliate programs; trust that a few are right for you. First, go to the industry experts. Table 13.1 provides the names of Web sites that can help you learn about and locate a good affiliate network.

## Table 13.1    Affiliate Network Resources

| Company | Web Site |
|---|---|
| Refer-It | www.refer-it.com |
| Associate Programs | www.associateprograms.com |
| Now Stores | www.top-affiliate-programs.com |

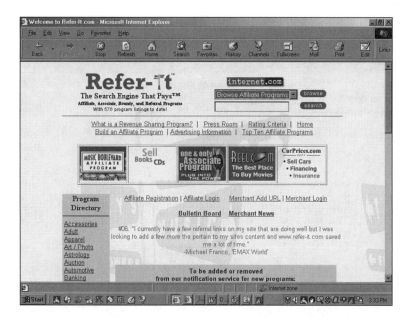

*Refer-It measures hundreds of affiliate programs against its own rating system and lets you search the entire database.*

Refer-It CEO James Marciano expects to feature 1,000 programs by the end of 1999. Marciano recommends that you evaluate the nominal differences among the programs. He strongly suggests that you negotiate on terms and invest time in reading contracts. Nowstores.com also provides a search engine and a rating service to recommend sites by category. Nowstores.com is an Internet marketing organization with Web site analysis, site registration, promotion, and <META> tag services.

### Third-Party Options: The Big Guys in Affiliate Networks

At press time, there are close to 600 affiliate programs, most of which are designed for a particular industry sector or category such as music at Music Boulevard and cars at AutoFusion's CarPrices.com. Many programs offer full-service packages to affiliates to monitor, track, and report sales activity as well as distribute the commission checks. Companies such as BeFree and LinkShare sell their technology separately so you can set up and run your own affiliate network. Following are reviews of a few of the industry leaders and a summary of their services:

➤ **Be Free! Inc.** (http://www.befree.com)    Be Free is one of the leading providers of online affiliate sales channel technology, services, and knowledge.

**231**

Be Free's merchant-branded affiliate sales channel model helps online retailers capture revenue by selling products in context on affiliate Web sites. President and CEO Gordon Hoffstein says that is the key. "Users are four to six times more likely to respond to a call to action when the links are in context," he notes. The Be Free model lets the merchant (that's you and your online business) have the affiliate relationship. The Be Free network doesn't own or control the relationship. With Be Free, it's like having your own sales force versus using a rep firm, Hoffstein says.

*Be Free offers a merchant-branded affiliate channel.*

➤ **LinkShare** (http://www.linkshare.com)  As many as 1,500 new affiliates join the LinkShare Network every week. The company services more than 200 retailers and manages a network of more than 100,000 affiliate sites. LinkShare services include third-party tracking and verifying customer referrals and transactions, and managing the related revenue and commission distribution.

Dell chose LinkShare to broaden its customer base. Dell's affiliate program is expected to generate additional purchases through links on LinkShare's network of general and special-interest content hubs, including those in the technology, home/family, and small business areas.

➤ **Commission Junction** (http://www.commission-junction.com)  According to its promotional material, Commission Junction is the only revenue-sharing network that provides "multiple high-paying programs under one roof, through our centralized, consolidated payment system. We also offer a suite of complementary services designed to increase business opportunities in the Web marketplace."

### How Do I Choose an Affiliate Network?

Start by using some of the research sites previously mentioned. Take a look at the larger Network Affiliate firms. Visit the Web sites of companies that offer affiliate programs. Compare and contrast; look for commonalties with your own marketing focus. Talk to their customers. Most sites have a client section: Call and ask about the service. Finally, in addition to your business-specific goals, ask the following questions before you sign up:

➤ How long has this network been around? How many sites and how many merchants are in the network?

➤ What are the particulars about the design of links and support of the sales process?

➤ What kind of tracking and activity reports will you receive and how often?

➤ How much customer support can you expect? Is a specific person assigned to your program?

➤ What are the terms, the duration, and the conditions of the business agreement?

➤ How do you get paid, and what are the conditions?

# Swap Advertising: Anybody Wanna Trade a Link?

Site cross-promotion is an excellent way to increase traffic and sales. Many companies facilitate promotional exchange. LinkExchange (`http://www.linkexchange.com`) started the trend of swapping links between sites with complementary products in order to share traffic. LinkExchange is best known for its Banner Network, a free service in which member sites display banners for other members to generate traffic and revenues. A portion of the banner space is sold to sponsors to keep the network free to member sites.

LinkExchange's ClickTrade product enables advertisers and direct marketers to create their own customer-referral networks; companies pay referring sites on a per-visitor, lead, or sale basis.

Most advertising exchange services operate on a barter basis. For example, with CyberLink Exchange (`http://cyberlinkexchange.com`), every time a person visits your Web site, which displays a CyberLink Exchange member banner, your account receives one credit. Your account is charged two credits every time your banner is displayed on another member's site. Link Trader (`http://linktrader.com`) exchanges seven credits for every 10 impressions. The advantage here, of course, is that no money changes hands. Many of the link and ad barter services offer other site-promotion opportunities, including the ability to purchase banners. Table 13.2 lists some sites that can help you get started with advertising cross-promotion.

**233**

## Table 13.2   Advertising Cross-Promotion Sites

| Cross-Promotion Site | Web Address |
| --- | --- |
| CyberLink Exchange | `http://cyberlinkexchange.com` |
| Link-O-Matic | `http://www.linkomatic.com` |
| LinkExchange | `http://www.linkexchange.com` |
| Link Trader | `http://linktrader.com` |

*Link-O-Matic represents the free-for-all banner model.*

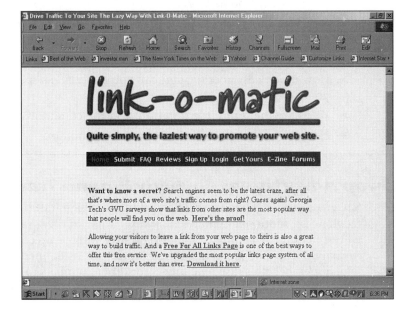

### Portals

The major portal Web sites are beginning to see the benefits in banner and ad exchanges. Microsoft acquired LinkExchange in late 1998 to expand its online business services and generate more traffic for the Microsoft Network (`http://www.msn.com`). Meanwhile, Netscape Communications (`http://www.netscape.com`) announced its intent to acquire AtWeb—a publisher of software tools that also offers an advertising banner exchange program.

# Do It Yourself—With Laser-Like Focus

If you don't have a large budget or you are the kind of person who likes to do things yourself, you can always create your own advertising exchange program or network. This is ideal if your company or organization focuses on niche markets.

To create a simple exchange program, you first want to find other Web sites that reach your target audience without representing direct competition. So, if you sell coffee on your Web site, a site that sells espresso machines might be great for cross-promotion. You need to do a little old-fashioned Web research to find the best cross-promotion sites and companies. Next, contact the Webmaster (usually the email address is listed on the site) and ask whether your two sites might exchange promotion.

The cross-promotion can range from a simple exchange of links to the exchange of banner advertising or even content. If you are exchanging advertising, be sure that you both know exactly what you're getting—in other words, know how long and how many times the ad will appear on the other site. You want a fair exchange. Also, carefully track the results of cross-promotion to determine the sites with which you want to continue to work.

You could also join or even establish a more comprehensive network that reaches a very specific target market. As an example, NewcityNet (http://www.newcitynet.com) was created as a means to help smaller, alternative newspapers enhance advertising revenues. More than 36 sites affiliated with alternative newspapers joined together as part of NewcityNet as a way to reach a larger audience and enhance both regional and national advertising. By joining forces, they enhance content, readership, and ad revenue.

The Christpages Banner Exchange caters to Christian-owned sites or those with Christian content. Ad Archer is a network that seeks to swap banners between sites that support collectibles, especially aviation-related content. The Fishing World Network swaps banners among participants in its industry sector. And, in an unusual twist on the global nature of the Internet, the Canada HyperBanner Network promotes itself as "the Canadian one-stop-shop solution for productivity and financial benefits for the Canadian Web site owners."

*The Fishing World Network swaps banners among participants in their industry sector.*

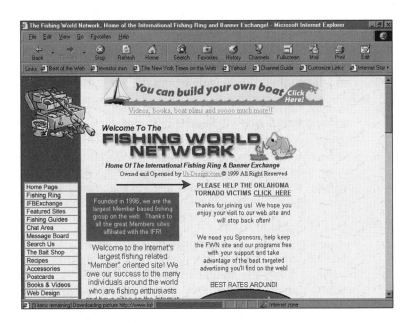

# Customer Loyalty Programs for the Web

There are many successful *offline* marketing programs and the airline and hospitality industries have mastered one of the best: the customer loyalty program. Very simply, a customer loyalty program creates benefits or awards for customers who regularly use or shop at one vendor. Airlines give out frequent flyer miles to people when they fly on their planes. The "miles" translate into awards ranging from special membership to free trips to gifts. Hotels, car rental companies, and other companies are now seeing the benefits of loyalty programs.

Loyalty programs succeed because you can reward your good customers and be sure they know you appreciate them. Even grocery stores have started reward programs that give customers special discounts based on spending above a certain level. That makes customers spend more and feel better about doing it. It doesn't get much better than that for marketing folks. The generally accepted principles of loyalty marketing include the following:

➤ Use incentives and awards to obtain a customer for life.

➤ Enhance the share of the customer (that is, the percent of the customer's total purchases of products in your product category).

➤ Recognize that it is less expensive to keep a customer than acquire a new one.

Of course, customer loyalty programs have made their way to the Web. And many companies are tying into and enhancing existing loyalty programs from the airlines and hospitality industries because they are well established. MSNBC, for example, is one of the most popular news destination sites. One incentive it offers to build its

## 236

customers' loyalty is an opportunity for site users to win frequent-flyer miles when they visit the Web site every day.

*MSNBC provides an opportunity to win frequent-flyer miles awarded to people who visit the site every day.*

It is also possible to create an entirely new form of awards for frequent visitors or customers. CBS SportsLine (`http://www.sportsline.com`) takes advantage of sports fans' fanaticism with contests, free email, sweepstakes, and lots of free stuff. Registered members receive award points for visiting and using various aspects of the Web site. These points can then be redeemed for awards such as a Joe Namath Autographed Wheaties Box.

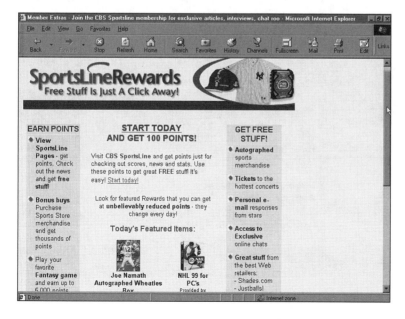

*CBS SportsLine rewards visiting sports fans.*

*ClickRewards from Netcentives drives traffic to some of the top online retailers (e-tailers) with a traditional frequent-shopper program.*

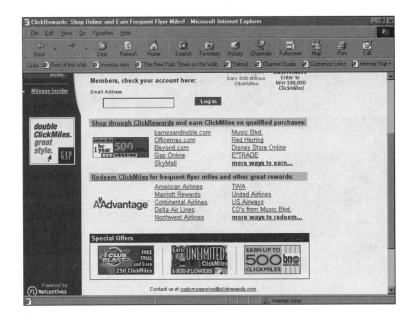

## CyberGold: The New Frontier

CyberGold (http://www.cybergold.com) offers a variation on the frequent-flyer program based on creating a new marketplace and new currency on the Internet that bypasses the costs merchants incur processing sales via credit cards. In CyberGold's Earn & Spend Community, money that customers "earn" online through various purchases can be spent online on digital goods and services.

*CyberGold promotes its "true Internet-based economy," where money earned both online and in the physical world can be spent online.*

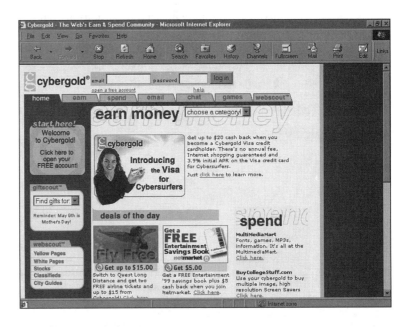

## Create Your Own Loyalty Program

Yes, YOU can have your own loyalty marketing program! You have a couple of different options in setting one up. One way is to build one from the ground up. A customer buys five bags of coffee and receives the sixth bag free. In other words, create an award system based either on people visiting your site or purchasing your products. Then, carefully track this information and give away awards.

A second option is to use a company that sets up a loyalty program (including awards) for you. MyPoints (`http://www.mypoints.com`) offers direct marketing programs and sells a technology package to customize private label programs. These programs contain several options. The MyPoints Network is a group of marketers that use MyPoints currency to drive repeat transactions to their site. Private label programs help large marketers create their own loyalty programs using MyPoints tools and technologies.

Points earned through MyPoints programs can be redeemed for a wide variety of products and services. Options include credit in other prominent loyalty programs such as Hilton Honors, travel awards (including frequent-flyer miles, cruises, free hotel stays and car rentals), free long distance from Sprint FonPromotions, and free merchandise from premium brands, such as Barnes & Noble, Blockbuster, and Eddie Bauer.

The private label loyalty programs are not for small businesses. For example, MyPoints offers a license to their software solution and a service-bureau approach for the not-as-big guys. The service bureau solutions require a commitment to a minimum 250,000 membership base, and $250,000 in Point purchases during the first year of the program.

By the way, MyPoints has been acquired by LinkShare, the affiliate program service. Consolidation in this industry confirms the presumption that affinity marketing and loyalty marketing are old-fashioned, tried-and-true offline marketing tactics that have their place on the Internet.

## Clipping Coupons on the Net

Grocers and packaged goods manufacturers have been doing it for years. Clip 'n save. Some days are double-coupon days. Oprah even has shows about the ladies who save hundreds of dollars (and overstock their pantry shelves) by redeeming coupons. So move it on over to the Internet.

As you've seen with other kinds of online advertising, coupons enable marketers to accomplish two enviable goals.

➤ They measure the success of a campaign.

➤ They target messages to a specific audience.

Coupons are frequently used to give prospective customers an incentive to switch brands or try a new product. On top of these benefits, with Internet-based coupons,

**239**

customers print the coupons on *their* printers, so your direct mail and printing costs are capped.

The coupon(s) can be a simple graphic that is presented on a Web page. The graphic has all of the terms and conditions for people who use the coupon.

Again, you can go at the "coupons" technique either by yourself, or with the help of another company. If you decide to do it yourself, consider exactly what you want the coupon to do for your business. You can limit the time period during which a coupon is valid (that is, until December 1999), but it is almost impossible to limit the number of coupons that your Web audience creates. In fact, you probably don't want to limit the number of coupons printed and used. If your coupon offers a 10% discount on a product or service, you WANT as many people as possible to use it because you want to increase sales. Even with the 10% hit, you have a profit margin.

*Example of an online coupon from coupon-surfer.com that lets users save $5 on a purchase of $50–99 and $10 with a purchase of $100 or more at the OfficeMax.com Web site.*

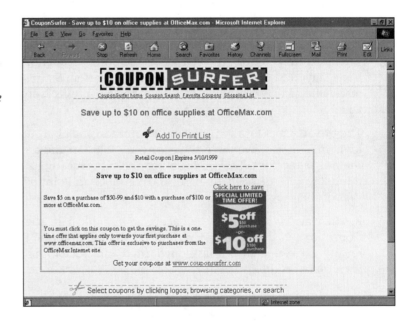

Most coupons are offered completely free, but you could also set up a coupon offer that requires users to answer a few questions (and you collect their email address) before you give away the coupon. Here are a few considerations when creating your own coupon program.

➤ Determine whether your coupon offers a discount percentage (10% off) or a specific dollar discount ($5 off).

➤ Determine the expiration date and other rules for the offer.

➤ Determine whether it is an unlimited or one-time offer (applies only the first time you purchase something via a Web site).

➤ Is the coupon available on your Web site for all users, or do users have to register to access the coupon?

➤ How will you track usage of your Internet coupons (that is, collect them at the stores)?

➤ Determine whether the coupon promotes one specific product (for example, staplers) or all products (for example, anything in the store). This can help with tracking.

➤ Determine whether you promote your coupons in your Internet advertising.

➤ Determine how you will redeem your coupon. Will it be at your store? Via mail-in rebate? Or via your Web site?

**Check This Out**

**Track Coupons!**

You'll want to track how many people actually use your Web coupons to learn how effective the program is.

You might consider having an Internet coupon company help you with your coupon program. Why? Because some coupon sites attract a significant audience specifically looking for coupons. For example, CoolSavings offers advertisers several promotional options: in-store coupons, sales notices, online coupons, mail-in rebates, and special shopping reminders. More than 40 national advertisers have used CoolSavings to target special offers to a rapidly growing membership of more than one million registered members.

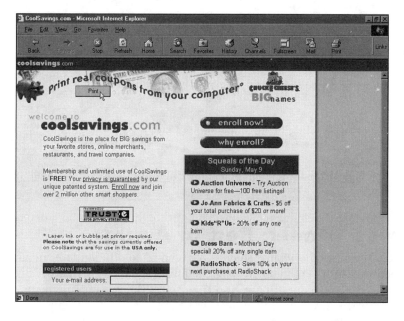

*CoolSavings is one of the top 200 most visited sites on the Internet.*

Most online coupons are offered through banner ads placed by one of several networks. For example, SuperMarkets Online and Planet U are two services that distribute coupons for packaged goods manufacturers. H.O.T! Coupons works with independent retailers, such as a local dry cleaner or an eyeglass shop. Many of these companies create the paper-based coupons that we all receive in the mail, and now offer both online and paper-based coupon programs for retailers. Table 13.3 lists a few companies that can help you with your online coupon programs.

### Table 13.3    Online Coupon Sites

| Company | Web Site |
| --- | --- |
| Coupon Depot | www.coupondepot.com |
| CoolSavings | www.coolsavings.com |
| Coupon Surfer | www.couponsurfer.com |
| H.O.T! Coupons | www.hotcoupons.com |
| Planet U | www.planetu.com |

*Free muffins, free cream cheese, free coffee. Coupons can promote local stores and businesses as well as national ones.*

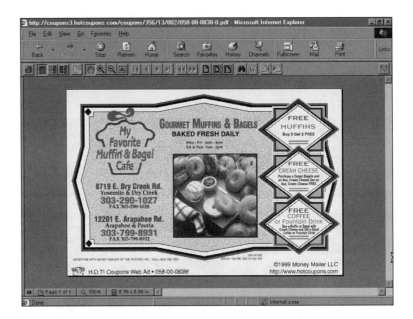

## Everybody Loves a Winner: Best of Awards

Many Web sites proudly promote the awards they have received to differentiate themselves from the competition. Okay, many of these Web "awards" are kinda rigged. There's no academy whose members nominate, and then select the coolest site or the best site of the month. But there is value in submitting your site to sites that give awards because awards can offer credibility, word-of-mouth marketing, and all for zero dollars! Most awards provide a graphic image that you can put on your site to claim that you've received the award.

Sometimes Web awards represent a win-win for both the company that gives the award and the company that receives the award. For example, if your site uses

Macromedia tools such as Shockwave, Macromedia lets you submit your site to be a "Shocked Site of the Day." If your site is chosen, Macromedia promotes your site on its site. The nice thing about winning this honor is that hundreds of thousands of people visit the Macromedia Web site, and you gain free exposure if your site is selected!

Ironically, two of the most popular award categories seem to be "cool" and "hot" sites of the day or week. Go to any search site and check out the various pages you get when you search Cool Site or Hot Site to identify awards that might be up your alley. There are also listings on Yahoo! that might guide your efforts. It's a long Web address but we'll give it to you anyway:

```
http://dir.yahoo.com/Computers_and_Internet/Internet/World_Wide_Web/
Best_of_the_Web/Sites_of_the___/Day/
```

Give a few of these a try, monitor the response, and try a few new ones. This is one of those iffy areas where you can spend a lot of time (even though you'll spend no money) and get little return. So watch out.

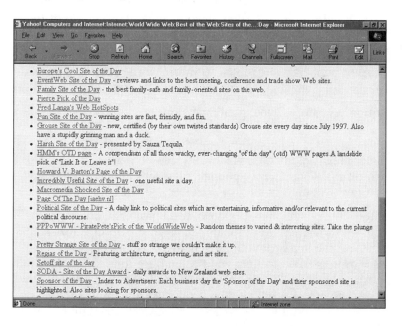

*Even Yahoo! has a category of sites that award "best of" awards.*

Fred Langa of *Windows Magazine* has pulled together some good data regarding types of Internet awards. He identifies the following categories:

➤ The really big, established awards that everyone wants to win at some point in their career. Getting a Starting Point Hot Site award or being selected by Point as a Top 5% of the Web award is hard to do. They get an unbelievable number of submissions every day, and they have only so many awards to give out.

➤ Next come the really serious, but not as fiercely competitive awards. There are hundreds of these. They are awards such as the Way Cool Hot Site award. When

**243**

you earn one from this category, you have accomplished just as much as if you had won in the first group.

➤ Next come the Promotional awards. Webmasters set up awards to help attract traffic to their sites. That doesn't mean that the awards are meaningless. Most are very valid awards. It does mean they tend to give out more awards than the previous categories.

➤ Next come the Everybody Wins awards that are given out by Webmasters that are only interested in building traffic. They give almost everybody who applies an award so that they can get as much traffic as possible.

➤ Now for the last in the food chain: the Let's Trade Awards awards. There are thousands of these. All you have to do is give them an award, or buy advertising on their site, and you get their award. Enough said.

# Media Relations: Oh Contact, My Contact

Pub-lic-i-ty, n. [Fr. Publicite] 1. The state of being public, or commonly known or observed 2. a) any information, promotional material, and so on, which brings a person, place, or product to the notice of the public b) the work or business of preparing and disseminating such material.

Okay, that's one definition of publicity. The thesaurus in the word processing software offers another:

advertising, promotion, exposure, hype, public relations, and press coverage.

These are good, too.

But we know that publicity means many different things to each person. In fact, this chapter and others touch on many varieties of publicity. But let's look at online publicity opportunities, starting with building a list of contacts and working your list.

Your first assignment is to find out who are the editors and reporters who cover your industry and your customers' industries. You probably have your own directories, but the Web has a great many resources for you, as well. MediaFinder (http:// mediafinder.com) offers resources that can help you find publications, media kits, and mailing lists. You want to create a list of publications (and names of editors and writers) that relate to your industry or products. You probably know most of them already, but a little online research might uncover a few more. New magazines seem to appear weekly. What you will discover is that many "real world" magazines also have Web sites. You might be able to get publicity for your company, products, or services in both places!

## Content Is King in PR, Too

After you create your contact list, what should you send them? Remember the currency of the Internet is information, and that is exactly what you can deliver to gain exposure. Here are some ideas that can help you get publicity both online and offline in publications:

➤ Announce your new customers, trade show appearances, strategic partnerships, and upcoming online promotions such as sponsored chats and forums.

➤ Distribute your releases through the extensive media network of reporters that cover online activities and newswire services. (It's that list you compiled after reading the previous section.)

➤ Find the specific online forums attended by your target audience and prepare content or topics for the discussion.

➤ Make it easy for reporters—write stories and pitch them. Track the editorial calendars (this is the list of major topics that a publication covers each month) and special editions; they will be very glad to get targeted pieces from you.

➤ Publish educational materials and white papers and deliver these feature stories to reporters, analysts, and conference planners.

➤ Create online events around new content or updated products on your site, contests or sweepstakes, or games.

➤ Establish yourself as an industry expert in your field with quotes, attribution, and interviews with the press

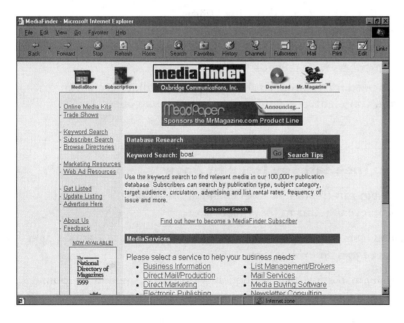

*MediaFinder is a resource to find publications, media kits, and mailing lists.*

# E-Zines: What Are They? Do I Need One?

Does absolutely everything on the Internet start with the letter E followed by a hyphen? An *e-zine* is really nothing more than an electronic newsletter distributed to an email list that has been purchased or created from subscribers who have opted in. (See Chapter 10, "How to Use (but Not Abuse) Email Marketing.") There are two things to do with an e-zine: Publish one yourself or advertise or sponsor an appropriate newsletter already designed for and subscribed to by your target audience.

Now, now, we know you're not in the journalism business or the publishing business, but all the publicity tools you created in the previous section provide you with most of the content you need for your newsletter. They don't have to be long. Most contain only 400–500 words. In addition to articles and white papers you've written for the press, your Web site has lots of content. Include testimonials or a Q&A session about the industry or product performance or whatever you know.

You can charge for your newsletter or not. You can sell advertising in your newsletter or not. Just keep a few things in mind:

➤ Make it easy for subscribers to join. The subscription form should be easy to navigate and should be available from lots of places on your site.

➤ Promote your e-zine everywhere you market your site—in ads, affiliate programs, sponsorships, even in your offline materials.

➤ Always deliver material that is valuable and timely for your subscribers.

➤ Use loyalty marketing tactics to leverage your current subscribers and get them to sign up new subscribers with rewards.

➤ Be sensitive to the need for voluntary subscriptions. We call it permission marketing. Privacy and confidentiality continue to be end-user concerns.

---

### The Least You Need to Know

➤ An affiliate program can create new sales channels for an online merchant and can add new revenue streams for affiliate sites.

➤ An online business can create its own affiliate network with as few as one or two relationships or join an existing one.

➤ Affinity and loyalty marketing such as frequent visitor programs and coupons can be as effective online as offline.

➤ E-zines are online newsletters that can serve as promotional, educational, or customer service marketing tools for prospective and existing customers.

# Chapter 14

# Precision, Targeted, One-to-One Marketing

---

### In This Chapter

➤ Learn how to use Web technologies to develop relationships with customers

➤ Tailor information and offerings to the needs of individuals

➤ Personalize the sales process at lower costs

➤ Create customer loyalty and improve customer satisfaction

---

Sally Johnson likes music. Not just any type of music—romantic music from the 1940s and 1950s performed by female vocalists. How do you know this? She's told you. Now you can recommend Natalie Cole's CD titled "Unforgettable." And she buys it. Companies with online businesses have good reason to collect information about customers and prospects. After you understand what your customers really like and want, and you can serve them better—and probably sell more products. Chapter 2, "Who's Out There and What Are They Doing? Profiles of Internet Users," provides information about large groups of Internet users. In this chapter, you will learn how you can obtain useful information about individual users and use this information to your marketing (and sales) advantage.

## One-on-One Marketing

Traditional marketing focuses on creating and distributing messages to large groups of people—mass marketing (such as television ads) or narrowcast marketing to a specific audience (such as radio ads). One-on-one marketing focuses on the creation of messages for individuals. You can't get much more targeted than this.

The Internet is the best medium available for one-on-one marketing. Why? Because the Internet uses computers. Web sites "sit" on computers. And computers can use databases to collect, store, and retrieve data. As a result, your Web site becomes a powerful marketing tool for one-on-one marketing. You can ask a visitor specific questions about his or her preferences. Then, again using databases, you can create a personalized page of information designed just for that individual. In other words, your Web site asks Sally Johnson about her musical preferences, and then creates a page that recommends Natalie Cole's CD. It's like having a sales clerk who really wants to help your customers find what they want. You build a relationship with each customer that you have.

Don Peppers and Martha Rogers, marketing consultants and champions of the principles of one-to-one marketing, have built a business out of this concept of customer relationship management (CRM). Some call it precision or *targeted marketing*; Peppers and Rogers refer to it as *1:1 marketing*. Most of their work is based on the age-old principles of database marketing that have been upgraded with new data-warehousing and data-mining techniques. These new technologies merely enhance a business' ability to get to know its customers, serve them better, and maintain the relationship. Visit the Peppers and Rogers site at `http://www.1to1marketing.com` to learn more about their common-sense theories.

Techno Talk

### Terminology

*Database marketing* refers to creating a database of information about your customers (such as names and addresses), and using the database for future marketing—such as a direct-mail campaign. A *data warehouse* is an electronic system that stores data from transactions and is designed in such a way that it can be queried (asked questions) and can generate reports. *Data mining* refers to taking a database that has perhaps hundreds of thousands of records and "mining" this data to find out specific things—perhaps the percentage of your customers who like red automobiles.

The Peppers and Rogers Group identifies four steps an enterprise must take put establish powerful 1:1 relationships with customers:

➤ Identify customers, as best you can, on a one-on-one basis. Get to know them and what they buy.

➤ Differentiate among your customers. Learn which ones are more valuable to you than others. Figure out what percent of your customers generate what percent of sales and profits. Find out who your best customers are and how to keep them. Evaluate whether or not you might have to "fire" some of your customers. (In other words, some customers might actually be bad for business.) Differentiate among your customers' needs. Do they all need the same products, or does each one need a unique version?

➤ Interact and communicate effectively with your customers. Develop a relationship with each one. The more information you gather, the better the relationship. Don't be afraid to test, retool, and test again.

➤ Customize your products and services to make each customer happy. This means you must evaluate how flexible your organization and production facilities are.

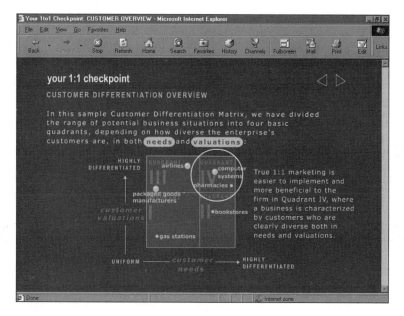

*Peppers and Rogers have pioneered the concept of one-to-one marketing.*

# Permission–Based Marketing

You're jazzed about the idea of collecting lots of useful information about your customers, then using it to enhance marketing. But there's one catch: They have to give it to you.

Spam—unwanted, unsolicited email from people you don't know and don't want to know—has given all types of Internet marketing a bad name. In addition to Internet-based spam, we live in a world where advertising messages are spammed upon us literally thousands of times every day. There's a growing landslide of clutter (that is, too many email messages). Typical mass media uses "interruption marketing." TV ads, radio ads, and billboards interrupt our day (or our program) and try to get us to take notice. At the same time we are bombarded with messages, our lives have less and less free time. So the marketing interruptions become increasingly annoying. These days might be soon over. Kaput.

In an attempt to solve this problem, we must to go back to one of the lessons we learned in kindergarten. If you want something, be polite and ask permission. Permission marketers ask their customers to raise their hands and volunteer to be marketed to. And, people will provide personal information for your database and give permission for marketing information if they know that the messages you send them will be

➤ Anticipated (not spammed)

➤ Relevant to their interests, lifestyle, and needs

➤ Of value (save them time or money)

➤ Personal in nature

# Why These Concepts Work

The principles of 1:1 and permission marketing have been proven to work. The Internet environment greatly enhances the effectiveness of these marketing concepts with technology every online marketer can put to work. And, the Internet dramatically changes the economics involved in identifying your best customers. This makes it easy for you to ask for their permission to market to them and deliver personalized messages. Basically, software does it for you.

The proof is in the pudding. Targeted product recommendations increase point of purchase sales. Personalized content and services increase viewer loyalty and create a strong brand experience. We know consumers are desperate to get out from under information overload. Users are swamped with opportunities to read and receive information. They just get too many impersonal messages.

Customers will volunteer to receive your marketing messages because you give them something of value and relevance, because they have a strong affinity or interest, or because there's a chance to win a contest or sweepstakes, all of which are pretty good reasons.

Online music store CDnow (http://www.cdnow.com) uses both 1:1 and permission marketing techniques to help customers and enhance marketing efforts. When you join their "My CDnow" program, you receive the following features (which all provide useful information to CDnow):

➤ **A wish list**   A registry of your favorite music so your friends can buy you presents.

➤ **Order history**   Track your purchases online.

➤ **Favorite artists**   Stay abreast of the latest releases from your favorite artists.

➤ **Rewards program**   Earn points toward free music CDs every time you make a purchase.

➤ **Account information**   Update your billing and shipping information.

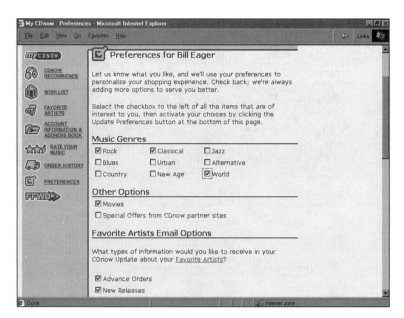

*CDnow uses both 1:1 and permission-based marketing techniques to collect data and serve customers.*

# Gamesville USA

The Gamesville Web site (http://www.gamesville.com) is touted as the game show site and entertainment destination on the Internet that has been wasting your time since 1996. In fact, the "Stat-O-Matic" on the start page tracks the number of players and cash prizes as well as the total number of minutes wasted. This site features lots of cash prizes and games such as Acey Deucy, Multimedia Celebrity Trivia, and the World's Biggest Office Pool—No Office Required in the SportsMadness family of prediction games. There's a shopping center, a chat program, player feature stories, and a winner's showcase. There's even a panic button you can click at work when people pass by, looking over your shoulder at your screen. The button launches a very businesslike page that disguises the fact that you're playing Gridiron Madness. And this site really works. Players spend an average of 4.1 hours per month at the site.

In spite of all the fun touted on the home page, Gamesville is really a database marketing company and an excellent example of 1:1 marketing and permission marketing in action. You see, the games are simply the Trojan Horse used to get consumers to fill out a registration form, says CEO and cofounder Steven Kane. And consumers consent, up front, to watch ads and receive email and other separate ads in exchange for the opportunity to play games and win prizes.

Because Gamesville requires registration, the site obtains considerable specific demographic, geographic, and psychographic data on each person in its fast growing user base—and microtargets all advertising (banners, buttons, e-mercials, email) on an individual by individual basis in real-time.

*Gamesville profitably practices permission marketing.*

Consumers gladly give their permission to be presented e-mercials for a couple of minutes between games. And two minutes is too short a break for the player to get up and do something else; it's just the right amount of time to sit there and watch the ads. These are not just little pop-ups that flash and quickly disappear. Gamesville serves up full-screen, rich media ads based on the user's profile. Gamesville proves the theory that the Internet is the best medium for specificity, for targeted marketing. The Web lets you go nuclear in the 1:1 marketing game.

## Advice from a Real Player, CEO Steve Kane

CEO and cofounder Steve Kane's business really is all fun and games, but he knows that the Internet requires a few adjustments to your thinking. "Be prepared to lose margin," Kane says. "Consumers expect your costs to be lower than bricks-and-mortar stores, so prices must be competitive. It's hard to define value-add."

"Don't believe the hype. What used to be common sense is now considered a trade secret," Kane says. "The old rules still apply. Understand your customer, craft a strong marketing message, and execute on your plan. Don't be seduced by the technology. It's bunk to think that software or programming can do your work for you."

# Tools to Collect Data from Visitors

In traditional database marketing, many data points are gathered, sliced, and diced to create a profile of customers, their buying patterns and preferences. And there are many kinds of data, such as psychographic (what you like) and demographic (age, income, and so on). Data can be collected from people in two ways:

➤ **Self-reported** You know the warranty card you fill out when you buy a new blender or microwave? That's an example of self-reported data. The response cards that fall out of magazines that ask about your interests, income, and preferences? That's self-reported data. A telemarketer asks you a few questions for a survey—self-reported data.

➤ **Behavioral activity** Behavioral data, on the other hand, is data that is "automatically" collected based upon what you do, your behavior. The next section tells you more about how the Internet can track what people do when they visit your Web site.

## Collecting Self-Reported Data

For self-reported data, your Web site can collect a variety of information from individual customers and prospects. Here are a few additions to your site that help users give you the information you want:

➤ **Registration page** You must have a registration page for visitors to your site! From this registration page, you can compile both a "real-world" and email list for targeted marketing messages. The great thing about a registration page is that the information can automatically be sent to and stored in a database for future use.

Remember, you can ask for more specific information (and expect it) after you figure out what the consumer would find of value in return. Maybe instead of urging visitors to register, you should persuade them to join your club, with the promise to make it worth their while by providing special information that only club members receive.

Here is a short list of the minimum information you will want to collect with a registration or joining page. Get the information you need, but don't ask for so much data that the user gets sick of the process. The following list shows important information that a user might be prepared to share with you:

First name

Last name

Address

City

State

Zip code

Email address

Preferences (based upon what you are selling)

*MetLife asks for your personal data to be able to suggest the right personal and business insurance products.*

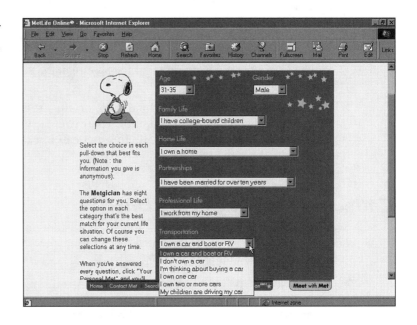

## Make It Easy

Make it easy for people to give you data. If you can, have a drop-down box where users can easily select one option—or use check boxes that simply require a click of the mouse for entry. Also, be sure that if you have data fields (first name, last name) that the page is programmed in such a way that the user can easily use the Tab key to move from one field to the next (as opposed to requiring that they use their mouse).

➤ **Surveys**   Everybody has an opinion, and asking Web visitors for their opinions is a great way to gather information about their preferences. Many sites use surveys to ask questions about customer service, or even ask about the features and effectiveness of the Web site itself.

➤ **Reminder Services**   There are hundreds of things about which you might remind your customers. It's time to give the old clunker a checkup or change the oil. It's time to replace the air filter in the furnace. It's time to get your teeth cleaned. Customers are happy to tell you things they need a little nudge about.

Sears effectively uses the concept of a reminder service. On its Web site, visitors can enter important dates such as birthdays, weddings, and anniversaries into the database. Then, the Sears reminder service sends reminder email messages prior to the events. Naturally, a visitor might take the opportunity to purchase some additional Sears products.

➤ **Gift Registry** For e-tail sites, a gift registry takes the reminder service one step further. Whether it is for weddings, birthdays, graduations, or holidays, why not let visitors enter a list of the products you sell that they wish someone would buy them? It can revolutionize holiday shopping. Go to a Web site and find out exactly what type of sweater or tool your brother-in-law really wants!

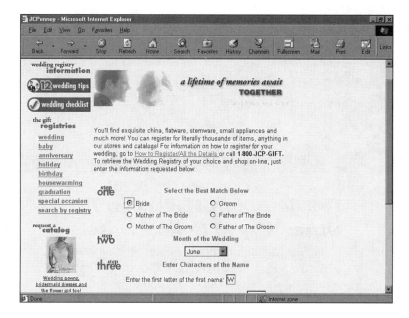

*JC Penney makes it easy to find what people want with an online gift registry.*

➤ **Polls** Like a survey, a poll is a good method to ask for an opinion, ask for permission, and offer to display the results to all participants. What's the difference between a survey and a poll? A survey asks an individual questions that are specific to his or her life. A poll focuses on opinions. A survey question would be, "How many times a week do you eat chicken?" A poll question would be, "Do you think chicken tastes better than beef?" Surveys usually collect information that the participant wants kept private, such as the amount of his or her income. A poll, on the other hand, usually collects information that can instantly generate an opinion chart for everyone to see, as in "Who do you think will win the Super Bowl?"

Many software programs make it easy to collect and analyze the information that users submit; using these types of programs makes great sense for polling and surveys. For example, Inquisite (`http://www.instapoll.com`) is a software program that enables you to quickly build a poll for deployment online or via email with an easy-to-use wizard. Results are created by accessing the data stored in a database. Most polling software does not require a license for each person who responds—but be sure before you purchase it.

*Catapult Systems' product, Inquisite, creates online surveys and polls and displays results graphically.*

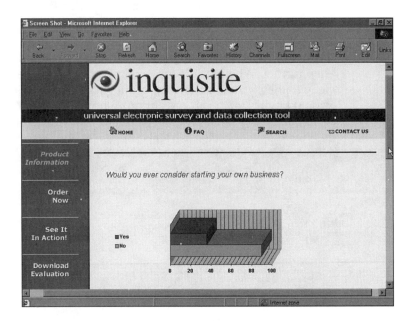

## The Downside

There is a downside to using declared or self-reported data to make marketing decisions. With no malicious intent, some users might submit information that might not be, um, entirely true. There's no substitute for getting to know your customers, especially after they've volunteered information about themselves. That way, you can weigh the answers one-on-one.

# The Behavioral Sciences: The Other Way to Collect Data

So far, our data collection has been self-reported. Now let's take a look at behavioral collection. What better way to figure out a customer's preferences than to actually observe his or her behavior? Good clothing store clerks watch which racks you visit and which articles you pick up. The best ones remember what you bought on previous visits. Based on current and past experience, a good salesperson will use that information to predict what else you might like to buy.

There are software tools that can help track a visitor's behavior at your Web site. But remember, no technology has all the answers. Tracking your customers' behaviors requires a combination of knowing what you want to collect and how you will use it, and then selecting the best technology for the job.

## Cookies

A *cookie* is a piece of data that is stored on your hard drive by a Web site that you have visited using your Web browser. That stored data is then sent back to the Web site every time you visit. It might include information such as a username and password for the site, or items you have previously put into a "shopping cart" at a shopping site.

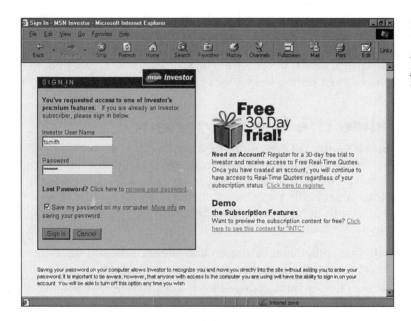

*The Microsoft Investor Web site uses a cookie to store your username and password, making it easier to log in to the site.*

Web sites also use cookies to collect data about the pages you visit. The good news is that cookies let Web sites customize your visits. If you go to a site such as Yahoo! and ask for bond prices, weather forecasts for France, and business headlines, Yahoo! stores these preferences. Next time you return, the Web site will "read" the cookie that is on your PC, see what you like, and customize the site accordingly.

The bad news is that you've just entered the land of no privacy. How do you know what will be done with your information? There is the potential that user information could be sold or rented without authorization. In fact, both Netscape and Explorer give users the option to refuse cookies. (More about privacy later.)

## Clickstream Data

You can learn about a person's behavior by tracking the way they move through your Web site—or how they click. Do most people go right from the home page to your press release section, or the contest page? It's important to track the content that users visit and click, where it is, and how long they take to view it.

## Putting It All Together

You might want to combine both declared data and behavioral data. In fact, it is recommended. The goal is to understand enough about your visitor that you can make a real-time offer directed specifically to him or her.

Products such as ProfileServer from Massachusetts-based Engage (`http://www.engagetech.com`) do just that. ProfileServer combines observed behavior, give-and-take interaction, and declared data to develop individual profiles, each associated with over 800 attributes. The software helps you get answers to questions you create with registration forms and surveys. The software also tracks where visitors come from. You can then make special offers, target advertising, or customize content based on a profile of the visitor obtained during the visitor's first visit.

# Tools to Personalize the User Experience

We've already entered into a significant period on the Internet called *personalization*. The theory is that giving the user the ability to customize his or her Web experience will increase loyalty and the probability he or she will return. Personalization takes many forms, including individual home pages, recommendations for specific products and services, and stock portfolios. There are actually two ways you can use data that you collect to personalize information:

➤ One is to collect data from individual customers and site visitors, and then use this information to create personalized Web pages for these people.

➤ A second technique uses information gathered from a large group of customers or visitors to create pages of information that should be of interest to certain segments of your online population. This concept is called *collaborative filtering*, and employs a technique in which a site combines the preferences and interactions of similar, like-minded users. Your preferences are merged with others and analyzed, and the site suggests recommendations. The more the site learns about the customers, the more valuable its recommendations can be.

**Check This Out**

**In the Old Days...**

Collaborative filtering is really a new way of talking about an old marketing technique. Remember the neighborhood grocer who would position all the ingredients for an entire meal in a single area and tell you that everybody in the neighborhood was enjoying all of those courses for Thanksgiving? It's making recommendations based on the collective behavior and preferences of like-minded individuals.

The clever people at Andromedia (http://www.andromedia.com) named their patented collaborative filtering technology LikeMinds. LikeMinds uses individual purchase history or preferences to find people with similar tastes, and predicts what each person will like, based on the collective wisdom of other like-minded individuals. At Levi's, the LikeMinds technology is used to predict which Levi's products are most likely to fit the customer's individual style and needs. You take a little "quiz" that asks you what kind of music you enjoy, what you like to do for fun, and what style of appearance you prefer. The site then provides clothing recommendations.

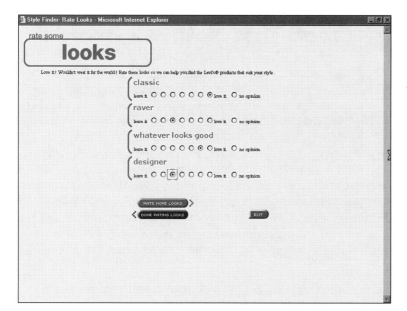

*Levi's uses collaborative filtering to make recommendations about the best fit of style with preference.*

# Tools to Build a Personalized Community

In other chapters, we talked about creating a sense of community with email messages, e-zines, chats, and forums. The recent successes of the community-based Web sites The Globe (http://www.theglobe.com) and GeoCities (http://www.geocities.com) show that you can leverage an online community to create new revenues from advertising and sales. The value of a personalized community is clear: It enables people to meet others with shared interests while serving very human needs such as ego, and the desire to be needed, to belong, and to be admired and respected.

Because communities form the personal relationships that are at the core of one-to-one marketing, let's recap some of the categories of communities that you want to consider creating for your Web site:

➤ **Demographic communities**  For people with common characteristics.

➤ **Professional communities**  For people who share similar professions.

➤ **Personal interest communities**   For people who share similar hobbies.

➤ **Psychographic communities**   For people who have common likes and dislikes.

**Check This Out**

Chapter 15, "The Value of a Virtual Community," provides more extensive coverage of the benefits and options involved in creating a successful online community.

Koz.com (http://www.koz.com) takes the concept of personalized communities and offers software that gives you tools to build communities that generate traffic, loyalty, and new revenue streams.

## Tools That Notify Customers

Personal notification is a great way to provide an incentive to have your customers return to your site. But in addition to dates on a calendar, there are other things about which you can notify customers. Based on NetMind Technologies' (http://www.netmind.com) Minder solution, the popular auction Web site, eBay (http://www.ebay.com), notifies users through email when an item in which they are interested comes up for bid. Before this service was available, users had to manually search for new information each time they logged on to eBay. Users can track individual items by keyword, description, and/or price range as well as specify how often they would like to receive email notifications for new listings. Perhaps you are temporarily out of stock on an item; use a notification service to let your customers know when the product is available.

Advanced "digital agent" software can even help your Web site notify customers via other types of media besides the Internet, such as the telephone, pager, and fax. Let's be honest; we don't spend all day surfing the Web. A digital agent is nothing more than a software program that can do things that humans usually do. Like what? Well, you could go to a Web site for a bank and tell the digital agent that you want to be notified the minute your checking account drops below $100 so you don't bounce any checks. You sign off the Web site. Two weeks later, you are on the golf course and you get a call on your cell phone. It's not a person; it's a computer voice that says, "Your account is now at $85. What do you want to do? Press 1 to transfer funds." So the software simply monitors (on a regular basis) your account balance. It can then notify you via phone, pager, or fax when an event (a balance of less than $100) occurs. Edify (http://www.edify.com) is an example of a company that makes digital agent software used by the financial and other industries.

## Privacy Is Important

Okay. Web sites are collecting information about where you live, what you like to do, your opinions, your friends' birthdays, and how you use the sites. There are databases that know more about you than your parents do. A little scary, isn't it?

Online privacy isn't a new concept, but it is a hotly debated one. According to the Direct Marketing Association, there are currently more than 80 bills related to privacy policy in Congress. There are two drivers of the controversy:

➤ **Electronic commerce**   Potential customers fear fraud on the Internet. They are afraid to enter their credit card numbers into a page on a Web site.

➤ **Spam**   Spam has inundated our hard drives with unsolicited messages.

If you expect a customer or visitor to tell you personal, private information, then you must tell them what you plan to do with this information. You need to both adopt and publish a privacy policy for your visitors that assures them that the information they provide will be kept private (for example, you won't be selling it to direct-mail companies), and you should make this privacy policy easy for your users to find. This is essential.

The Disney Web site (`http://www.disney.com`) is a popular destination for children. Disney has an extensive privacy policy that provides details about how they use (and don't use) information that is collected on their site. The policy is available from a link on their home page. For children, the policy is quite clear, including this:

"No information collected from guests under 13 years of age is used for any marketing or promotional purposes whatsoever, either inside or outside Disney."

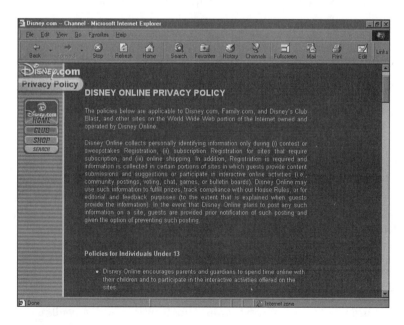

*Disney makes it easy to locate and read its privacy policy.*

## TRUSTe Program

TRUSTe is an independent, nonprofit privacy initiative dedicated to building users' trust and confidence on the Internet and accelerating growth of the Internet industry.

The organization has developed a third-party oversight "seal" program that can help alleviate your users' concerns about online privacy, while meeting the specific business needs of each of the licensed, member Web site. Visit the site at http:// www.truste.org to stay current and review the program for your own business. Here are its principles and license fee schedule:

➤ Adopting and implementing a privacy policy that factors in the goals of your individual Web site as well as consumer anxiety over sharing personal information online.

➤ Posting notice and disclosure of collection and use practices regarding personally identifiable information (data used to identify, contact, or locate a person), via a posted privacy statement.

➤ Giving users choice and consent over how their personal information is used and shared.

➤ Putting data security and quality, and access measures in place to safeguard, update, and correct personally identifiable information.

## Table 14.1   License Structure for TRUSTe

| Your Company's Annual Revenue | Annual License Fee |
| --- | --- |
| $0–$1 million | $299 |
| $1–$5 million | $399 |
| $5–$10 million | $499 |
| $10–$25 million | $1,499 |
| $25–$50 million | $2,499 |
| $50–$75 million | $3,499 |
| $75 million and over | $4,999 |

### The Least You Need to Know

➤ One-to-one marketing works to improve relationships with customers and improve sales.

➤ Permission marketing means that customers have given you permission to deliver your messages; that means they're more receptive to them.

➤ Collect data from site visitors with surveys, polls, and questionnaires as well as collect shopping and buying behavior data to better target your message.

➤ Privacy is still a huge issue; display your policy and walk your talk.

# The Value of a Virtual Community

In the real world, there are two types of communities:

➤ **Geographic communities**   Everyone who lives in a neighborhood or town is part of a geographic community. You share interests and concerns with the other people who live in your geographic community. Common interests might include diverse topics such as the weather, local taxes, entertainment, and land development. This community is created and exists largely because of geography. You might not share these interests and concerns with someone who lives in a different county, state, or country.

➤ **Common-interest communities**   A second type of community is one in which you gather with people who share more personal concerns and interests. You are a member of a scuba diving club, an investment group, an industry trade association, or the Boy Scouts. This is a community that exists because of common interests that are based not on geography, but on enthusiasm for a topic or hobby. You might even travel several times a year to participate in events with other people who share these interests.

The Internet provides many opportunities for both types communities, enabling people to join and participate in an online space where they can meet and share common interests and ideas. This chapter focuses on what has been appropriately termed the *virtual community*. You'll see how you can use a virtual community as an effective tool to attract and keep current and prospective customers at your Web site.

# What Exactly Is a Virtual Community?

Online or virtual communities share many traits with their physical counterparts. Think for a moment about what people (that includes you) who belong to a community do. They talk, express themselves, make new friends, ask questions, share ideas and knowledge, share experiences, leave messages, and participate in events. A virtual community enables people to engage in these same activities—only they do most of them via their computer screens and an Internet Web site. Table 15.1 shows how the virtual community mirrors these common activities with specific Internet technologies—specifically, chats, forums, personal Web pages, and events calendars. We will learn more about these virtual community technologies later in this chapter.

### Table 15.1   Activities That Take Place in the Real World and Online

| Activity | Virtual Community |
| --- | --- |
| Talk | Chat rooms |
| Express yourself | Personal Web pages |
| Make new friends | Chat rooms |
| Ask questions | Chats and forums |
| Share ideas | Forums |
| Participate in events | Event calendars |

The average Web site, with its pages of text and graphics and perhaps even electronic commerce, does not constitute a virtual community. With the exception of email, most Web sites do not encourage a lot of interaction between visitors and the Web site owner, and literally no interaction between the visitors themselves.

This overlooks the capability of the Internet to truly connect people. An online community presents a tremendous opportunity to enhance marketing efforts. How? An online community creates a terrific reason for people to return to a Web site. Members of any community enjoy the ability to gather, communicate, and participate. And, after relationships are created, these individuals return again and again to both the community and the Web site that offers the community. The Web site becomes an electronic community center.

Let's consider virtual communities that focus on people who live in a geographic area. Possibly one of the most wired communities in the entire world is Blacksburg,

Virginia. The concept of the Blacksburg Electronic Village (BEV) began in 1991, when Virginia Tech joined forces with the Town of Blacksburg and Bell Atlantic to offer Internet access to every citizen in town. Many office buildings in the area are completely wired for direct high-speed access, and dorm rooms and apartments are wired with Ethernet (high-speed) connections. By 1997, more than 60% of Blacksburg's 36,000 citizens were using the Internet on a regular basis. The BEV project is unique because it focuses on both access and content. Currently, more than 250 local businesses advertise online. The BEV Web site creates a virtual community that complements and enhances the physical community. People can use the BEV Web site to learn about local events, participate in political debates, access educational services, and tap into an online shopping mall.

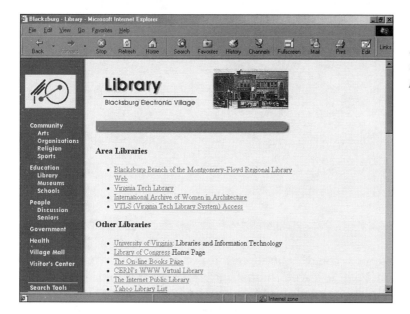

*The Blacksburg Electronic Village creates a virtual community that complements and enhances the physical community.*

# How a Virtual Community Benefits Your Business

A virtual community can become an essential aspect of your Web site. It encompasses a variety of services that help the people who are part of "your" community. Indeed, over time, it is possible for the community to become a major attraction for your Web site. This is a good thing, because when your customers and prospects and other visitors are "in" your community, they have the opportunity to learn more about your company and its products and services. And, there is a good chance that the communication between individuals relates to your company's products and services. The virtual community helps your business in at least four ways:

➤ The members of your community learn more about your products and services when they are in the community.

➤ The members of your community can help one another with ideas and questions related to your products and services. You help these people help themselves, thereby enhancing customer-support services.

➤ You will gain valuable insight into the needs and concerns of people who belong to the community (read: cost-effective market research).

➤ Members of your community generate content that adds value to your Web site.

*The Kodak Web site has a variety of online forums where people who share an interest in photography and Kodak products can share information and experiences.*

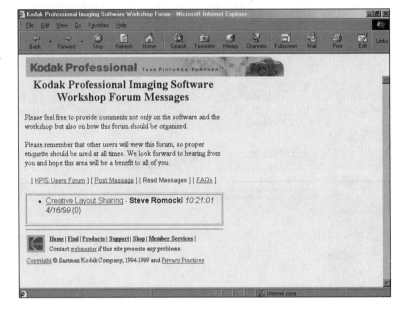

Indeed, user-generated content could, by itself, be a reason to create a virtual community. Think about how difficult, time-consuming, and expensive it is to constantly generate new and interesting information and content on your Web site. And you know that without new content there is very little reason for people to continue to return to the Web site.

A virtual community can eliminate this catch-22 as the members of your community begin to create new messages, conduct chats, create Web pages, add events—basically providing free content for your Web site. And, there's a very good chance that the content will be of interest to other people who visit your site. As an example, the Web site Airbrush.com (http://www.airbrush.com) has several features that support communications in a virtual community including chats and forums. The messages and discussion among the members create useful information that draws people to the site.

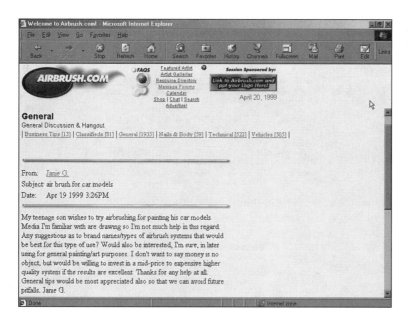

*At Airbrush.com, members contribute to the content of the site with their ongoing conversations.*

# The Power of Portals

One of the big trends on the Internet is the creation of Web sites known as *portals*. The dictionary definition of a portal is *a doorway, gate, or entrance*, which pretty much defines what an Internet portal site is. These sites want to become the starting point for a large number of Web users, to be the first Web site people use when they jump onto the Internet, and to be the default start page or home page (the page that your Web browser loads when you launch it). The concept is quite clever: If you can become a portal site, you will have a large number of people who always return to your site.

Most portal sites are really jumping-off places. In other words, the Web user goes to the portal site to find useful information that might be available on other sites. Thus, the site is a portal to other places. Search engine sites (such as Yahoo! and Lycos) have made significant efforts to become widely popular portal sites, and they've even added a large number of community features such as online chatting, game rooms, email, and forums to keep visitors from even leaving the portal.

With a search engine and site directory, headline news, personalized email, chat, message boards, shopping, and directories to locate people, Lycos (http://www.lycos.com) has assembled services and information that create a powerful portal site.

*Lycos is a portal site that offers users a variety of information and community features.*

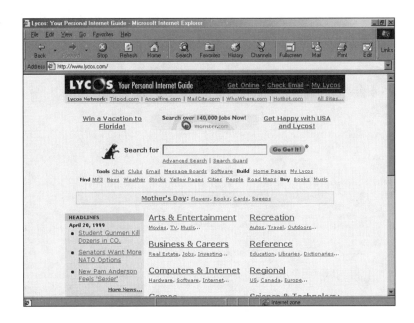

A portal site is different from a virtual community; a portal site might or might not have features that create a community. Yahoo! and Lycos are portal sites for the general public, but it is also possible to create a portal site for a narrower target audience, such as a portal site for cable television engineers, forest rangers, or teenagers. However, for marketing purposes, you are better off adding elements to create a virtual community on your site than trying to become a portal site, because a portal site is a tool for the users that takes them to other Web sites. Portal sites are great if your revenue model is advertising. But a virtual community might support your products and services in a better fashion.

## What Type of Community Do You Want?

As previously mentioned, a virtual community can (like its real-world counterpart) represent a group of people who share a geographic bond or a set of common personal interests. You can create either type of virtual community. Most Web sites that represent businesses, organizations, or associations can benefit from a virtual community based upon the personal interests of the visitors.

I cannot think of a business that could not benefit from the creation of a virtual community, because every business offers a product or service that caters to the needs of people that share common interests. If you have a sports store, or manufacture sporting goods, your customers share a common interest in sports. And if you manufacture only volleyballs, you still reach a target audience that shares an avid interest in the sport. Don't forget—the great thing about the Internet is that it is a global communications system. So, there might not be enough volleyball enthusiasts in Topeka, Kansas, to create an active community of volleyball lovers, but when you enlarge the potential size of the community to encompass the entire world, you can definitely create an active and exciting online community.

The people who use online communities (your Web site visitors) are known as *members*. Sometimes membership requires that the members either register or possibly even pay membership dues (monthly subscription fees) for the privilege of having access to the community.

There are four levels, or types, of virtual communities. Each level offers more interaction and open communication between members or visitors to your community:

➤ **Level One**   You let visitors only communicate with your company, and you post content that you think will be interesting for other visitors.

➤ **Level Two**   You moderate the content between members. People enter their communication among one another, but you post only the information that you feel is useful.

➤ **Level Three**   Full interaction among members. You allow people to register at your site to become a member of the community. If they break any community rules (perhaps submitting offensive material), they are not allowed to participate in the future. Membership can either be free or subscription based.

➤ **Level Four**   Full interaction among members and visitors. Anyone who comes to the site can participate in the community, and there is no registration requirement.

All these levels open the door to creating a community at your Web site. There is really no right or wrong way to create a virtual community; the only word of caution is that creating a virtual community that involves moderation of content considerably increases the time and effort required to manage the community.

We worked with Kryptonics (`http://www.kryptonics.com`), a company that manufactures high-quality wheels for inline skating, roller skating, and skateboarding. Its Web site has useful features such as a searchable database of stores, a directory of wheels, and the ability for skaters to submit photos for possible inclusion in an online photo gallery. It presents an opportunity for members of this global community to gain a little exposure. This is a good example of a "level one"-type community.

*The Kryptonics Web site features pictures of skaters.*

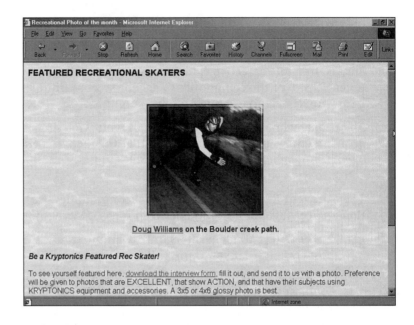

## Chat Gets Them Talking

Chat is probably the most popular form of real-time communication on the Internet. With chat, members of your community use their keyboards to type in messages that are shared instantaneously with one person or a group of people. Chatting offers a fun opportunity to have a spontaneous dialog with a friend or colleague from a distance over the Internet.

Chat on the Internet is very similar to what it is in everyday life. We talk with friends, family, even strangers. The biggest difference with Internet chat is that you don't use your voice—you use your keyboard. You type in your thoughts, and your words are viewed instantly by other people on their computer screens. They see what you type, and you see what they type. Of course, with the Internet, you can chat with one, two, or even hundreds of other people simultaneously. Technically, you visit a Web site or an online service (such as America Online) and enter an area devoted to chat. Most chat areas are categorized by topic, so you can chat with other people who share a common interest.

First-time chat users might be a little overwhelmed by what they see on their computer screens. Sometimes a chat session has 30 or more people "talking." Some people are talking to the group, and others are essentially having private conversations that the group can view. So it is a little confusing until you jump in.

You can also offer scheduled chats. These are chats in which a famous person or an authority on a subject chats at a specific time. This is great for marketing. You can schedule a chat about new products or customer-support issues, or perhaps have your company president chat with your customers. Sometimes chats are moderated, and a moderator filters questions that go to the "speaker." Following are definitions of some common chat terms to keep in mind:

➤ **Chat room**   A place where people chat, usually about a specific topic.

➤ **Chat window**   The onscreen window where chat messages are seen.

➤ **Instant message**   A private message that one chatter sends to another.

➤ **Moderated chat**   A chat where questions are filtered before being answered.

➤ **Private chat**   A one-on-one chat.

➤ **Profile**   The publicly available information that describes a certain user.

➤ **Scheduled chat**   A chat that occurs at a specific time.

➤ **Screen name**   The identification or name that a person uses when chatting.

An increasing number of Web sites offer chats. Usually, a visitor must become a member of the Web site to enter a chat, although some sites let visitors chat as guests. The only challenge with Web-based chat is that you have to locate a site where other people are actually online. If there's no one there, chatting with yourself gets boring pretty fast. It's like having a party where no one shows up.

If you are going to add chat to your virtual community, you should consider how many people currently use your Web site. If you don't have a lot of visitors, then chat can actually become a negative community service. Most people won't try a chat too often if no one is ever there.

Ivillage (`http://www.ivillage.com`) is a Web site devoted to women and women's issues. The site has regularly scheduled chats on a wide variety of topics including health.

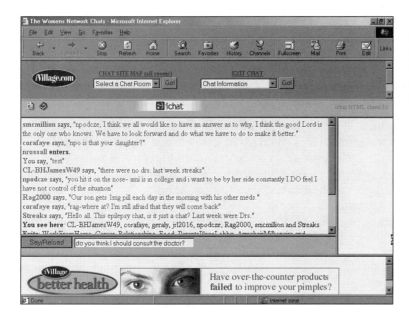

*The iVillage site has numerous chat rooms that focus on topics of interest to women, including chat about serious health topics such as cancer.*

The FreeZone (http://www.freezone.com) is a Web site devoted to kids. There is online chatting, where kids can talk with one another. Parents don't need to worry, because a chat-room monitor ensures that the chatters stay within the rules of the site and kicks off anyone that gets out of hand.

*FreeZone is a Web site where kids can meet online friends and chat.*

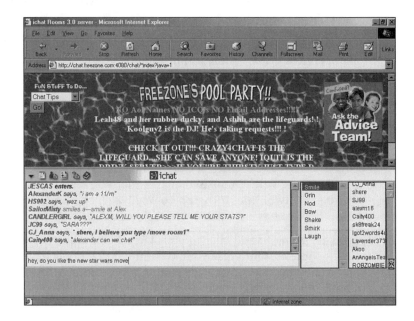

## Forums Present Useful Messages

Chat is a real-time activity. In other words, it takes place live. At any moment, people are either chatting or not chatting in the community. A *forum* is a different type of communication system. Forums are Web-based versions of newsgroups (see Chapter 11, "Marketing with Newsgroups," for specifics about how forums work). Members of the community enter messages about specific topics, and other members can see and respond to these messages. Because messages are stored on the Web site, members can jump in and share their thoughts at any time—it doesn't have to be in real time.

Let's consider some examples. The Web site Power Online (http://www.poweronline.com) creates a virtual community, a marketplace for professionals in the power industry. The site includes several community-building features such as a career center with job opportunities, a product center with information, and a buyers' guide for products and supplies used in the power industry, industry news, and chat sessions; an industry events calendar, and forums. (The following figure shows a forum message where the author is requesting information about monitoring oil debris on a gas turbine.)

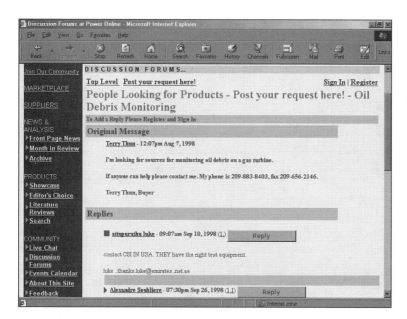

*The Power Online site includes a forum discussion area where members of the site can post questions and answers about the power industry.*

Most forums are divided into subject areas so people can quickly find messages that are of interest. For example, if you own an outdoor gear store and have a online forum, you might create "subforums" for backpacking, camping, fishing, hiking, kayaking, swimming—whatever subcategories are appropriate for members of your community. For example, the Lipton Kitchens Food Forum includes three different forum areas:

➤ Recipe recommendations

➤ New ways to cook with Lipton Secrets

➤ General cooking tips

Messages posted to the forums are moderated, and there can be some delay between the time a visitor posts a message and when it appears on the forum. Nonetheless, this is a great example of how forums can be used to simultaneously create a community and promote company products.

Another way you can use forums for marketing is to establish special forum topics related to your products. Let your customers post questions and the answers (that you provide) will be seen by everyone. Create a forum for tips, advice, case studies—any topic that adds both credibility and practical advice about your products and services.

*The Lipton Kitchens Food Forum enables members to share messages, including recipes that use Lipton products.*

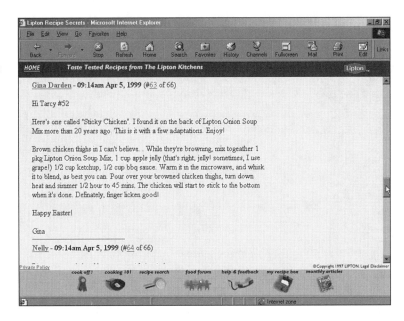

# Let Members Publish with Personal Web Pages

Another community-building feature for your virtual community is to let your members create their own Web pages. Why is this a good idea? Because people love to share their Web creations with friends, family, and colleagues. If they have a Web site that also happens to be part of your Web site, you automatically generate additional traffic to your site. Naturally, every member's Web page will have a link back to your company's home page!

The concept of letting members create Web pages is epitomized by GeoCities (http://www.geocities.com), which was acquired by Yahoo!. Why? Because with more than 3.5 million sites authored and hosted on GeoCities, the company has created one of the Web's largest communities. GeoCities' Web-based publishing tools enable nontechnical users to create, publish, and update content on the Web. Members must register. Indeed, the 3.5 million GeoCities members have created more than 32 million pages of personalized Web content! GeoCities offers both free sites and sites with advanced features such as additional storage space and electronic commerce. Additional fees are required for these features. One of the revenue models for GeoCities is that when you visit a page or site created by one of the members, you will automatically see banner ads or pop-up ads.

Your site can also offer the "create-a-Web-page" service to enhance the online community. For example, suppose your company manufactures plumbing supplies or fixtures. Why not let plumbers create their own Web pages for their businesses on your site? It would be a valuable service, and it would help brand your products. The plumbers' customers would go to their Web pages and have the opportunity to learn about your products, and which they would want the plumber to use.

Crafters Network (http://www.crafters.net) is billed as "The Virtual Community for Crafters, Artists, Collectors, and Hobbyists!" This site lures in both people and companies in the world of crafts by creating a virtual community. The following figure shows the Web wizard (a simple onscreen form) that helps members create their pages. Here are some of the other community-building features they promote:

> "Become part of a global community of friendly people with like interests in arts and crafts. Enter a comprehensive and highly visible listing in our Huge International Craft Fair for Free. Participate in our Top 100 Craft Sites list or post a classified ad free! Create your own Web page instantly if you don't have one. Our Web Wizard makes it easy! Join in on friendly discussions about arts and crafts, and related topics in our forums! Gain access to Internet-related information and resources in our Members Area and more!"

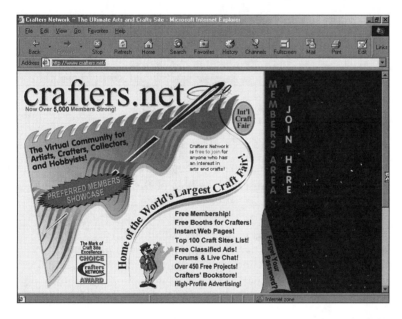

*Crafters Network creates a virtual community by offering members a variety of community-building and communications tools.*

*Crafters Network uses simple, onscreen forms to help members create their own Web pages.*

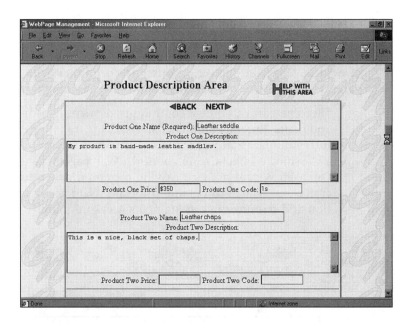

## What's Happening: The Value of an Event Calendar

Another community-building feature is an event calendar. Every town and every industry has ongoing events that are of interest to members of the community. The events could be a list of medical conferences for physicians, trade shows for cable television engineers, or NASCAR races for auto racing enthusiasts. Naturally, if your company offers any special events or training sessions for customers, you'll want to include these in the calendar. An event calendar can simply be a Web page that lists upcoming events, or it can be a database-driven system where members can search for events that occur on specific dates. The following are two ways to create a useful event calendar:

➤ Simply conduct research on your industry and create a one-year event list.

➤ A more powerful method is to allow members of your community to submit or add their own events to the list.

We worked with a Denver, Colorado, arts organization called Arts to Zoo during the initial development their Internet presence. The nonprofit organization helps local arts organizations get information about their services, activities, and events out to the public. Their Web site (http://www.artstozoo.org) provides information about the various organizations, as well as access to a comprehensive events database. Member organizations can submit upcoming events via a secure Web form; therefore, they participate in the content of the Web site itself. The events become part of an ever-expanding database of events through which users can search. The site has become a popular destination for people in Denver and Colorado who want to find out what's happening in the arts scene.

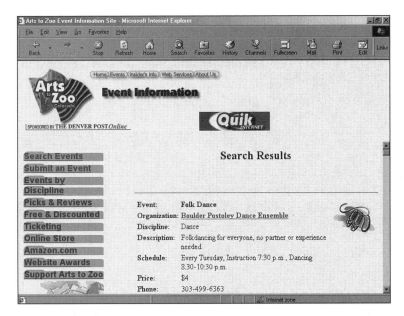

*Members can submit events to the Arts to Zoo Web site, which provides a searchable database of cultural events.*

On the Web site for the National Tour Association, visitors can search a database of festivals, fairs, and events. After you conduct a search, you get a list of events with links to more Web pages that have additional information.

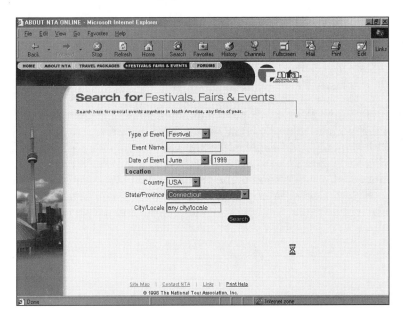

*The National Tour Association helps both members and visitors with a searchable database of events.*

**277**

# Creating Your Virtual Community

Okay. You're sold on the idea of creating a virtual community to enhance your marketing efforts. But how do you actually create one? The company that you use to create your Web site (or your Webmaster) should be able to integrate the various community-building services into your Web site. There are a variety of software programs that create chat rooms, forums, and event calendars.

How much should you expect to pay to establish a virtual community? Somewhere between $5,000 and $20,000 to create and customize chat and forum functionality. Like everything else related to the Web, price depends upon exactly what you want to do and how much custom work needs to be done to achieve your goals.

More importantly, how do you launch these services and actually build the community? We recommend that you phase in various aspects of the community. In other words, don't launch them all at once. Some virtual community services, such as chat, require a substantial audience before they become effective. Also, by phasing in these features, you have an opportunity to fine-tune them (for example, you could create new forum topics), and to see what works and what doesn't. Table 15.2 provides a launch plan for features of a virtual community.

### Table 15.2 Phase In Features of Your Virtual Community

| Month | Virtual Community Feature |
|---|---|
| One | Member registration form (collect email address and other member information)<br>Forums<br>Events calendar |
| Two | Personal Web pages<br>Email newsletter |
| Three | Chat<br>Industry news<br>Member directory |

Other community-building features that you could add include industry news, a directory of members with brief bios and email addresses (you'll have to ask people for permission to include them), and links to other useful Web sites or reference materials. If you are charging members to access the virtual community, you could add additional business services such as Internet fax (where they can send a fax from your Web site) or a career center (where job opportunities in your industry could be posted).

# Don't Stop Now: The Commitment to Your Community

You might consider having someone on your staff jump-start and monitor the content aspects of your community—create useful forum topics, add a few initial forum messages that will spark further discussion and add new messages weekly, and reply to messages that relate to your company or products. In other words, get involved in your community. If you don't use it, why should anyone else?

Many of the large virtual community sites use volunteers and staff to both monitor community content and to create new content that keeps the community alive. For example, The Mining Company (http://www.theminingcompany.com) has 690 "guides" who develop and administer different topical sections of the search site. The company pays people as contractors, and they get a percentage of the revenue. GeoCities has more than 1,500 volunteers who function as community leaders and liaisons to help new members with questions. And America Online uses more than 10,000 volunteers to help administer chats and answer questions. If you use the volunteer technique, be warned that you should give the volunteers something in exchange for their time—if not money, pay for their Internet access, or give them discounts on your products...anything that provides enough incentive to keep them happy. It's probably a wise idea to create a simple contract for volunteers or contractors that defines the terms of their activities.

*The Mining Company uses independent contractors called "guides" to help administer sections of the virtual community.*

But don't stop there. You *want* members. The more, the merrier. In fact, you can develop the greatest virtual community in the world, but if you don't have members, the community will fail. Use all of the Internet (and non-Internet) marketing tactics described in this book to market your virtual community. Place banner ads announcing your community, send out a targeted email marketing campaign, and post an announcement on select newsgroups. If your community offers true value to members, the word will spread quickly.

And, use the communication aspects of your community to regularly ask your members about new features they would like to see. Don't forget to use the power of the community to interact with members to get ideas about new products, product features, and services that your members would like to see your company offer. The community might take on a life of its own, but you can use the features of the community to simultaneously conduct marketing and market research.

Long known as a creative pioneer in music, films, and theater, David Bowie jumped onto the Internet. He created BowieNet. This is a virtual community devoted to (you guessed it) David Bowie. What's unique about BowieNet is that the service sells its members both Internet access as well as access to content on the site. A brilliant marketer, Bowie uses the site as a vehicle for communication, product improvement, and publicity. He regularly adds content such as a diary of his thoughts to the site. He also had a contest where fans submitted lyrics for his song "What's Really Happening"; the winner received a $15,000 publishing contract and a weekend in New York City. Naturally, thousands of people entered the contest, which generated interest in the song and publicity for BowieNet!

*BowieNet is a virtual community that supports and enhances David Bowie and his songs, and makes money.*

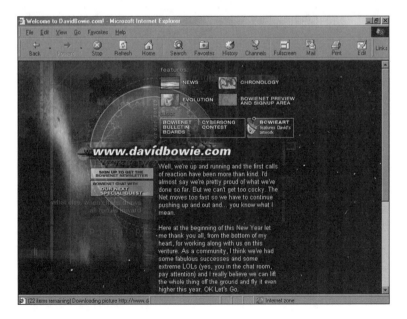

We will certainly see an increasing number of companies take their Web sites to the next level by creating a virtual community. The first and foremost goal of the community is to support your marketing efforts by providing a useful service to customers and prospective customers. And, if the community becomes wildly successful, you can consider charging monthly access fees, or providing Internet access and other value-added services. There's nothing wrong with creating additional revenue streams (money that can enhance your Internet activities) as long as it doesn't interfere with your strategic goals.

---

### The Least You Need to Know

➤ In this chapter, we explored how a virtual community can enhance both your Web site and your marketing efforts.

➤ The ability of a virtual community to entice customers and prospective customers to return again-and-again to your site is one of its greatest assets.

➤ Enabling your customers to share ideas and to interact with one another can be a very powerful addition to your marketing arsenal.

---

# Speak Like a Marketing Geek: Online Marketing Terms

**animated GIF**   A GIF file that is composed of two or more individual GIF images, also known as *frames* (as in an animation). Each frame appears on the Web page for a specific length of time and a specific number of cycles (or repetitions). Both the times and cycles are determined by the creator of the ad.

**attrition**   Also known as *churn*. Occurs when a customer cancels his or her account with an Internet service provider. Marketing efforts focus on minimizing churn because the cost of getting a new customer is usually much greater than the cost of retaining a customer.

**banner ad**   A graphic element on a Web page that promotes a product or service and opens a new Web page when a user clicks it. There are several different sizes of banner ads.

**branding**   Branding as it relates to marketing is the science or process by which your company (corporate branding) or your products (product branding) establish themselves in the minds of your customers, your investors, and your employees. Customers recognize brands and they often choose products and companies that have brand-recognition over those that do not. You can use your online marketing efforts to solidify your brand(s).

**chat**   Communicating online by typing your comments, then responding to other people who are doing the same thing. For marketing, online chat can be used for product promotion or to answer customer service questions.

**churn**   See *attrition*.

**clickstreams**   The electronic path that is created as a user navigates from one site to another, within a site, and from page to page.

**clickthrough**   The act of clicking a banner or other ad, which takes the user through to the advertiser's Web site.

**clickthrough rate (CTR)**   The response rate of an online advertisement, typically expressed as a percentage and calculated by dividing the number of clickthroughs the ad received by the number of impressions, and multiplying by 100 to obtain a percentage. (Example: 20 clicks/1,000 impressions = .02 × 100 = 2% CTR)

Historically used as a measurement of ad effectiveness based on the idea that online promotions do what they're intended to do—get you to click.

**cookie**   A cookie is a very small text file that is placed on a user's hard drive when he or she visits certain Web pages. The cookie file helps the site track visits to the site, and can store other information that users volunteer (such as user names or passwords). When the user returns to the Web site, the site retrieves the cookie file from his or her PC and uses the information obtained to target content and advertising to the user's stated preferences. Cookies are used to store items in electronic shopping bags.

**cost per action (CPA)**   The price paid by an advertiser for each action that a content site delivers. The action might be a sale, a lead, a successful form fill-out, a download of a software program, or an e-commerce sale of a product. The action, price, and terms of a CPA purchase are mutually agreed upon by the advertiser and content site.

**cost per click (CPC)**   The price paid by an advertiser to a content site. When buying on a CPC model, the advertiser and content site have mutually agreed that the content site will continue to display the advertiser's ad creative until $X$ number of clicks have been delivered—the amount purchased. This pricing model typically ranges between 10¢ CPC up to $2 CPC, and, as with other forms of online advertising, is dependent on content, audience reached, and targeted delivery (untargeted being lower priced, targeted to an affluent audience being at the high end of the rate scale).

**cost per sale (CPS)**   The price paid by an advertiser to a content site for each sale that results from a visitor who is referred from the content site to the advertiser's site. This type of buying model is typically tracked with cookies, where the cookie is offered on the content site and read on the advertiser's site at the success page after successful completion of one transaction/sale.

**cost per thousand impressions (CPM)**   As an advertiser, the price you pay a site to display your banner ad 1,000 times. In traditional media (TV, radio, print), CPM is based on viewership.

**customer segment**   A group of prospects or customers who are selected from a database based on characteristics they possess or exhibit.

**data mining**   Data mining refers to taking a database that has perhaps hundreds of thousands of records and "mining" this data to find out specific things, such as the percentage of your customers who like red automobiles.

**data warehouse**   A data warehouse is an electronic system that stores data from transactions and is designed in such a way that it can be queried (asked questions) and generate reports.

**database marketing**   Database marketing refers to creating a database of information about your customers (such as name and address), and using the database for future marketing, such as a direct-mail campaign.

**demographics**   Characteristics of a group of people, including (but not limited to) age, location, and income.

**domain name**   The IP (Internet Protocol) address for a Web site. In addition to the numerical identification, Web sites also have "plain English" names. You must register your domain name with Network Solutions for a two-year registration.

**e-tailer**   An online retailer. A "real" e-tailer not only promotes and shows products on its Web site, but also offers full electronic commerce to enable customers to make purchases online.

**e-zine**   An Internet-based magazine that can be used to send subscribers both useful content as well as marketing messages.

**effective frequency**   The number of times an ad should be shown to one person to realize the highest impact of the ad without wasting impressions on that individual.

**effective reach**   The number of people who will see an ad the most effective number of times.

**embedded HTML ad**   An embedded HTML banner ad is (as it suggests) a banner ad embedded in a Web page. HTML code enables the banner ad to accomplish tasks that you can create with HTML. It creates a banner ad that a viewer can actually interact with (as opposed to simply clicking).

**extranet**   A Web site that reaches several different audiences. Usually an extranet connects directly into specific existing computer systems at a company to enable suppliers, distributors, and customers to interact with the company.

**forum**   Web-based forums are similar to newsgroups, whereby users can submit and respond to messages that are categorized by subject, and remain available for all users to see for a specific period of time.

**frequently asked questions**   A list of common questions (and answers) that your customers or prospects might have. Generally put up on a Web site as a page of FAQs.

**hit**   A downloaded file as recorded in a server log. It is probably the least valuable and most misunderstood metric around. A hit is not a pair of eyeballs or even one eyeball. A hit is a downloaded file, and a downloaded file is any graphic or any page. Therefore, a page with eight graphics would equal eight hits.

**impression**   A unit of measure. One set of eyeballs glancing over one banner counts as one impression, whether it is the same pair of eyeballs or not.

**interstitial ad**   A class of ad that pops up in a window between page loads. The window can display for a given time and then go away without annoying the viewers by making them close the window manually.

**Java**   Created by Sun Microsystems, Java is a computer language that can create programs (and just like any software, the programs can run a wide variety of applications). Java programs run over networks (including the Internet), run on any computer, and do not use a tremendous amount of space.

**marketing**   A textbook definition of marketing encompasses the entire process of creating and executing a plan to develop and sell your product or service. Marketing can play a role in product definition and development, packaging, pricing, promotion, and distribution—in other words, all aspects of successfully getting a product or service into the marketplace.

**newsgroup**   There are more than 20,000 different newsgroups. Users participate in newsgroups by submitting and responding to messages sent by other users. Although blatant commercials are generally not appreciated by users, marketers can use newsgroups to promote useful Web sites and general information that will be of interest to the users.

**one-on-one marketing**   When marketing efforts can be specifically tailored to reach individual users. The Internet is ideal for one-on-one marketing because database profiles of users can be used to create customized Web pages that present information that is created specifically for an individual customer.

**opportunity to see (OTS)**   Also known as *page view*. A page view is an OTS, but not necessarily an impression. The page can be downloaded, but if the banner is located at the bottom of the page and the visitor does not scroll down, the banner is not seen.

**opt-in mail list**   A list of Internet users who have agreed to receive email, sometimes about specific topics. With opt-in, the email recipient tells you (or an email list-gathering company) that it's okay to send him or her email. It is a consent for future mail. Opt-in mailing lists generate better response from users because they have requested the information and it is not considered spam.

**page view**   When a browser retrieves a Web page. Page views are often used to track the number of impressions a banner gets.

**portal site**   A Web site that offers users enough valuable services and information that they will either make it their Internet start page, or go to the site regularly to begin their Internet exploration. Although sites such as Yahoo! and MS/NBC are portal sites for large audiences, it is possible to create a portal site for a very narrow audience—such as people who collect stamps.

**privacy policy**   A written policy that states your company's position on exactly how it will use information provided by users of the Web site. It is a good idea to make it easy for users to access your privacy policy from the home page.

**registration**   The process whereby users are asked to submit information about themselves (email address and so on) to be permitted to access certain useful features of a Web site. Registration is an excellent way to build a useful Internet marketing database.

**ROI (return on investment)**   All business people understand this concept; it's evaluated to make decisions about virtually every activity, whether buying a backhoe or leasing a plane. And every ad agency has adopted this concept as the measurement of a campaign's efficacy, finally overcoming some of the shortfalls of the click-through. It will be a different calculation for your business than it is for your neighbor's.

**search engine**   A Web site that helps users locate information (and other sites) on the Internet. Many popular search engines (such as Yahoo! and Lycos) have expanded to become portal sites that offer many additional features including news, email, and chat. Because of the large number of users, search engines have been popular sites for placement of advertising.

**spam**   Unsolicited email that is sent to large numbers of people. Spam mail is usually sent anonymously, can involve scams, and usually will not honor a user's request to be removed from future mailings.

**sponsorship**   A form of advertising in which a content site such as chat, forum, newsletter, and so on, is sponsored by an advertiser targeting the same audience as the content publisher.

**stickiness**   A measure used to gauge how effective a Web site is in retaining individual users or providing information or tools that make users want to return to the site on a regular basis.

**streaming media**   Audio or video that is streamed to a user's PC. Unlike a file that must completely download before it plays, streaming media usually can begin playing within 10 seconds—even if the user has a 28.8Kbps modem.

**U-pon**   An Internet coupon that offers a discount on products or services. U-pons can help businesses obtain new customers or have customers switch their brands. U-pons can either be made available on Web pages or sent to users via email.

**unsolicited email (UCE)**   Unsolicited email is email that has not been requested. Unlike spam, UCE will have legitimate content and honor a request to be removed from future mailings, the sender uses a valid FROM: field and senders pay for transmission and use their own ISP.

**virtual community**   When a Web site uses community-creating features such as forums and chats to create a site where users can communicate with one another. The advantage of a virtual community for the online marketer is that it provides user-generated content on the Web site and gives users a good reason to return to the site.

**visit**   Also *session*. A completed visit to a Web site by a surfer/viewer/visitor.

# Index